Danger Zones

MEMOIRS AND OCCASIONAL PAPERS

Association for Diplomatic Studies and Training

In 2003, the Association for Diplomatic Studies and Training (ADST) created the Memoirs and Occasional Papers Series to preserve firsthand accounts and other informed observations on foreign affairs for scholars, journalists, and the general public. Sponsoring publication of the series is one of numerous ways in which ADST, a nonprofit organization founded in 1986, seeks to promote understanding of American diplomacy and those who conduct it. Together with the Foreign Affairs Oral History program and ADST's support for the training of foreign affairs personnel at the State Department's Foreign Service Institute, these efforts constitute the Association's fundamental purposes.

Danger Zones

A Diplomat's Fight for America's Interests

John Gunther Dean

Association for Diplomatic Studies and Training
Memoirs and Occasional Papers Series

Washington, DC

Copyright © 2009 by John Gunther Dean

VELLUM/New Academia Publishing, 2009

The opinions and characterizations in this book are those of the author and do not necessarily represent official positions of the Government of the United States or the Association for Diplomatic Studies and Training.

All rights reserved. No part of this book may be reproduced or transmitted in any form or by any means, electronic or mechanical, including photocopying, recording, or by any information storage and retrieval system.

Printed in the United States of America

Library of Congress Control Number: 2009925224
ISBN 978-0-9823867-0-5 paperback (alk. paper)
ISBN 978-0-9823867-1-2 hardcover (alk. paper)

New Academia Publishing
P.O. Box 24720, Washington, DC 20038-7420
info@newacademia.com - www.newacademia.com

To Martine

Contents

Preface ix
Acknowledgments xv

1. Born German, Thoroughly American 1
2. The Power of Knowledge 13
3. Colonial Turns 25
4. Quagmire 47
5. War, Peace, Coup, Peace 65
6. From Shangri-La to Hell 83

Photo Gallery 115

7. The Crucible of Lebanon 131
8. Asian Tiger 149
9. Fatal Embraces 169

A Final Word 205
Index 211

Preface

"John, all your appointments with the top U.S. officials have been cancelled. Why don't you come over to my house and we'll just have dinner?"

I was tired after a long flight from New Delhi to Washington's Dulles International Airport, and I was anxious about this trip. My wife asked me not to take it—the first time in my long career as a diplomat that she advised against doing something risky. "You have already told them your concerns," she said. "No good can come of a trip to Washington."

But I felt that I had to go. My job as ambassador was to tell the truth as I saw it—the whole truth—to my superiors in Washington. If the president and his top advisors were to make the best decisions about global hot spots, they needed to get direct and honest accounts of events in the field.

The flight from New Delhi to Washington was strange. An official from the Central Intelligence Agency escorted me. Rather than traveling under my own name, as I always did, my tickets were made out to my first two names, John Gunther. The CIA representative seemed on edge, as if he could not afford to let me out of his sight.

I came to Washington in my capacity as the U.S. ambassador to India, a country caught in a constant state of tension with its neighbor Pakistan. Less than a month before, on August 17, 1988, the president of Pakistan, General Muhammad Zia ul Haq, had been killed in an airplane explosion. Everything about the explosion seemed suspicious. Zia had reluctantly accompanied a group of Pakistani generals and the U.S. ambassador to Pakistan to a tank demonstration. Zia did not want to buy the tank, manufactured by an American company, but members of Pakistan's army and a number of interest groups prevailed on him to go to the demonstration to see how well the tank worked—which, as it turned out, was not very well. Following the demonstration, he boarded a plane for the return journey, and in a flash, he was dead.

Zia's death was troubling, not just because a leader in an unstable region of the world had been violently eliminated or even that a high-level American official had been killed with him. It was also troubling because it affected a chain of interests in the region. What would happen to Pakistan? How would Pakistan's new leadership deal with the most explosive issue of the day, Pakistan's efforts to develop a nuclear bomb? How would those efforts affect India, which had already achieved nuclear capability? Would India go on nuclear alert?

And what about neighboring Afghanistan? After nine years of bitter war between Muslim guerillas and the Soviet Union, negotiations were under way to create a coalition government. Soviet President Mikhail Gorbachev had pledged to withdraw Soviet troops from Afghanistan over a period agreed to by all parties. But what kind of Afghan government would take the place of the government imposed by the Soviets? The battle for the control of Afghanistan pitted India and the Soviet Union against Pakistan and the United States. What kind of coalition would each of these nations support? Who would control that coalition? Would they be secular Muslims or fundamentalist ones? Already concern had risen that the fundamentalist mujahidin, supported for years by American aid, would turn against the West. They supported themselves, in part, by trafficking drugs on the world market—a major concern since the Iran-Contra scandal of just a few years before. A key group in the fundamentalist army was the Taliban. What would happen if the Taliban or a like-minded group took over Afghanistan?

Something else was going on as well. Vice President George H. W. Bush was running for president against the Democrats' candidate, Governor Michael Dukakis, and seemed to be holding a strong lead. After falling behind in the summer polls, Bush had devastated Dukakis with a series of attacks on Dukakis's supposed lack of patriotism and judgment. But major events could change the presidential election. For years, both parties worried obsessively about an "October surprise," a major event that would deal one of the candidates a devastating blow. Candidates leading in the polls usually try to run out the clock in the last weeks of a campaign. Like a college basketball team trying to hold a lead in the last minutes of a championship game, candidates concentrate on not making mistakes, not arousing the public to think again about their allegiances.

I had come to Washington to meet with Secretary of State George Shultz and the director of the Central Intelligence Agency, William Webster. I also thought I might get some time with Vice President Bush, who may well have played a role in getting me appointed ambassador to India three years earlier.

I wanted to talk face to face with the highest officials in the Reagan administration about my concern that events were spiraling out of control in one of the most important regions of the world. I did not know exactly why General Zia's plane exploded, but I was convinced that it was an assassination carried out with the help of at least one of the world's intelligence agencies. Because the region was so dangerous—and because several Americans were on the plane—I thought the people making foreign policy in Washington should have a direct and honest conversation with one of their veteran diplomats. When leaders get assassinated, the world's institutions become more fragile. We needed to get to the bottom of the suspected plot that led to Zia's killing.

When Mort Abramowitz, the head of Research and Intelligence at the State Department and an old friend, greeted me at Dulles, I was surprised that my prearranged appointments with top U.S. government officials had been canceled. Abramowitz and later other State Department officials told me that my prearranged meetings were off. I would not be meeting with Bush or Shultz or Webster. Instead I would be meeting with Assistant Secretary Richard Murphy and George Vest, the director general of the Foreign Service.

When I met my friend and former boss George Vest, I finally understood all this puzzling behavior.

To this day, I am still stunned by the message that George Vest gave me. Doctors in the State Department, Vest said, had determined that I was under such stress in my position that I had become mentally deranged and had a "personality change." As a result, I would not be allowed to return to the American embassy in India. Rather than send me to a mental institution, George Vest had suggested to the department that I be allowed to go to my wife's family ski cottage in Switzerland.

I stayed at the house in Switzerland for six weeks before returning to New Delhi to pack my personal effects and return to Washington. When I realized that the State Department had no further assignment for me, I told them that I was resigning from the Foreign Service. Right away, my medical status was cleared. I was not mentally incompetent—in any way—after all.

Once I decided to leave the government, the kind words flowed. I got effusive letters of thanks and congratulations from President Ronald Reagan, Vice President Bush, Secretary of State Shultz, and others as well. Rajiv Gandhi praised me, too. All very nice. But not nice enough for someone who had worked honorably for the U.S. government since 1950. I needed to find out what happened.

Clearly, someone in Washington needed to get me out of the way. Figuring out who was like an Agatha Christie mystery. Was it the vice president, concerned that an international firestorm would threaten his election prospects? Was it the secretary of state or other members of the foreign-policy establishment, eager to tamp down rhetoric they considered provocative on issues connected with the Zia assassination? Was it the pro-Pakistan lobby inside (or outside) the United States? Was it the military-industrial complex that made fortunes selling weapons to all of the warring factions in the Middle East? Was it the Israeli government or its intelligence service, scared about Pakistan's acquisition of the "Muslim bomb"?

Over the course of my career, I found myself involved in controversy in a number of hot spots in the world. I had several stints in Vietnam, Laos, and Cambodia. In the 1950s, I worked on development projects in all three countries. I then worked with the U.S. military in Central Vietnam in the early 1970s.

Then, I brokered the deal that ended the war in Laos. After years of resisting the idea, the State Department allowed me to work with all of the parties in that long and bitter struggle. We worked out a deal that allowed a neutralist government to take over initially. I also faced down an attempted coup d'état in 1973 against the neutralist regime of Prime Minister Souvanna Phouma. After the fall of Saigon and Phnom Penh, a communist government took over in Laos. But Laos had avoided the wholesale violence of Vietnam and Cambodia.

I was not successful in Cambodia. Although I argued passionately that we needed to bring all parties together to end the war in Cambodia, Secretary of State Henry Kissinger rejected my efforts. I was the last man out of Cambodia on April 12, 1975. I appeared on the cover of *Newsweek* carrying the American flag as the last helicopter left Phnom Penh and Khmer Rouge forces approached the city.

Years later, in Thailand, I worked closely with HM King Bhumibol on a number of development projects as well as projects to provide military training to the Thai army and secure military bases for the United States.

I also served as ambassador to Lebanon, where I worked hard to get to know all the factions in that divided nation. I promoted the idea of one Lebanon— one nation, with many factions. At the instruction of the Carter administration, I successfully worked with Palestinian leaders to help free the first group of American hostages in Iran. I was also the target of an assassination plot. My motorcade was ambushed en route from the Embassy to the American University of Beirut.

At various times I had less controversial stints in the African nations of Togo and Mali, and I enjoyed three lovely years as ambassador to Denmark.

I was best known for my willingness to work with anyone and everyone—Communists and capitalists, diplomats and spies, urbanites and peasants, entrenched leaders and emerging reformers, Christians, Jews, Muslims, Hindus, and Buddhists. I always considered the work of diplomacy was to talk with—and listen to—everyone involved in a country. The more people you talk with—and the sooner you do it—the more options you have. I was an activist diplomat—I worked hard to bring people together rather than have them killing each other.

I always followed orders from Washington, whether I served a Republican president like Richard Nixon, Gerald Ford, or Ronald Reagan or a Democratic president like Jimmy Carter. I always placed American interests first. I worked hard for U.S. corporate interests, labor interests, religious groups, and others—but my total allegiance was to the United States as a whole.

Now my career is over. When I reached Washington on September 10, 1988, for meetings on the volatile situation in India, Pakistan, and Afghanistan, events and players were suddenly too big—and too invisible—for me to handle. What happened and what lessons my career may offer for American foreign policy in the twenty-first century are questions I hope to explore in this brief memoir.

Acknowledgements

This book is based on the oral history I recorded over a period of seven years (1996–2003) with Stuart Kennedy of the Association for Diplomatic Studies and Training (ADST). It covers the period from my birth in 1926 to my retirement from the U.S. Foreign Service in 1989.

In 2003, I received a request from former president Jimmy Carter, later supported by a second former president, Gerald Ford, to donate the papers and documents related to my Foreign Service career and in my possession to the U.S. National Archives. In response, I donated more than 12 linear feet of documents and messages to the Archives, which housed them at the Jimmy Carter Library in Atlanta, Georgia. In 2004, the director general of the Foreign Service, Ambassador W. Robert Pearson, sent the oral history I had recorded with ADST to the Archives at the Carter Library, which has put it on the Internet. As of 2008, the Archives have released my papers covering the years up to 1981 to the public. Documents covering my ambassadorship to Thailand (1981–85) and to India (1985–88) have not yet been declassified or released.

A special thanks goes to ADST, including its president, former ambassador Kenneth L. Brown, and to Stuart Kennedy, director of ADST's Oral History Program, which makes available to the public the experiences and views of the diplomats who have represented the United States abroad since the end of World War II and before. Some 1500 of these oral histories are now accessible through the Library of Congress Web site, identified as "Frontline Diplomacy."

Finally, I would like to acknowledge my friendship and gratitude to the many Foreign Service officers with whom I worked over the years, many of whom are no longer alive. From them I learned how to represent our country with honesty and respect for friend and foe alike. Among them I would like to single out Ambassador Charles Bohlen and Averell Harriman. But the one Foreign Service officer from whom I learned the most is my friend and colleague, former ambassador Robert Keeley. We worked together twice in our careers, and I remain grateful to him today for his advice and guidance.

Serving a cause bigger than oneself is a great privilege. Thank you, America.

John Gunther Dean

Danger Zones

1
Born German, Thoroughly American

I was born in Germany and now live in Paris. I have lived in many countries as a representative of the United States, but what defines me is that I am an American. Outside of my family, I care most about living according to accepted universal values, which I would like the United States to project abroad. I have devoted my life to defending American interests.

I was born Gunther Dienstfertig in the industrial city of Breslau, in the Ruhr Valley of Silesia, on February 24, 1926. When I lived there, Breslau was a German city of about 600,000 people. Over the previous millennium, the control of Breslau had shifted from Poland to Austria to Prussia and then to Germany. Breslau was a vital intellectual place, the home of nine Nobel Prize winners in the first three decades of the twentieth century. Protestants and Catholics made up all but the roughly five percent of the population who were Jews. Churches and other grand gothic buildings dominated the landscape, especially in the ancient city center. It was a jumping off point for the Teutonic Knights to bring Christianity to Eastern Europe in the Middle Ages.

Breslau's rich intellectual life—its university, medical institutions, botanical gardens, observatory, seminary, charitable organizations—went far beyond the city's economic dynamism. In addition to their native German, many educated people spoke French, an essential language in the world at the time. Located near coal and iron fields, at the convergence of rail lines, linked also by the deep waterway of the Oder River and close to Czechoslovakia and Poland, Breslau was an industrial power where airplanes and locomotives were built. Like some but not all industrial centers, Breslau translated its economic power and diverse cultural history into a cosmopolitan city with a first-rate university.

My father, Josef Dienstfertig, was a lawyer who sat on numerous corporate boards, including banks, machine tool factories, and mining concerns. What was perhaps unusual was that though he was a Jew, he sat on the board of directors of the Princes Hohenlohe, a powerful aristocratic family. The Hohenlohe family had vast estates in Silesia, owned mines and lumber mills, and included the last chancellor of Kaiser Wilhelm's imperial Germany before the First World War.

My father's family had lived in Silesia for five centuries. He was active in the civic affairs of the city. He was a Jew who considered his religious life to be a personal matter. Even though he was the president of the Jewish community for a while between the wars, he derived his deepest identity from his nationality. When asked to attend the opening of the Hebrew University in Jerusalem in 1929, he and other Jewish leaders agreed, but also said, in so many words, "I am a German citizen of Jewish faith. I am not a Zionist. I believe in the assimilation of Jews and all others into a larger community. Our faith is between ourselves and our maker."

Papa looked like the classic German burgher of his time. He was a round man of medium height. a ruddy complexion, and dark brown hair and wore elegant clothes—I still have a photograph of him wearing a beautiful three-piece suit, standing proudly, his short hair combed back off his high forehead, his soft stomach centering his body. He was an intellectual in all ways and a self-made man. He collected objects that expressed his refined tastes—first-edition books, paintings by the leading artists of Europe, sculpture, rugs, and graceful eighteenth-century furniture. He cared about things, but only when those things expressed his values and culture.

My mother, the former Lucy Ashkenaczy, had more of an international identity. Her father was a banker who prospered in the Austro-Hungarian Empire but whose family was dispersed all over Europe and America. Some members of the family converted to Catholicism; others remained Jewish. Many of her family members rose to prominence in their fields. One became chairman of British Petroleum Chemicals; another was the Polish ambassador to the Court of St. James's and later representative to the League of Nations; and another became chairman of Harvard University's medical school. Her brother fought for the French in World War I, and his son fought in the French Resistance during World War II. She grew up speaking Polish but spoke excellent German and French as well. Later she learned English.

What mattered most to me—and my friends—was that my mother was a tender and loving woman. She loved her life with her two boys and her husband, living in an elite community with a grand apartment filled with beautiful antiques and art. Mutti, as I called her, had brown hair that was fuller than my father's. Her body was slender, her skin fair. She wore the best clothes of her time. She loved fashion and surrounded herself with clothes her whole life, first as an affluent consumer in Europe and later as a middle-class sales clerk in America. But her most important quality was her openness. More international than my father, she was adventurous about exploring ideas from all cultures.

I aspired to many of my parents' qualities. I looked to them as an example of living a good and decent life. I imitated their behavior and sought to understand their values. That was not hard, because my parents lived vivid lives and made time to explain the values that governed their choices. The earliest lesson I learned was tolerance. My parents never cared about a person's religion or nationality, only that the person be industrious, fair, and honest.

Tolerance was the central value of my parents and their community. Prejudice existed, but people knew how to stand up to it. I remember the mother of a playmate telling her boy not to play with me because I was a Jew. "You're not going to tell me not to go with him," my friend retorted. "He's my buddy. I don't care if he's a Jew or not." We continued to play together. Some people understood, even at a young age, that personal and civic virtues mattered more than the ways people differed. My parents always taught me—with words and by example—not to judge people except by their deeds.

I attended school until 1936, when the Nuremberg laws made it difficult for a Jewish family to maintain normal routines in school and society. Von Zawatzki, my school, had about twenty students per class, a total of eighty; there were only two Jews in the school. I felt as welcome in the school as any other kid—I felt no stigma about being a Jew. The school demanded hard work, and I had plenty of homework. Study and sports, especially soccer, which we played often, are what mattered day in and day out, not the politics of religion. The first time I remember getting excluded because of religion was when my teacher took me out of a school play. "It's probably best that he not participate," my teacher told my father, "on account of the Nuremburg laws." I always felt a great desire to be part of the gang, and I felt left out for the first time in my life. But still, it didn't mean very much to me.

In 1938, my mother's brother-in-law, Paul Stern, was sent to a concentration camp at Buchenwald. The family worked to get him out. Everyone had to contribute money for his release, and the state requisitioned his flour mill in Brandenburg, not far from Berlin. He was allowed to take only some of his Impressionist and other great paintings when he departed for England. His first cousin, Otto Stern, won the Nobel Prize in physics.

I did not see much of my parents during the time we lived in Germany. I saw them mostly on Sundays, when we shared a big Sunday dinner. The rest of the week I saw my father when he came home and kissed me goodnight. A tutor, Herr Pezet, and an English lady named Eleanor Mary McCarthy came in 1936 to teach me English at home; between them they looked after my education. A German governess cared for me throughout the day. I studied—English, arithmetic, science, German, civics, literature, and music—and I played with boys my own age. I lived a strict, disciplined life, but it was a life of fun and adventure as well. My favorite game was soccer. Every day I could, I went to a park in the neighborhood and kicked the ball around with other children, older and younger. I was a good athlete.

My older brother, Wolfgang, was not as intellectual as others in the family. As a teenager, he began to prepare for a career in the department store owned by my mother's brother-in-law across town. That was the way things worked in Germany. One made early assessments about a child's aptitude and forged a life for the child according to that evaluation. We all loved Wolfgang. He had a mischievous way about him, less impressed by books and high culture but always easy with a laugh and roughhousing. He was handsome and girls sought him out.

At first Hitler's rise to power was not considered terribly alarming, especially among the business class to which my father belonged. Hitler argued—rightly—that Germany could never live up to the terms of the Versailles Treaty after World War I. In the Weimar Republic, Germany suffered crippling inflation and unemployment. Hitler promised to renounce the treaty and to revive the nation's industrial and military power.

In *Mein Kampf*, Hitler expressed his vile hatred of Jews, but the bourgeoisie did not take that political tract into account as he rose to power. The democratic Weimar Republic had many excellent features, but it was nonetheless unable to cope with the problems of postwar Germany. Fascists on the right and communists on the left competed for German sympathies.

It became ever clearer that Hitler would target the Jews economically and socially as he consolidated his power as chancellor. Jews were forced to sell their businesses for temporary reprieves from arrest. In exchange for their factories and warehouses, Jews were allowed to leave the country with their belongings. This was the case of my uncle Petersdorf, who had to sell his large, elegant department store (which still stands today). Jews could not take German marks out of Germany in any significant amount. In addition, Hitler had cut off the German currency from the international monetary system. Some people had been able to store money in foreign banks in Switzerland or elsewhere; my mother urged my father to do so, but he refused. "How can I not bring my money home?" he said. "I am a lawyer and a public notary, a government-appointed position. How can I not follow the law?" He was a German nationalist, a patriot, to his core.

My father continued to believe that he could and should stay in Germany, that the Jews' worst fears would not be realized. Some of my father's business associates supported Hitler, confident that they could control his fanaticism and that they had no acceptable alternatives in Germany. Papa used to say that the troubles facing Jews in Germany would "blow over." But that was becoming harder and harder to believe, and my mother began to argue for leaving. Her relatives had moved to New York in the early 1930s, and she had visited them in March 1938.

On that visit, my mother learned that my brother had died from an infection. It was before the discovery of antibiotics, and his heart gave out. He was only sixteen. My mother was so distraught that she began to talk about moving to New York as well. While there, she had the foresight to get our relatives to write an affidavit saying that they would care for me, which would allow me to get papers to come there. After her return to Breslau, she ordered smaller furniture in anticipation of emigration to the United States. The Bauhaus furniture made for us was designed to fit the narrow staircase of a New York apartment building. I still own the Bauhaus desk we brought to New York when we fled Germany. In November 1938, the police came for my father. The concierge of our apartment building raced up the stairs to warn us that the Gestapo had come to arrest him. "*Herr Doktor, Herr Doktor! Sie kommen! Schnell!!*" he cried. My father fled down the back stairs. He went to Berlin where an American lawyer named Jazelli got the American consulate to add my parents' names to the affidavit my mother had gotten for me in New York. Within two weeks, we were on our way to America.

In November, we took the furniture, some clothes, and some of our priceless art that the Nazis had not commandeered. We did not have much cash to take, since my nationalist father refused to keep his money in foreign banks. We went first to Holland, where we were hosted by a business associate with whom my father had worked on a mining company in Greece and then to England. Finally, we traveled to New York aboard the S.S. *Queen Mary*.

I fell in love with America right away. The first day I stepped outside our apartment in Kew Gardens, Queens, I saw some boys playing stickball and ran over to join them. I learned how to throw a baseball and swing a bat. People were nice to me, and I fit in. I felt at home. Even though I would not become a naturalized citizen until I joined the war effort in 1944, I became an American in mind and spirit that afternoon.

Like other immigrants, my family adopted a shorter, Americanized name upon our arrival in our new country. Instead of Dienstfertig, we now called ourselves Dean. We had the change approved by a court in New York. I changed my own first name after a talk with my school's principal. "Hey, kid, you don't want to be called Gunther! You want an American first name. What name do you want?" I said I liked the sound of the name Tom. "No, that's not right. Why don't you call yourself John?" I agreed. He suggested John Gunther, after the journalist who would later write the bestseller *Death Be Not Proud*. My parents soon allowed me to change my name to John Gunther Dean.

All I wanted was to fit in. I wanted to be with the others and to be like them. The boys made fun of my English accent, which I got from my British tutor. "Hey, it's the Limey!" I immediately set to work to plane down the ornamental British edges and to give my speech the roughness and plainness of the American dialect.

I went to grammar school in Kew Gardens at P.S. 99. My mother and I were happy with our new home. She had always loved fashion and found work in a clothing store. But my father, once a respected and important man in a sophisticated community, struggled to find work as a lawyer.

My cousin Henry Stern—my father's godson—soon sent word that Kansas City offered more opportunities for my father. Kansas City was an agricultural center, and Stern's family had worked in the milling industry in Brandenburg. He had come to the United States in 1937. The milling business is a small world, and he quickly found his way to Missouri. He told my father he could find work as a bookkeeper. We moved west by Greyhound after living in New York for five months.

Living in Kansas City had a profound impact on me. We took an apartment in a four-unit building at 4211 Harrison Avenue. We were different from our neighbors, who found us peculiar from the start but accepted us completely. They tilted their heads in puzzlement as we moved antiques, paintings, and sculptures into our modest little home. But before long, we became part of the life of the community.

In our four-family apartment building, we had a porch where we slept during the summer to beat the heat. Few people owned air-conditioning in those days. Harrison Avenue was home to a striving middle class in Kansas City. The neighborhood was part of the same, regular street grid that has defined the contours of so much of America—regular, straight, and predictable. People there were very nice. The neighbors knew something about our past.

My father and mother both worked, and I went to school. I made fast friends with other boys in the neighborhood. My father established a new network of friends and business associates in the city. He became the head of a local German immigrant group. We became part of a local Reform Jewish congregation, which lent its building to the congregation of a Christian church that had burned down.

I felt terribly sorry for my father. He had been a large figure back in Germany but was reduced to rather ordinary work in the United States. When we left Germany, the life he had lived was over. He worked for Crown Drug Store as an accountant. For a while, he was a guest lecturer in international law at the University of Kansas in Lawrence. But he lost that position in 1940 when he spoke out against Charles Lindbergh, who was opposing American entry into World War II and was sympathetic to the Nazis.

Without his old prestige, my father devoted himself to me selflessly and cheerfully. He had dreams for me—he wanted me to be a banker. Very early, I told him I wanted to be in the diplomatic service. "You? You want to be in the diplomatic service in the United States?" The tone of his voice implied that my foreign birth would afford me little chance of achieving such a goal. But he embraced my choice and dedicated himself to ensuring my pursuit of the life I wanted.

I did all the things American boys did in the Midwest. I played sports. I joined the Boy Scouts and embraced its motto. I took up a newspaper delivery route for the *Kansas City Star*. I learned how to take responsibility for a small business, deal with customer complaints, and manage money. I also worked at the Kroger food store bagging groceries. I packed clothing for shipment at Hartsfeld Department Store. Then I worked at Railway Express, hustling trunks onto trains. When I finished working, I found lots of time to play with a band of boys in the neighborhood. I dreamed of one day going to Harvard University and later joining the Foreign Service.

I was lucky that my family moved to Kansas City. In New York, the immigrants clustered among their own kind, spoke their old language, and built an intense world as devoted to the past as the present. But in America's heartland, immigrants like us had to become part of a larger community. We had to speak English and adapt to our new life. Life in the Midwest reinforced my family's assimilationist inclinations in every way. Although Kansas City, Missouri, retained the ugliness of racial segregation and discrimination, the community overall was tolerant of different ideas and people.

The big change for me in America was that I now spent a lot of time with my parents. Instead of living a busy business and social life and leaving the care of their child to nannies and tutors, they now spent most of their time near home and with me. When I came home from school, my mother gave me the quintessentially American snack of a cupcake and a glass of milk, and we talked about the day. At home we talked around the kitchen table, and we talked as we did errands around town. I talked about everything with my parents—school, playmates, politics, work, what I wanted to be when I grew up. We talked a lot about morality, about the right way to live a life. The words were so meaningful to me because they were part of a loving, ongoing conversation. The life I lived in Germany—cosseted in a world of tutors and servants—became transformed into a life in the warm embrace of my parents. There was no way my father was going to recover the style and grandeur of his life in Breslau, so he and my mother devoted themselves to me. Whatever it took to teach me, care for me, and pay for my education at Harvard or anywhere else they were determined to do.

My father taught by both example and exhortation. I remember vividly sitting in a streetcar with him in downtown Kansas City when a black woman, obviously tired from a long day's work, climbed aboard. My father stood up, tipped his hat, and gave his seat to her. A white passenger became irate and cursed at my father. I can still hear the harshness in her voice: "You nigger lover, you getting up for this gal here. What is this here?"

The streetcar driver then turned to my father: "Listen, old man, you take your boy and get off this streetcar. I don't want any trouble here." I didn't completely understand what was going on, but I looked up to my father and knew he must be right. To this day, I find it completely incomprehensible that people can think less of others because of their skin color, religion, level of education, or any other factor besides their character.

Our modest circumstances did not dampen my parents' enthusiasm for good things. We simply had to make choices about what things were most important. My father still wanted books and cigars. Since he didn't have much money anymore, he was happy to give up a cigar for a book. They were always sacrificing because they wanted to send Johnny to college. If they had a dollar, they saved ten cents.

My father regularly quoted poetry, literature, and philosophy to give me rules to live by. Whether he knew it or not, he was acting in the spirit of self-help that Benjamin Franklin made such a distinctive part of the American idiom. Just before I left for Harvard, he wrote down for me the following fragments of wisdom:

To be and not to seem; to do and not simply to talk.
Love your neighbor as yourself.
Be orderly; it will save you a lot of problems.
Love as long as you can, because the hour approaches when you stand at the graveside and grieve.
Whatever you do, be prudent and respect the end.
Use the day.
The fact that you are a human being—that very thought—should make you humble.
That you are a human being, that fact should make you raise your head again.
If you bring to the world heaven on earth, you will not be rewarded. Therefore think of yourself and your family.

These passages express universal truths that apply to situations all over the world. They provide a guide for living. They tell you that you owe something to the world. I tried to follow these truths because I wanted to have my father's approval. Still today, some sixty years later, I'm seeking my father's approval. I still have that collection of quotations.

I spent hours at the public library. I read history and philosophy. I talked with my parents about what I was learning. I developed friendships with teachers and librarians, neighbors and shopkeepers. I told a librarian once that I wanted to learn more about America and was interested in the life of Alexander Hamilton. She told me she thought Hamilton was too authoritarian and that I should consider learning about Thomas Jefferson and James Madison as well, which is what I did. Today my political ideals have at their core the wisdom of Madison, who argued for a system of dispersed power, checks and balances, and joint responsibility, for not only acting modestly but also taking responsibility for countering the improper use of power by others in the system. When I read *The Federalist Papers*—the articles that Hamilton, Madison, and John Jay wrote to promote adoption of the U.S. Constitution—they became an essential part of who I am and what I believe.

As I studied the stories of great Americans, they became part of my heritage. People sometimes forget that when you become American, you become part of a national lineage, just as if your family had always been in the United States. I consider George Washington to be my spiritual ancestor. I consider Thomas Jefferson, Abraham Lincoln, Teddy Roosevelt, Franklin D. Roosevelt—all of them—to be part of my intellectual lineage. My first fight in America was defending Franklin Roosevelt. A kid was saying something nasty about FDR. I came home with a black eye, but I was defending *my* president.

As a youth, I looked for every way possible to prepare for Harvard. My parents gave me an ongoing tutorial about philosophy, history, art, and culture. I asked teachers, Boy Scout leaders, everyone, for advice about how to improve myself. One teacher told me to read a different play by Shakespeare every week, and I followed her advice. When I came across a word I did not know, I looked it up in the dictionary and wrote out the definition. The lessons of Shakespeare stayed with me. Somehow, he captured all of the contradictions of man's nature and condition. Man is smart and blind, loving and jealous, powerful and pitiful, tender and violent, poetic and inarticulate, modest and bombastic, redeemable and hopeless. I was lucky to be guided to Shakespeare at a young age, and I have lived a full enough life to see all of his lessons play out before my eyes.

We watched events in Europe with great interest. I remember listening to the radio in May 1940 when news came that France had surrendered to the Germans. H. V. Kaltenborn, one of the pioneers of radio news, broadcast France's surrender from the same railroad car in which Germany surrendered to France in 1918. My mother was crying.

The average person in the Midwest did not pay too much attention to the war. In Kansas City, people talked about the minor-league baseball team, the Pendergast political machine, controversies over burlesque parlors, and why the schools had to close a month early because of fiscal shortfalls. Most people who paid attention to the war were neutral. It was not until the devastation the Germans wrought with their blitzkriegs that many people awakened to the Nazis' ruthless ambitions. As we had family members all over Europe—including some in concentration camps—we followed the war closely. We knew the towns involved and got letters from France, England, and Belgium, all commenting on the war and conditions in Europe.

As I grew older, I decided I wanted to fight in the war. We knew the United States would be part of the Allied cause before long, and it finally entered the war when the Japanese bombed Pearl Harbor on December 7, 1941.

My parents lost almost everything when the Nazis forced them to flee Germany, but they never expressed resentment or bitterness about their experience. I owe all my loyalty toward America, but I cannot hate Germany. It has been two generations since the evil of Nazism took over Germany and threatened Europe and the world. Some people cannot let go of their losses and pain, but I cannot hold such negative feelings. New generations have risen in Germany, and my native country is more democratic and open than it has ever been. I cannot tell other people how to feel, but I have always thought it better to live in the present, building upon the past rather than longing for what has been lost. We need to heal wounds rather than rub them raw.

Whenever the subject of the past came up—how much we lost when we were forced to flee Germany—my mother often told me: "You cannot look back. Look at what lies ahead."

Looking ahead to me meant going to Harvard University and preparing for a career in public service. I graduated from Westport High School as a sixteen-year-old in June 1942.

2
The Power of Knowledge

My father had a friend from Germany named Heinrich Brüning who taught at Harvard. Brüning, a devout Catholic, had been head of a moderate conservative party and became chancellor of Germany in 1930, remaining in power until 1932. Governing by decree, Brüning took drastic—and unpopular—measures against inflation, but was forced out of office in 1932 when President Paul von Hindenburg named Franz von Papen chancellor. Brüning left Germany in 1934 and joined the Harvard faculty in the Government Department in 1937.

When I applied to Harvard in 1942, my father wrote to his friend Dr. Brüning in the hope that he might explain my background to the Harvard Board of Admission. I had passed the eastern College Board examination, which made me eligible for admission. But what chance did an immigrant public school kid from a small midwestern high school have to get into Harvard? Nobody from Westport High School had ever attended Harvard College, as Westport's principal reminded me. But after an interview in Kansas City with a traveling member of the Harvard Board of Admission, I was the first applicant in my city to be notified that I had been accepted. It was a great day for me, but even greater for my parents, for whom my life's goals were paramount.

I was so intent on attending Harvard that I did not think to apply to other schools. I did everything I could to prepare for the university. I became fluent in several languages, studied American history and culture, read philosophy and literature, and burned with desire to achieve.

In those days, Harvard students were required to take courses in six different areas—history, humanities, mathematics, science, and others—and to take six courses in one area of concentration. This "concentration and distribution" curriculum was a forerunner of the core curriculum that sought to give Harvard students the broadest possible understanding of Western civilization and knowledge.

In my first year I lived at Wigglesworth, a freshman dormitory in the Harvard Yard. Since my parents could only afford to finance a portion of what it cost to attend Harvard, I worked as a student waiter in Winthrop House, which helped cover my meals. Then I sold laundry and pressing contracts to the more affluent students for an establishment near Harvard Square. I earned a commission for every contract sold. My classmate and later colleague Arthur Hartman, who became U.S. ambassador to France and the Soviet Union, still remembers me in this capacity. I earned enough to pay for two tickets to the movies, beautiful Radcliffe or Wellesley girls were eager to meet Harvard boys, and life was great.

In 1942–1943, young males were becoming scarce as the draft called up more and more men. One day in early 1943 at the Harvard Square movie house, watching the newsreel, I saw Field Marshal Von Paulus surrendering an entire German army corps to the Soviets at Stalingrad. The picture of Von Paulus holding high his marshal's baton still sticks in my mind more than sixty-five years later. Perhaps this episode even enhanced my desire to enter the American military as early as possible.

Harvard houses students in residence halls so that they develop a stable social community. Adams House, where I lived my second year, was one of the college's more storied houses. In previous years it was home to Franklin D. Roosevelt, Buckminster Fuller, and William Randolph Hearst, Jr.

World War II shaped the environment of life at Harvard. With men fighting in Europe and the Pacific, the ranks of the student body were thinning. For generations, Harvard had been home to prep school boys with connections in business and government, but when I attended, refugees from war-torn nations—like me—gave Harvard a more international atmosphere.

The provost of the university, Paul Buck, told incoming students that they had "no right" to university life unless they considered their duties to serve in the war effort. The academic calendar was changed to keep the university running twelve months a year, with a twelve-week summer semester added to the standard fall and spring terms. Harvard Yard became the training ground for military programs similar to ROTC, with daily drills starting at six in the morning. Adams House was one of the few campus buildings not turned over to the war effort. The usual university pranks and campus politics almost disappeared. The traditional Harvard-Yale football rivalry was temporarily suspended to cut down on travel costs—Harvard played Boston College instead. Academic courses placed more emphasis than ever on science and technology, as well as intensive training in foreign languages that might be useful to the war effort.

After two years, I left Harvard to enlist in the Army. I had to volunteer for enlistment because I was still an "enemy alien," a German citizen, and hence could not be drafted.

My first action after enlistment was to become a naturalized citizen. I had never doubted that I would one day become an American citizen. Sent to Fort Belvoir, near the nation's capital, for basic training, I went to a federal courthouse in Washington for the ceremony with about twenty other servicemen who wanted to become American citizens, including one who was rejected because he had been a member of Fritz Kuhn's anti-American German Bund. My picture for the naturalization certificate shows me in uniform looking like a young kid. It was a big moment for me. I was going to become part of the United States! The ceremony was short and uneventful, unlike some of the elaborate ceremonies that INS holds today at places like Faneuil Hall or Ellis Island. We took our oaths, had lunch together, and went back to the base.

Life as a private in basic military training at Fort Belvoir provided yet another lesson in working with people from different backgrounds. I met a lot of young men from the Appalachian Mountains who could not read or write. They were good people, but we had little in common. I remember making a deal with Private Corvin, an illiterate boy from Appalachia. He was eighteen years old and married. In exchange for my reading and writing his letters, he cleaned my rifle. He became my friend, but we received different orders at the end of camp. Corvin was later killed in the Battle of the Bulge in the Ardennes in late 1944.

After four months of training, at the "graduation ceremony" on the parade ground, the commander called individual recruits one by one and asked them to step forward for their assignments overseas. I was the only recruit whose name was not called. Because of my language skills, I was sent to a top-secret intelligence operation just outside Washington, known as Post Office Box 1142. It was my first exposure to the importance of intelligence-gathering. I was a small part of the operation, but all of us felt we were making a contribution to the war effort. One of my buddies there was Alexander Dallin, who later became a professor at Columbia and Stanford, where he wrote two books with a promising student on international affairs, Condoleezza Rice.

One of my later assignments was to work with Dr. Heinz Schlicke, a German scientist. The Allied forces had captured Schlicke when his submarine, headed for Tokyo and carrying precious metals, surrendered off the coast of Uruguay in May 1945, when the war with Japan was still on. Those on board the sub included two Japanese military officers who committed *hara-kiri* when the submarine surrendered to the Allies.

Schlicke had worked on infrared technology at Peenemünde, where Werner Von Braun had developed the German V-1 and V-2 missiles used against England. Infrared enabled German aircraft to see through obstacles like clouds, woods, and darkness to identify the location of enemy troops by the heat given off by human bodies. When Schlicke was captured, the sub had been en route to deliver to the Japanese the secrets of infrared technology, which the Allied Forces did not yet possess. Military officials with a scientific background persuaded Schlicke to work with American scientists so that the United States could learn about the infrared technology.

My assignment was to keep Schlicke company and become his friend. I hiked with him, ate with him, and played sports with him. When he became convinced to share his know-how with us, he asked us to help get his wife and children out of the Russian zone in Germany. The war had ended in Europe and all the Allies were trying to learn all they could about German technology and science. I was sent to Germany to get Schlicke's wife and two children out of the Russian zone of occupation into the American zone, and succeeded in doing so.

In later years in embassies, I spent much time establishing competent science and technology sections. Sometimes it was a matter of sharing knowledge with friendly nations. At other times it was finding out what stage foreign countries had reached in developing new technologies, as most technological and scientific inventions can be used for dual purposes. For example, atomic rays can be used to destroy certain malignant growths. These rays can also be used to kill enemy soldiers. Some chemicals can heal specific ailments, while the same chemical in different doses can be used to destroy life.

Obtaining the secrets of science and technology would lie at the cutting edge of intelligence in the second half of the twentieth century—knowledge is power. Later in my Foreign Service career, I often urged innovative foreign scientists to work in the United States, because it would encourage scientific progress in my country. In return, I helped to establish links between well-known U.S. scientific and technological universities and their counterparts in countries where I was stationed. I also tried to find funds to send American professors to work in foreign scientific establishments. I succeeded in this endeavor in such places as Thailand and India.

I did not know exactly what it meant in October 1944, when I first heard the term *atomzertrümmerung*—the splitting of the atom—from one of the German "guests" at P.O. Box 1142. Almost a year later everyone in the world would know what it meant. The United States dropped the atomic bomb on Hiroshima and Nagasaki on August 6 and 9 of 1945. The bomb hastened the Japanese surrender and the end of the war. It also ushered in the nuclear arms race and an age of nuclear danger, in which any nation with the bomb could blow up the world. Now, in the early days of the twenty-first century, the "nuclear club" has expanded beyond the United States, Russia, Great Britain, and France to include China, India, Pakistan, Israel, and North Korea, with Iran seeking to join. The nuclear threat remains one of humanity's greatest challenges. The attacks of September 11, 2001, have given rise to new fears that terrorists will one day possess the technology to set off a bomb. And still the world community has not found a way to significantly reduce the stockpile of weapons materials vulnerable to rogue groups. While I was in the military at Post Office Box 1142, my education in *Realpolitik* included long conversations with some outstanding personalities from Germany and Russia, one of whom, Gustave Hilger, had been a German diplomat stationed in the Soviet Union. Born to a well-to-do German family that had lived in Russia for a couple of centuries, Hilger had a profound knowledge of Russia's past and present, more than anyone in the United States possessed at the time. He was a highly educated man, erudite, honest, and tolerant, equally at home in German culture and Russian civilization, with a high regard for both. Around 1924, the Weimar Republic asked him to represent the German Red Cross in the Soviet Union. When the German government established diplomatic relations with the Soviet Union in the early thirties—before Hitler came to power—he was asked to join the German embassy as counselor.

Hilger participated in the 1939 negotiations that led to the German-Soviet treaty that divided Poland between the two countries. The picture commemorating their momentous event was carried in newspapers around the world. It showed German Foreign Minister Von Ribbentrop sitting next to Soviet Foreign Minister Molotov. Right behind Ribbentrop stood Gustave Hilger.

In late 1944, after the Allied landing in Normandy, Hilger gave himself up to American authorities and was taken to the United States. His only child had been killed at Stalingrad, and he had become completely disillusioned with both Hitler's National Socialism and Stalin's communism. Hilger tried to help Americans understand Stalin's Soviet Union and the problems that lay ahead for the democratic West after the war. He remained in the United States with his wife for almost five years before returning to Germany.

As Hilger could not speak English, but spoke German and French, I was assigned to him, spending hours entertaining him during his leisure hours. Other high-ranking American civilian and military officers worked with him professionally. As we drank coffee or tea, Hilger explained to me the character of the Soviet regime, including the full extent of the horrors of Stalinism—the millions killed from starvation and forced movement, the millions more killed in the war. He told me how the Ukrainians received the German invaders joyously with arches made of flowers, grateful to be freed from the misery and violence of Stalin. He told me about the wretched life of Russians in the cities and the countryside. None of this excused the Nazi atrocities, but it did teach me about the awful choices that you face in foreign affairs. As terrible as Stalin was, the Russians played the key role in winning the war for the Allies. Revisionists now attack Roosevelt and Churchill for caving in to Stalin at Yalta. How could the Allies have capitulated to Stalin on Germany? On Poland? On Yugoslavia? Did we really have a choice? We did as well as we could at Yalta. Yalta may have also forced America's decision to use the atomic bomb. Stalin told his partners that he would finish off Japan. Was our only hope for beating the Soviets to use an atomic bomb on Japan? If so, that was an awful choice. That was *realpolitik*.

Everyday life at our military installation at P.O. Box 1142 was slow. I quickly got a reputation for my love of sports, and one day someone challenged me to swim across the Potomac River and back again. We bet twenty dollars that I couldn't do it—a lot of money to me. I dove right in, but then discovered two things I hadn't counted on. First, the river had a strong current. I was being pushed down and had to swim against the tide just to stay in the same part of the river. Even more daunting, the river was a sewer—literally. In those days, the Potomac was where the toilets emptied out from Washington and other communities. I felt sick as I swam amidst floating debris across the river. But getting across was not enough—I also had to swim back. I did it, and got my twenty dollars, but I vowed never again to take a wager without knowing everything about the challenge.

A recent development linked to my Army service during World War II occurred on October 17, 2007. The U.S. House of Representatives passed Resolution 753, honoring those who had served at Fort Hunt, Virginia, in the Post Office Box 1142 unit more than sixty years earlier! The resolution reads as follows: "Resolved, that the House of Representatives honors and extends its sincere appreciation to the soldiers of Post Office Box 1142 for their sacrifice to our Nation during a time of war, their pursuit of necessary intelligence through humane means and their service that went too long unacknowledged." I deeply appreciated this recognition by our country so many years after World War II.

I got out of the Army in 1946 and returned to Harvard for the fall semester. Gone were the financial constraints I had lived under during my first two years in college. The G.I. Bill of Rights now paid my tuition. My parents were also more financially secure after my father had gotten a job—thanks to his friend Max Warburg—in a New York bank. I remained serious about my studies but decided to have a good time, too. I liked girls, parties, and going to the movies. I thought I deserved to enjoy myself.

My father wanted me to remember German civilization, so I took a one-semester course on Goethe's *Faust*. I never regretted it. Aren't the temptations described in Goethe's *Faust* the same ones we all face in life? Isn't there something of Jekyll and Hyde in every one of us? When Goethe writes that a man's salvation lies in his using his own powers to achieve his aims, I can only admit that the very same ideas became the leitmotif in my own behavior in life.

Another great intellectual treat was a course on religion and ethics at the Divinity School taught by George La Piana, which I was allowed to audit in my last year at Harvard. When I returned to postwar Harvard, I felt confused. I needed some kind of moral and intellectual guidance.

When I had gone to Europe to pick up Heinz Schlicke's family, I was shocked by the war's devastation. Everywhere I went whole neighborhoods and cities were blown up beyond recognition. Often buildings had turned into rubble and people walked aimlessly, with worries and concern written on their faces. As the war drew to a close in Europe, both sides had unleashed lethal force on communities populated only by women, children, and old people—people who posed no military threat, people who had already suffered from war for too long.

I also saw soldiers take advantage of their power in communities they occupied. Some Russian soldiers raped German women until their officers arrived on the scene and stopped them. No one was without fault. American soldiers used nylons and coffee for sexual favors from young German women and girls. It was nothing like rape, but it was the exploitation of one side by the other. Like all Americans—especially like all victims of the Nazi regime—I wanted to defeat the Germans. But at the same time, I also felt sorry for ordinary Germans.

La Piana's course provided the guidance I needed. Every lecture was packed. La Piana was an authority on church history and a leading figure in the debates about whether and how to modernize the Roman Catholic Church. Born in Palermo, Sicily, he was an ordained priest who had taught at Harvard since 1916.

La Piana was not only brilliant but also courageous. He spoke up on the political issues of the day. He criticized the Vatican over its agreement with Italy's dictator, Benito Mussolini, giving the church power over Italy's educational system. He also took up the issues of censorship and academic freedom, abortion, and population control, as well as the church's role as an interest group in a democratic age. La Piana was involved in the life of the university, participating in debates over Harvard's tutorial system and bringing speakers and debates about contemporary issues to Harvard. In those days, colleges did not have the wealth of speakers and organizations that they do today. People like La Piana played an important role in the democratic education of students.

On the day of his last lecture before retiring in 1947, La Piana talked about Albertus Magnus, a thirteenth-century scientist, theologian, and student of St. Thomas Aquinas. Albertus held that the only way to discover scientific truth is through experimentation. That was a radical notion at the time—and when one thinks about it, it is one of the most world-changing ideas of all time. Magnus gathered together all the known truths of scientific inquiry into a single volume, but he was humble and modest. He had a sense of just how much was unknown to humans, and that humility not only kept the Catholic establishment from denouncing his work but also deepened his sense of awe about God's work. At the end of the lecture, La Piana noted that his career as a teacher was ending and concluded with a passage from the second book of Corinthians: "*Dominus autem Spiritus est ubi autem Spiritus Domini ibi libertas,*" meaning "Now the Lord is that Spirit: and where the Spirit of the Lord is, there is liberty." Though not a religious man, I understand the limits of human understanding and the largeness of the forces that move us—ever more, as I grow older.

Graduation day arrived on June 5, 1947. The commencement speaker was Secretary of State George Marshall. His twelve-minute address outlined the radical idea of using American economic might to rebuild the countries that experienced the devastation of World War II. Delivered in a flat monotone, Marshall announced that the United States would provide massive aid to rebuild Europe's economies. Marshall said that the wholesale destruction of factories, mines, railroads, cities, and towns cost more than any European country could afford to pay without resorting to dangerous borrowing. The war had not only destroyed physical assets but also wreaked havoc on the legal and social underpinnings of the economy. Only a major international effort could restore Europe to prosperity and allow free institutions to thrive. "The remedy," he said, "lies in breaking the vicious circle and restoring the confidence of the European people in the economic future of their own countries and of Europe as a whole." Marshall warned against a resurgence of profiteering from Europe's misery: "Governments, political parties, or groups which seek to perpetuate human misery in order to profit there politically or otherwise will encounter the opposition of the United States."

Thus began the Marshall Plan that would spend billions of dollars in the reconstruction of Europe and thereby inject renewed confidence in the future of those European nations that chose to participate in this American initiative.

At the time, Marshall's speech attracted little attention. The audience at Harvard greeted Marshall enthusiastically before and after his address but did not interrupt it with applause. The enthusiasm was for Marshall the man. Few newspapers seemed to apprehend the importance of this announcement. The *New York Times* emphasized the importance of "European unity" in reconstructing the continent rather than the prospect of a major U.S. initiative. Only the New York *Herald-Tribune* and Boston *Globe* seemed to understand that the speech heralded a major initiative. Even James B. Conant, Harvard's president, acknowledged years later that he had missed the magnitude of that speech. Soon enough, the Marshall Plan would offer me a place to begin my career in foreign affairs.

After obtaining my bachelor's degree from Harvard, I continued my studies at the Institut des hautes études internationales at the University of Paris and then returned to the Harvard Graduate School for a master's degree in international relations.

Studies in Paris were the result of a detour arranged by my parents. My best friend Max Petschek and I had met two beautiful women and decided to get married. I told my parents of my plans, and they did something very smart. Rather than arguing against marriage on the grounds that I was too young—which would have only made me more stubborn and sure of myself—they expressed delight at the news. "Just one thing," my father said, like television's Colombo leaving an interview with a suspect. "Why don't you bring your girl to see us on a summer vacation? And why don't you go to school abroad for a year and give yourself greater opportunities to care for yourself and your future wife?" I agreed.

On the boat trip across the Atlantic Ocean, I was dazzled by other beautiful women on board. After five weeks in Paris, I wrote to my father: "You know, Papa, I think I might be too young to get married."

In Paris, I studied international law and wrote my thesis on the Austro-German Customs Union of 1931. I took on the issue mostly because it was of interest to my Harvard mentor, Heinrich Brüning. The subject involved questions of international cooperation—always an interest for me—and provided a complex real-world problem to analyze. Working in a French university, I applied a more rigorous approach to the problem than I had used before. The French understood all problems to arise from the inherent contradictions of existing arrangements, which created tension that needed to be resolved by integrating different aspects of a problem. Like the Germans operating in the tradition of Kant, Hegel, and Marx, the French solved the problem by understanding how thesis and antithesis had to be overcome by developing a new synthesis. That's how I began to analyze problems.

After earning a doctorate degree in Paris in 1949, I returned to Harvard for further graduate studies, receiving a master's degree in 1950. I attended an international affairs program at the Graduate School headed by Dr. Dan Cheever. Some of the fellow students I met there remained friends for life: John Brademas, who became the Democratic whip in the U.S. House of Representatives; Robert Miller and Thomas Shoesmith, who became U.S. ambassadors; and Herbert Goodman, who entered the private sector and rose to the top ranks in the petroleum business. The program honed whatever talents I had acquired in foreign affairs, with emphasis on international economics.

I was now ready to begin my life in diplomacy. It was time to take up the challenge of building the new world that George Marshall had outlined in his commencement address three years before.

In 1951, I borrowed money from my good friend Max Petschek to take my parents on a grand vacation. I wanted to show them that I was on my way. We traveled to the south of France and stayed in the best hotels and ate at the best restaurants. We visited Monte Carlo. My father thought I had made it. I had not, but I was on my way. He died three weeks later, a happy man.

3
Colonial Turns

My introduction to world affairs began with service in World War II, one of the greatest and most tragic events of modern times. My introduction to the world of diplomacy began with the end of colonialism in Indochina, with the French decision to leave and the costly American decision to take it over from the French. But there was a difference between the policies behind the two decisions. The French were beginning a process of decolonization, while the United States was applying their policy of containing communism in Southeast Asia and preventing communist encroachment in Africa. In both areas, the United States and France had to cope with rising nationalism.

After finishing my graduate studies at Harvard in 1950, I received two job offers—one to work at the Central Intelligence Agency and one to work in Paris with the European headquarters of the Economic Cooperation Administration (ECA) established to carry out the Marshall Plan. Averell Harriman, one of the great figures in American foreign policy, needed someone to go to Paris to work on economic development projects in Europe.

My father convinced me to take the job in Paris. "John, as a human being, you need applause," he said. "When you work for the CIA, you can't get applause. If something works, they will never admit it. If it fails, you might get the blame."

It was wise advice. Over the years, I have worked with hundreds of intelligence people. They cannot share what they do even with their immediate families. They have no way of processing their day-to-day frustrations. Nothing is ever at face value in the world of intelligence. If you don't have the right mindset for living a life of secrecy, you would feel smothered and invisible at times.

The team that Harriman assembled in Paris included some of the leading figures in academic and public service for the next generation. Thomas Schelling, a political scientist whose work in game theory would have a powerful influence on foreign policy theorizing, was there. In 2005, he shared in the Nobel Prize for economics. Also part of the team were Henry Tasca, who later became ambassador to Greece; Arthur Hartman, who later served as assistant secretary of state for European Affairs and ambassador to France and the Soviet Union; and Lincoln Gordon, who left Harvard to serve in the Marshall Plan and later became assistant secretary for Latin America.

The Marshall Plan took shape in an unsettled and polarized period of the Cold War. Originally, the United States offered assistance to the Soviet Union as well as other European nations devastated by the war. But the Soviets immediately opted out, rejecting the very premises of the plan, which for them made sense. George Marshall always spoke bluntly that the goal of the effort was to revive the market economies of the area, and the Soviet Union was in the thick of its most collectivist approach to developing heavy industry and mass agriculture.

The specter of Soviet communism was everywhere—including France, Greece, Italy, and Belgium. Many Europeans, overwhelmed with the task of rebuilding their economies from scratch, found the centralized mobilization of the Soviet model attractive. Some also believed the Soviet rhetoric about the proletarian revolution. Organized labor was strong in Europe, and communist rhetoric about class solidarity was appealing to factory workers in Manchester, dockworkers in Marseilles, and hill farmers in Greece. The coalitions of many European governments included Communist parties. The challenge for the Marshall Plan team was how to provide aid that would revive the economies and the market system.

At Marshall Plan headquarters for Europe in Paris, I worked closely with officials of Greece and Turkey on development programs. These two countries provided a telling window on the problems of postwar Europe. Aid to both nations underscored the connection between military and economic security. Greece was in the middle of a civil war, and Turkey had been friendly to the Nazis during the Second World War. Looking back, many people think of Turkey and Greece as footnotes in the Marshall Plan. But they were among the first nations to get our aid and in many ways the most strategic. Both were teetering politically and economically at the time, and our assistance was critical in helping to keep them in the Western camp.

Turkey did not suffer physical devastation during the war, but its economy had been stretched perilously thin by its military budget. The country had a huge standing army, first to protect itself against foreign aggression and, after the war, against the Soviets. Roughly half of the nation's budget was devoted to the military. Almost a million men served in the military during the war and 600,000 after the war. By providing economic aid, the Marshall Plan aimed to expand the overall economy, enabling Turkey to afford its army and modern military equipment. Much of the aid was for agriculture, but money also went to roads and other infrastructure and to modernization of heavy industry. I worked on the steel mill at Zonguldak, a coal port on the Black Sea, where I concentrated on the modernization of the loading and docking facilities, which dramatically increased the productive capacity of the nearby mines.

We also had a huge ECA mission in Greece, both for economic aid and for military assistance to help the government put an end to the rebellion. I traveled twice to Greece from Paris and worked with the elder statesmen of that country, George Papandreou and Sophocles Venizelos. Both men had been on the political scene since the twenties and thirties. Neither spoke English, but both spoke fluent French and German, a reflection of the power situation in that part of the world in those years. It was easy for me to communicate with them. Today, more than fifty years later, most Greeks speak English. In those days, international tourism was still in its early stages. In my leisure, I had the Acropolis and other monuments of ancient Greece to myself. I witnessed the sun setting into the Aegean Sea from the glorious temple of Sounion, without hundreds of tourists moving around taking photographs.

After working on the Greece and Turkey projects, I was transferred to Brussels, where Robert Murphy was the American ambassador. The highlight of my time in Belgium was my marriage to Martine Duphenieux, a Frenchwoman. The ECA required both Martine and me to get background security checks. It was understandable that the French and American governments would want to check us both out. In one interesting twist of fate, my wife's family and Belgium played a role in reinforcing the Western alliance. In 1965, Charles de Gaulle asked NATO to leave Paris. My wife's family had owned a castle near Mons, Belgium. In World War II, the Germans took it over and used it as headquarters for the Luftwaffe until England bombed and destroyed the castle in January 1945. Because the Germans had built a good airstrip there, Belgians offered the site as the new home of NATO in the late 1960s.

During my posting with the Economic Assistance Mission to Belgium, I witnessed for the first time in my life the temptations of corruption. One of the tasks of my section was to give foreign firms an opportunity to earn hard currency—dollars—by manufacturing items needed by the U.S. military. One item for which the U.S. Navy had put out a tender was an antisubmarine wire net to be used in one of Belgium's deepwater ports. A firm in Flanders won the multimillion-dollar contract. After a few months, an American army officer investigating the contract came to my office and asked questions about my boss. Unbeknownst to me, the man had taken a substantial bribe in return for recommending that the contract be awarded to the Flemish firm constructing the antisubmarine net. It had never occurred to naïve me that somebody would engage in such dishonest behavior. My boss resigned, and I learned a lesson about government contracting. I also noticed a difference between a businessman turned government employee spending only a couple of years working with the government and a public servant who devotes his entire career to serving the nation. Isn't honor more precious than quick material gain obtained at the price of sacrificing one's integrity?

Starting in 1953, I became involved with the beauty and tragedy of one of the world's most exotic places—Southeast Asia. Like so many parts of the prewar European empires, Vietnam, Laos, and Cambodia posed one of the world's fundamental tests after World War II: What was the best way to deal with the colonies spread across the globe? Should colonial powers hold onto their vast holdings, or should they find a way to loosen their grip and provide a smooth transition to independence?

I volunteered to go to French Indochina for the Marshall Plan not long after my marriage in 1952. My fluency in French would help me deal with the people of Vietnam, Laos, and Cambodia since they had been under French domination for most of the twentieth century. My wife, too, was excited about seeing the world outside Europe. Stationed in Saigon—although accredited to all three countries of Indochina—we spent a lot of time in the field, visiting U.S.-financed projects throughout the region.

At the time, the United States had one ambassador for all three countries. Even though the three countries had important differences in culture, they were considered a kind of natural bloc. How the countries differed, and how their political dynamics got wedged into each other, would shape the region for generations.

After World War II countries outside the industrialized world were organized into colonial outposts of Europe's traditional powers—Great Britain, France, Spain, The Netherlands, and Portugal. Independence had come early to Latin America. Through military occupation or economic might, the United States and the European powers maintained control over a number of nations. In Africa, these powers controlled territories that now comprise fifty-four independent countries. In Asia, colonial powers controlled territories that now comprise twelve nations, including among them India, Pakistan, Malaysia, Laos, Cambodia, Vietnam, and Indonesia.

Postwar colonial arrangements were complicated by the beginning of the Cold War, which divided the globe into the first world (industrialized democracies), second world (Communist nations), and third world (developing countries). Issues of all sorts—territorial boundaries, military alliances, economic enterprises, educational systems—got defined by whether a nation or territory was allied with the United States and the West or with the Soviet Union and the communist world. Even when a community had no real stake in the U.S.-U.S.S.R. competition, it was forced to choose sides with far-reaching consequences. French Indochina provides the perfect case in point.

Since the eighteenth century, France had ruled an area known as Indochina in Southeast Asia. After the fall of France to the Nazis in 1940, Japan occupied Indochina in 1941. During the Second

World War, an American major named Petty had been parachuted into Vietnam and was acting as liaison with Ho Chi Minh. In anticipation of Japan's defeat, President Franklin D. Roosevelt casually offered control of the area to Chiang Kai-shek and China, but the Chinese leader declined the offer. He explained to FDR that the area's history and culture differed too much from that of China. After the war, the French regained control, but France remained weakened economically and militarily by years of warfare and occupation. Politically unstable and divided, French leadership was not strong enough or united enough to make the necessary concessions to Ho Chi Minh when he came to Fontainebleau in 1947. Ho wanted to work out a deal whereby France would grant Vietnam independence within the "French Union." There was no deal. Instead, the French brought back as chief of state Bao Dai, the former hereditary chief of Annam who had been living in exile. The French then reestablished three separate nations: Vietnam, Laos, and Cambodia. Perhaps as a "birthday present," France forced Thailand to return to Laos and Cambodia the territory west of the Mekong that Thailand had annexed during the Japanese occupation of French Indochina. France achieved this restitution by opposing Thailand's entry into the United Nations until the land had been returned.

France's return to Indochina created a nationalist revolution in Vietnam. Like Mao before him and Castro and Che after him, Ho used his charisma and outsider status to rally the people to his cause. The logic of insurgent warfare—developed during the American Revolution, when the military might of the British was vastly superior to that of the Americans—lies in the differential costs of warfare. Insurgents are willing to pay a higher price for victory because they have a higher emotional and ideological stake in victory. Occupiers and status-quo powers—accustomed to the comforts of dominance—feel the sting of financial and manpower losses more acutely. As a result, insurgents are often willing to stay in a fight for a very long time and thereby win a war of attrition.

I met Prince Norodom Sihanouk of Cambodia in 1953, and we eventually became friends, socializing at his palace and traveling together around Cambodia. From the early 1940s into the twenty-first century, Sihanouk would play a central role in the politics of Cambodia.

Because of his dazzling personality, Sihanouk became the very embodiment of the Cambodian people. He was a beloved figure with a unique kind of charisma—a playboy who also had the calm essence of a Buddhist, and a devoted nationalist who also played practical politics on all levels. He was faithful to the simple peasants of his country, but he also cut a figure on the national and international stage, spending years in France.

Sihanouk was a pleasant-looking man, with a round face and jet-black hair. He looked approachable and went out of his way to meet ordinary Cambodians, dropping by small rural communities without advance notice and speaking regularly on radio broadcasts. From his earliest days in public life, Sihanouk moved back and forth among his different personas—Francophile, playboy, jazz musician, film producer and actor, friend of America and friend of China, steadfast neutralist, and friend and foe of the communist Khmer Rouge insurgency. He could be soft and gentle, bombastic and angry, playful and creative, resentful and intransigent, ordinary and humane, superior and aloof.

Whatever Sihanouk's inscrutability, I always considered him the greatest hope for Cambodia to find peace and security in our lifetime. Above all else, he had guts. He knew that history was a long process and that his fortunes would experience countless ebbs and flows. The Buddhists have a sense of timelessness, an understanding that the events of history have their own force and that the best thing people can do is to be ready to act when opportunities present themselves. Sihanouk knew that he was a small actor and that Cambodia was a bit player in world affairs. But he also knew that if he asserted himself in the right way, he could turn history to his nation's favor. If superpowers were to turn Cambodia into a staging area for their global competition, Cambodia could be devastated. But if he could steer a neutral course, the simple agrarian nation could flourish.

In 1954, Sihanouk went to Bangkok and told the French he would not return home unless it declared Cambodia an independent nation. The French capitulated. At the Geneva Conference of 1954, Sihanouk refused to acknowledge the existence of the Khmer Rouge, the Communist resistance movement based in the Cambodian countryside. In the same conference, Vietnam acknowledged the existence of the Viet Minh and Laos acknowledged the Pathet Lao. Sihanouk had the guts to stand up for his country when others were treating old colonies like small pawns on a chessboard.

Cambodia was a slow, languid country, where people lived simple but peaceful lives. If you've ever seen the classic film *Lost Horizon*, you get a good idea of the nation's peacefulness and enchantment. Cambodia was a country of smiles, with a small class of wealthy and educated people, a large group of peasants who had enough to eat, and no pressing problems. There was no military insurgency in those days. The Cambodians were a happy people, protected by the French from Thailand in the west and Vietnam in the east. Cambodia's challenge was to find some way to modernize without upending centuries of traditions.

When we talked about topics other than movies and music, Sihanouk impressed me with his ideas about neutrality. The Cold War was a bitter reality around the world, but Sihanouk insisted that nations like Cambodia did not need to accept the Dulles dictum that either you're with the Americans or you're with the Soviets. Within a decade, Cambodia would become a "sideshow" to the central conflict of Vietnam. The nation of smiles would be turned into a nation of war, terror, and murder. But for the time being, life in this ancient civilization was peaceable and kind.

Vietnam was another matter. People sometimes forget the origins of American involvement in Vietnam. By understanding how we got there—the logic of our involvement, the decisions made and not made, the strategic choices we faced—we can better understand the choices American foreign policy makers face in other hot spots around the globe.

Actually, calling Vietnam a hot spot is not exactly accurate. It was as hot as we—and other international powers, like the Soviet Union and China—made it. Leaders as varied as Franklin Roosevelt and Harry Truman, Dwight Eisenhower and John Kennedy, Winston Churchill and Charles De Gaulle have stated that Vietnam was a place where the world could easily have avoided conflict and freed time and resources to engage real problems. But for various reasons, we chose to make a big deal out of Vietnam.

The origins of the modern Vietnam tragedy can be found in the humiliation of France during World War II. After France was liberated from the Nazis, Western leaders sought a way to bring France back to full strength as a political and economic power. One symbolic way to elevate France's stature was to let France work out its own future relations with its colonial empire. But French governments of the postwar Fourth Republic were too weak to offer meaningful independence to their possessions in Indochina. No single French leader of any political party had the support in the French National Assembly to make the kind of offer to the Vietnamese that Ho Chi Minh could accept. When Ho Chi Minh returned to the jungle and the French reinstated Emperor Bao Dai, the Soviets and Chinese began arming Ho's movement. In 1950, the United States and other countries recognized Vietnam, Laos, and Cambodia as three countries under the aegis of the French Union. Soon, even as France was operating as the lead power in the region, the United States was providing it hundreds of millions of dollars in military and economic support. By 1954, the United States was paying 80 percent of France's bill for maintaining its rule in Vietnam.

That would end, though. On May 7, 1954, the French suffered a catastrophic defeat at Dien Bien Phu and soon thereafter quit the region.

Dien Bien Phu was a village in the northwestern Vietnamese highlands, near the Chinese and Laotian borders. The French had gathered their military strength at a ten-mile-long bowl. The goal was to draw Viet Minh guerillas and regular troops to the enclave, and then achieve a decisive victory by cutting them off from their supply routes. By positioning troops along the lip of the bowl, the French thought they would be able to attack any attacking enemies. But the central position of the French army was at the bottom of the bowl, which meant that they would be trapped and exposed to fire if the enemy got control of the high ground, which they did. When the French troops surrendered on May 7, 1954, the French had lost 2,200 men, and the rebels 8,000. But it was the end to the war. Soon after their defeat, the French announced that they would leave Southeast Asia.

At the Geneva Conference in 1954, France agreed to withdraw from its colonies in Southeast Asia. The Geneva Accord divided Vietnam into North Vietnam and South Vietnam, with the promise of uniting the two regions into one nation and holding elections to select a government. The accord also provided for a limited time the free movement of people between the two regimes. The large Catholic community in Vietnam used the brief opportunity to leave North Vietnam to come to South Vietnam, where religious freedom prevailed. The United States refused to sign the Geneva Accord but instead adopted South Vietnam as the best hope for promoting democracy and averting a Communist takeover of all Southeast Asia.

Under the so-called "domino theory," if one nation fell to Communism, nearby states would quickly fall in succession. To prevent a broad takeover by Communists, the United States and its allies had to prevent any single nation from going Communist. For its part, France decided that holding onto colonial outposts in Asia was no longer worth it. With its loss at Dien Bien Phu, France understood that the stubbornness of the Vietnamese nationalists simply did not allow a continued colonial presence.

Over the years, I have come to understand that the way a colonial power leaves its outpost, the way it works with the forces of independence and nationalism, does much to determine the success of the new nation. Once they accepted that their destiny no longer lay in Vietnam, the French developed a constructive approach to getting out. They worked with the Vietnamese to make sure that all of their Vietnamese friends got safely out of the north, if possible with their property and dignity intact. They offered assistance to the new leaders in the south, holding out the prospect of a future as allies. And they left not as a defeated power, but as a power wise enough to understand the new realities of global politics.

The United States, committed to a Cold War view of the political balance of power across the world, could not accept leaving Indochina alone to possibly fall to the communists.

I left Saigon in 1956. After home leave I was assigned as political officer to Vientiane, capital of Laos, where I served for two years—1956–1958. My adventures there at that period of my career are combined with my second tour in Laos, in the early 1970s, in a separate chapter.

Colonial Turns   35

In March 1959, I was among the first group of American diplomats to open posts in Africa. The State Department's aim in sending us to Africa was to have an American diplomatic presence in place as the various territories and colonies became independent. My assignment was to help manage the transition to independence of two French-controlled territories: Togo and Mali. These two West African states, though with different cultures and histories, were both in the process of breaking away from their French masters and building their own political, economic, and social destinies.

Traveling to Togo, I routed myself via Senegal, Liberia, the Ivory Coast, and Ghana. These stopovers were to enable me to better understand the region and learn what I might do in Togo to avoid mistakes made elsewhere, or to imitate success in other parts of West Africa. In Liberia, I was surprised to see only one paved road from the capital, Monrovia, leading upcountry. That one road led to the Firestone plantation and was probably financed by the plantation owners.

Most of us selected for this job were either bachelors or left their wives and children at home until living conditions permitted families to join us. My wife and our children came to Togo six months after my arrival.

All the diplomatic "pioneers" in Africa had a lot of leeway to act on our own; our supervisors were usually far away in different countries or even on different continents. We had to use common sense and good judgment to buy or lease buildings for offices or for housing the American staff that would surely arrive with time. Hiring of local employees to staff the various sections of the post was another urgent duty. Also important was establishing a direct relationship with African leaders who would head the new nations, or with personalities who would be in opposition to the African "George Washingtons" once independence was proclaimed. Cultivating these contacts had to be accomplished while maintaining a good relationship with the colonial masters who still held the reins.

For the African posts I was asked to open, the prerequisite qualifications were to be able to speak and write French fluently and to be sufficiently versatile to operate in a country with no Americans present to give advice or guidance on how to get things done. The only Americans living in Togo were some Christian missionaries upcountry. There were no American business people, no banks, no oil or mining prospectors, no teachers, no representatives of NGOs like CARE or World Vision. For most of us rather young Foreign Service officers, opening posts in Africa was an exhilarating experience. We were eager to learn about Africa, its culture, its different races and traditions, and above all, its needs. We also realized we were forerunners of a new generation of American diplomats working with a continent that had not been involved in foreign affairs for a couple of hundred years.

The colonial division of Africa into separate possessions resulted primarily from the Berlin Conference of 1884–85, when fourteen European countries gathered at the invitation of German Chancellor Otto von Bismarck. At the time, Europe's control of the continent was mostly limited to coastal areas. When the conference started that November, some 80 percent of Africa remained under control of indigenous peoples. More than 1,000 tribes ruled the continent according to the traditions and systems native to the continent. They warred and made peace, and although not prosperous by Western standards, they fed their people and maintained some social and economic stability.

As a result of the Berlin conference—and two more decades of negotiations among the conference participants—by 1914 Africa was divided into fifty colonies, territories, and nations. England and France dominated the continent. Britain took control of the lands stretching from Egypt in the northeast of the continent down to South Africa. France dominated western Africa. Belgium took over the Congo in the center of Africa; Portugal took Mozambique in the east and Angola in the west; and Italy later took Somalia and Ethiopia. The problems, though, were many, most notably that the new nations did not coincide with tribal boundaries and realities. Tribes were often split between different countries, and incompatible tribes were put together under one nation's control. Too often, the colonial powers exploited the colonies for their material resources while neglecting to educate the people or allow them meaningful participation in their own rule.

The colonial legacy in Africa varied. The French built universities and trained military officers. The British did a good job creating a civil service and judicial system. The Belgians did nothing, concentrating only on exploiting a huge country with natural resources. The Portuguese intermarried, with one result being a general absence of racial prejudice. Some colonial powers provided infrastructure—roads, medical facilities, schools, etc.

But by the end of World War II, powerful movements for independence had taken hold across the continent. In 1958, Charles de Gaulle offered a deal to France's colonies: opt for independence with no aid or become part of the "French Community" and get economic and military aid. Guinea alone chose independence, and the French pulled out, taking all the assets they could and leaving the nation to fend for itself.

The independence movements of Africa had their share of prejudices and delusions, but for the most part the people in these lands simply wanted to have control of their own governments, schools, businesses, religions, and cultural life. Even if they did not live as well materially, Africans wanted to control their own destinies. "We would rather be poor in freedom than rich in slavery," Sékou Touré told de Gaulle. As for fear of the Soviet empire, many Africans found the idea perplexing after years of domination by Western powers. "Why should I fear what you call Russian imperialism? We in Africa have had the experience of French colonialism, of British colonialism, or Belgian and Portuguese colonialism," said one Guinean leader. "We have never experienced Russian colonialism or seen evidence of Russian imperialism. We can worry about Russia later."

Guinea turned to the Soviets for assistance and as a model for development. The Guinea experience introduced the Cold War into Africa. Rather than focusing exclusively on how to provide the emerging nations with the political and economic infrastructure they needed to join the community of nations, the United States got caught up in superpower competition.

I always thought the best way to deal with former colonial powers was to work with the nations having a stake in the old colonies and create joint development initiatives. If the French played a prominent role in the colony, why not see what the French were willing to contribute to the new nation? The United States did not have to do everything by itself. It mattered little who got the credit. If everyone contributed to a solution, there would be enough benefits for all parties. The main thing should be to help these new nations develop economically and socially as long as they also wanted to develop our values of democracy, free enterprise, cultural diversity, individual and property rights, and human rights. We wanted countries that would continue to look to the West, whether it was the British or the French or the Americans.

When I got the assignment to set up the American consulate in Togo, I told my mother I was going to Lomé. She said, "Wonderful! I've always loved Rome!"

I said, "No, Mutti, *Lomé*!"

"Where is Lomé?"

"It's near Upper Volta."

She said, "Hmm. Where is Lower Volta?"

When I went to Togo in March of 1959 to set up an American consulate, the area was still a United Nations Trust Territory under French administration. French officials with Togolese understudies held most of the top positions. My first call was on the French governor, whose office looked like a castle on the Rhine in Germany. The building had in fact been built by the German colonial administration prior to 1914, when Togo was a German colony. My position was consul, and the American Consulate in Togo was under the direct jurisdiction of the American Embassy in Paris.

My boss was the American ambassador to France, Amory Houghton, whom I met in Paris. He gave me a codebook, $5,000, and a flag the size appropriate to put on a car. I would only use the codebook if I thought I needed to send an urgent confidential message to Paris, Washington, or Accra, but that was unlikely—it was kind of like the bullet the fictional Mayberry deputy sheriff Barney Fife kept in his front pocket. I was thrilled to be working on my own, thousands of miles away from my boss. But this lasted only a few months, until an older, more senior colleague arrived as my resident boss.

Lomé was a small town. While still looking for the town, I asked directions from the car and was told I was there. On March 22, I went to the post office and registered the telegraphic address for public telegrams for the consulate. When I reached the hotel in Lomé and asked how to get into town, the concierge replied, "Oh, but Monsieur, we're in town now!" The hotel was the equivalent of an old-style motor lodge that had not been maintained for many years. Mosquitoes were everywhere, and the mosquito net in my room did not help much. No air conditioning. No private toilet. I complained to the management, but there was no alternative. A year later a modern hotel was built to house the guests for the independence ceremonies.

Sylvanus Olympio was being groomed to become president after independence. In the meantime, he was the acting prime minister under the French government. My first order of business was to buy a building that could serve as a consulate and a residence for me, and then look for other buildings for the additional officers who would staff the U.S. Consulate. Olympio's brother, a contractor, helped me. He first found a house on the ocean to rent, with an option to buy, and fixed it up as a residence within a few months. We then went looking for a building that would serve as a consulate and perhaps later as an embassy. We found a house for the consulate next to Sylvanus Olympio's residence. It was simple, like one of the houses in my neighborhood in Kansas City. Made of stone and brick, the one-story house had four rooms altogether. That was good enough for me to get back to work.

While Togo remained a United Nations trusteeship, Prime Minister Olympio worked under the leadership of a French governor. Olympio was a smart man, schooled in Western universities and the world of business. He attended a German school in Togo, then the London School of Economics, followed by the Sorbonne in Paris. He served on the board of directors of the United Africa Company, a British firm. Olympio's family was open, native, and educated. Olympio himself had a great presence. He was a distinguished-looking man in his fifties, grey haired, somewhat reserved, always well groomed, at ease in three major European languages—English, French, and German. His tribal affiliation was Ewe, the major African tribe in the coastal area of Togo and eastern Ghana. Olympio was well known at the United Nations, where he had strong support to lead Togo after the U.N. trusteeship came to an end.

Olympio and I discussed what the United States could do to help in the development of the country. We agreed that we should work closely with French officials stationed in the country. Our goal was not to pretend that the colonial era had not existed but to work with anyone who could help to build a new nation. Togo needed as much cooperation as it could get. After independence, a major American investment by W. R. Grace & Co. in potash and potassium created a major export commodity. The Germans modernized the port of Lomé. But the French remained the largest provider of assistance to the public sector and private investment.

So much of foreign policy is based on the destructive approach of divide and rule. I never saw any reason to cut someone else out of the picture if they did no harm to American interests—and especially if we could work with them constructively. If the French want to be part of the process, building schools or hospitals, or the Germans want to build a port, so much the better.

As we moved to independence—the formal ceremony was to take place in April 1960—the French government sent a man named the Baron de Testa as the diplomatic advisor to the president of Togo. But de Testa was perhaps the wrong person for the job. Olympio and de Testa did not get along. De Testa may not have taken into account that Olympio was going to be the head of an independent nation and would no longer be under colonial tutelage. In any case, Olympio asked the French government to replace de Testa with another advisor.

Awaiting the arrival of a different French official, Olympio wrote to my boss at the State Department, Christian Herter, asking if I could help him organize the independence ceremony for the new nation of Togo. Above all, Olympio wanted my help in setting up Togo's own Foreign Office. Secretary Herter agreed to put me at the disposal of the Togolese president for a limited period of time.

Attorney General William P. Rogers represented the United States at the colorful independence ceremony. Tribal chieftains in their native robes swore allegiance to the new president of Togo. Young maidens in African dress entertained the guests from around the world by dancing traditional dances to African music. Olympio spoke separately to every foreign delegation attending the ceremony, explaining how foreign lands could help Togo in its new role as an independent state.

After independence, I stayed on to set up the Togolese Foreign Office. This entailed registering incoming and outgoing mail, setting up a filing system, organizing the office and the new Togolese staff according to geographic areas, briefing newly assigned Togolese diplomatic officials on the country of their future accreditation, and preparing briefing papers for Olympio for meeting with newly accredited foreign diplomats. Above all, I had to prepare draft replies to the mountains of mail received on the occasion of Togo's accession to independence. As the transfer of power agreement between France and Togo provided that the official language of written communication would be French, all my draft letters had to be in that language. But these letters of reply by Olympio were not mere courtesy letters. They implied recognition of the nations initiating the correspondence, willingness to trade and accept investment from them, willingness to accredit foreign ambassadors or send Togolese diplomats abroad, establish consulates, and more. In my work with President Olympio, I tried to ascertain his attitude on specific issues before I submitted the draft, while at the same time trying to protect American interests.

At one time, I had to navigate my way through the politics of the communist People's Republic of China (PRC) on the mainland and the nationalist Republic of China on Taiwan. At the time, the United States did not recognize mainland China but only Taiwan, populated largely by the people who had fled the mainland under Chiang Kai-shek during the 1949 revolution. Communist China, however, claimed that Taiwan was legally part of its regime. Olympio got letters from leaders in both China and Taiwan, both saying that they would like to recognize Togo and set up missions in the new nation. I put the letter from Taiwan on top of the mail pile so Olympio's positive response to Taiwan would be sent out first. When the PRC found out, it retracted its invitation for relations.

Not all of the correspondence was that substantive. But official protocol had to be observed in every letter. I drafted the letters, my wife corrected my French as needed, the secretaries of the Togolese Foreign Office typed them, and then Olympio signed them. At first, Olympio refused to address the letter to the queen of England with the salutation of "Madame," but I showed him the protocol book and he soon agreed.

The letter to the pope was stickier. In Africa, the Catholic Church's laws on sexual relations were modified to allow polygamy, which was an old custom. Polygamists were allowed to go to church but could not take communion. Those who kept only one wife could. According to the protocol book, whether you could take communion determined how you could address the Pope. I did not feel comfortable asking Olympio whether he was a polygamist, so I asked him, "Mr. President, do you take communion when you go to church?"

He said, "Yes, of course I do." I knew by this that he wasn't a polygamist and I could write the letter so that Olympio could sign it, "Your devoted son."

Martine and I traveled widely when we were stationed in Togo. Since we departed from the west coast of Africa, the point of embarkation of slaves sold to North and South America, I was interested in exploring the complexities of the African slave trade, which so harmed and shaped the culture and economic life of the continent. One day we visited the house of a village chieftain on the coast of Dahomey, now known as Benin. His name, De Santos, indicated that he was of African/Brazilian extraction. He lived in a substantial Western-style house with elegant chandeliers, mirrors, and heavy wooden furniture. He explained to Martine and me that his family had been in the slave trade in the nineteenth century and opened files that recorded the numbers of Africans sold, the sex, age, and state of health of each captive, the price obtained, and the unfortunate person's destination. He also showed us the chandelier and large framed mirror his forebears had received as presents from the slave traders in recognition of their services. De Santos said that in his area most of the merchants buying slaves had been Portuguese and that the destination of those sold into slavery was mostly Brazil. He also explained that certain rituals and ceremonies still celebrated in Brazil by Brazilians of African descent are the very same as those performed some 150 years ago in the interior of West Africa. Some reminders of that sinister trade remain standing in the form of castles in Ghana and on the coast between Togo and Benin, which served as holding centers for the captives' embarkation.

In March 1960 I was assigned as Principal Officer in Bamako, French Sudan. At thirty-four years of age, I had my own post. The French Sudan was part of a federation with Senegal, which had its capital in Dakar. Hence I was heading a consulate under the jurisdiction of the American ambassador in Dakar. In that year African nationalism and the drive for self-determination and a separate identity was exploding not only against former colonial powers but even within newly independent African nations that had already received their freedom. This was the case with Senegal, where the eastern part of the federation that had formally been known as the French Sudan broke away and proclaimed its independence as the state of Mali. The name goes back to the middle ages. It is best known as the land of Timbuktu.

By the time I arrived in Bamako, the split-up of the federation had been consummated. Modibo Keita was declared president of the Mali Republic. I went to call on him. The American government followed suit by declaring the post of Bamako directly linked to Washington. All links between the American Consulate in Bamako and the American Embassy in Senegal were severed. My boss was now an official in the Department of State in Washington, and I received letters of credence as chargé d'affaires *à pieds*. This meant that I was chief of mission. For the foreseeable future Bamako would not have a resident U.S. ambassador, and I was "in charge."

Keita looked exactly like an Ohio State basketball champion. He was tall—six feet three inches—and was an excellent athlete. In fact, one of the ways we relaxed and got to know each other was to play volleyball with his staff and anyone else who happened to be around. Keita was a smart, well-educated man. He had been at one point in his career a member of the French government.

One of the highlights of my time as a chargé d'affaires was meeting the great French existentialist author André Malraux, who was serving as minister of culture for France. Malraux was in town to meet with Keita and steer him away from the Soviets.

Mali had remained in the West African French Franc Zone, making its currency convertible. Then the revolutionary shadow of Sékou Touré, president of Guinea, began to fall on Mali. Modibo Keita was flirting with the idea of establishing Mali's own currency, the Malian franc. Next he asked the French military forces to leave Mali. The Soviet mission in Bamako was quite popular among Mali politicians, and the Soviets offered aid and advisers from Guinea. Mali showed its political leanings by holding torchlight protest marches at night, objecting to the killing of Patrice Lumumba in the Congo. The Malians made it clear at the time that they thought foul play was involved in Lumumba's death and that the West was responsible. They were beginning to question their ties to the former colonial power—discussing whether to leave the West African French Franc Zone and discontinue membership in the French Union.

When I met Malraux in Bamako in the early morning hours at the airport, he thanked me for meeting his plane and revealed the reason for his coming to Mali. "We have to try to keep the Malians in the West African French Franc Zone. We don't want to repeat Guinea and be overrun by Soviet advisers and Soviet ideology in Mali." Malraux also stressed the "strategic location" of Mali. I had never thought of Mali in those terms. South of Algeria, Mali lies north of the Ivory Coast and Guinea, which both give access to the Atlantic Ocean. It is on the ancient trade route between Arab North Africa and the black tribes in West Africa. Malraux urged that the United States keep the French informed to avoid any duplication of effort.

Shortly thereafter, I went to see President Keita. He said he would like to establish his own currency. Instead of giving a negative or positive response, I took a piece of paper and drew up a balance sheet, with credits and debits on opposite sides. I showed what items to put under assets and what to list under debits in a Central Bank balance sheet. I explained that you could not just go down into the vault of the Central Bank and take banknotes as if you had earned them. We discussed the need for drawing up a national budget and the advantages of a convertible currency.

As a representative of the United States, I always wanted to cooperate with other nations—not only the host nation, but also other Western nations in the area. When Keita asked the United States to provide training for paratroopers, I agreed, but wanted first to check in with the French. At every step of the way, I kept the French informed. We signed military and economic aid agreements with Mali in 1961.

Like the leaders of many newly independent nations, Keita wanted all the visible trappings of nationhood. He wanted a national airline—Air Mali—but there just wasn't much of a market for business people or tourists to or from Mali. It made no sense.

Keita also wanted a national currency. But Mali was much better off tied to an existing international currency like the franc. If there's anything a new country like Mali needs, it's the stability that the franc or other international currency can offer.

Keita was staunchly nationalistic. He was attracted to simply saying *"Non"* to de Gaulle, but he also understood that he was part of a larger system. Ultimately, Keita's better judgment prevailed. When the French left Mali, Keita and the French authorities arranged for a ceremonial exit. General Charles, head of the French colonial forces in Mali, led his troops in a formal parade, after which they departed in style. Mali stayed in the West African French Franc Zone and remained strongly pro-Western.

While in Mali I spent a memorable twenty-four hours with one of the great post–World War II political personalities: Marshal Josip Broz Tito, president of Yugoslavia. Tito came to Mali with the laurels of a Marxist war hero who had succeeded in staying out of the Soviet orbit, had become one of the leaders of the nonaligned movement, and had kept together Yugoslavia's different ethnic and religious nations. Moreover, Yugoslavia was developing rapidly economically and socially while maintaining a number of individual freedoms such as foreign travel, religious tolerance, and peace. Strong-willed, nationalistic leaders attracted new African nations emerging from colonialism, and Tito fit that description.

Modibo Keita knew that I had worked with the Marshall Plan, in which Yugoslavia participated, and that the United States had good relations with Yugoslavia. He therefore asked me to accompany Tito during his brief visit to the various events that had been laid on for him. Tito's interpreter spoke French and German, making it easy for us to communicate. In addition, the attractive Yugoslav ambassador to Mali, a Muslim lady from Bosnia-Herzegovina, helped in showing Tito around.

What was Tito like? Short and stocky, he exuded physical power. In his questions he showed interest in the technical aspects of development projects in Mali. He was at ease with Africans and asked them how they saw their future. He asked to see wild animals roaming freely and, as a lover of hunting, probably regretted he could not bring back a trophy. He was a decidedly strong, outgoing personality. The Malians saw Tito as a political leader interested in helping the underprivileged, one who succeeded in foreign affairs by not transgressing others' spheres of influence but without sacrificing his nationalistic ambitions.

In conclusion, I would say that the timely, energetic U.S. presence prevented Mali from going communist, as Guinea had. Mali remained in the French Franc Zone, a part of West Africa, and maintained close links to the West. The United States had put its best foot forward in Mali, while the Communist countries were unable to subvert it or win it away from the path of democracy. Today, Mali remains one of the more open, tolerant societies in Africa.

By the time I returned to Washington to spend a few years at the State Department, I had received a good education on the new realities of global politics. I had met with some of the most compelling figures in the emerging world—from Olympio and Modibo Keita in Africa to Tito and André Malraux in Europe, to leading figures in American foreign policy. I saw the hope of newly independent nations and the new realism of old powers. I saw the possibility for peace and coexistence in places like Cambodia and Laos, but I also noted the preference of some elements in America for a policy of dividing the world into friend and foe, into those who are "for us" and those who are "against us." Why not, I thought, give more emphasis to a new, flexible approach that might prevent war and destruction?

4
Quagmire

In the early days of 1967, as the United States increased its bombing raids over North Vietnam, opposition to the war increased across America. But most people still supported President Lyndon Johnson's war efforts. Few questioned the domino theory, which held that the loss of one nation to communism would lead to a wave of losses across Asia, Africa, Latin America, and even Europe. But despite the consensus on the general themes of the Cold War, Americans grew uneasy about the scale of death in Southeast Asia.

And 1968 was a presidential election year. One of the leading contenders for the presidency on the Democratic side was Robert F. Kennedy. Now a senator from New York, Kennedy had made a major U-turn since his days as a hawk in the administration of his brother, John F. Kennedy. The senator was still searching for a meaningful purpose in the years following President Kennedy's assassination. He had a visceral mistrust of President Lyndon B. Johnson, whom he considered something of a usurper, and Johnson returned the mistrust. Even more important, Bobby Kennedy believed that American politics had taken dangerous turns in recent years. The assassination was just one symptom. So were the riots in the cities, the murders of Martin Luther King Jr. and Malcolm X, the growing racial tension that extended from the segregationist south to the northern cities and suburbs, the plight of migrant workers in the fields of California, and the scourge of drugs on campuses and on the streets.

And what seemed like an unwinnable war in Vietnam. In the previous year, Kennedy had made plans to tour the major capitals of Europe to size up the global issues facing America. One of his stops was Paris, where I would play a role.

Working with Bob Kennedy was a real education for me. He was smart, quick, and creative. On his own time, he acted like a playboy—but that was his business. What mattered for his work as a politician was that he had a 360-degree view of the world. He could see everything going on around him, even when just visiting a place for a few days.

When Kennedy arrived in Paris in late January 1967, France was mourning the death of Marshal Alphonse Juin, one of the great French military leaders of World War II. Kennedy did not know much about him, but instantly decided to make a public appearance at Les Invalides, the seventeenth-century building housing Napoleon's tomb, where Juin's body lay in state. Kennedy ordered a giant wreath to bring to Juin's bier, with a card reading "From the Kennedys." I accompanied him to Les Invalides, carrying the wreath. As we arrived at the casket, draped with the French flag, I gave Kennedy the wreath and he knelt in prayer, lightly crying. The act was political, dramatic, and compassionate, all at the same time. Television cameras captured the moment as Kennedy laid the wreath. The gesture not only elevated Kennedy in the eyes of the French, but also solidified his place as the keeper of the Kennedy name and strengthened the Kennedy family's mystical bond with people all over the world.

Kennedy arrived in Paris shortly after a leftist journalist in Australia had published an interview with North Vietnamese Foreign Minister Nguyen Duy Trinh. That interview opened new possibilities for a negotiated solution just at the moment that the United States and South Vietnam were wearying of the war.

For years, the two warring sides had shown no inclination to end the fighting through negotiations. Ho Chi Minh's mission was to defeat South Vietnam and unite the two states into a single communist nation. And the United States, deep into the Cold War, was unwilling to concede the possibility that South Vietnam would be absorbed by communist North Vietnam. The United States continued to pound North Vietnam with bombs—before the war ended, it would drop more tonnage on Vietnam than did all combatants in World War II—but the North persevered and even gained ground through guerrilla warfare. The Ho Chi Minh Trail, which twisted and turned through 12,000 miles of jungle, provided a supply route

Quagmire   49

into South Vietnam and a sanctuary from American bombs. As much as the United States wanted to see Vietnam as two distinct systems and cultures, the Viet Cong had thoroughly infiltrated the South—and the neighboring countries of Laos and Cambodia.

But Trinh said "if the bombings of the North cease completely, good and favorable conditions will be created for talks."

Since arriving in Paris in 1965, I had developed a close working relationship with Etienne Manac'h, head of the Asia Division of the French Foreign Office, who knew Indochina intimately. Manac'h represented the best of postcolonial France. He cared about the people of former colonies of Asia and wanted to do something to end the war that was ravaging the cities and the countryside. We talked frequently about Vietnam's culture, its politics, and the war. Manac'h believed that the war had little to do with the spread of communism across the globe, but rather with the desire for self-rule. It was a nationalist movement. The North Vietnamese were fighting for their own land, for their own way of life. The United States was an outsider without a tangible stake in Vietnam's well-being. The Vietnamese would fight forever. The United States, like France before it, had limits.

Manac'h read the interview with Trinh and thought it represented a major breakthrough. If the United States seized the opportunity early enough, it could broker an end to the war that was at that stage much less damaging than Dien Bien Phu had been for the French. He asked Mai Van Bo, North Vietnam's top diplomat in Paris, whether the interview was intended as a major overture to find a way to start negotiations with a view ending the war. Bo said it was.

Manac'h wanted to make sure the message got through to the United States as dramatically as possible. Thus when Kennedy arrived at the French Foreign Office in Paris, Manac'h was determined to convey the news to him. At their meeting, his friend William Van den Heuvel accompanied Kennedy, and I served as an interpreter and note-taker. Manac'h told Kennedy that the Trinh statement could create the opening for a negotiation to end the war. I was not sure Kennedy grasped what Manac'h was telling him, so I interrupted. Does this mean, I asked, that the North Vietnamese are willing to sit down and find a way to negotiate an end to the war? Yes, Manac'h said, absolutely.

I rushed back to the Embassy to write a top-secret cable to send to Washington on Kennedy's conversation with Manac'h. It was obvious that the war in Vietnam was not going well and could get worse, despite what the generals and the president and the hawks were saying. And now here was a way out—an honorable way out.

What I did not know was that *Newsweek* would obtain a copy of one of the cables I sent and report the overture in its next issue, and that the *New York Times* would put the breakthrough on the front page. Douglas MacArthur II, the assistant secretary of state for legislative affairs, had leaked the documents in an effort to undercut any movement toward peace talks. By leaking the sensitive information, MacArthur drove the Johnson administration into retreat, if it was ever inclined to pursue peace talks in the first place. If Robert Kennedy was *for* something, Lyndon Johnson was going to be against it.

The *Times* article reflected the period's confusion about how to get meaningful negotiations going: "By now, all sides agree that what the New York Senator heard from a French official in Paris was not a 'peace signal' from Hanoi, as reported in N*ewsweek* magazine a week ago, but rather a French official's appraisal of what Hanoi might be willing to do if the United States stopped bombing North Vietnam."

This dismissal of a real proposal—peace talks for a bombing halt—was mistaken. It was a genuine overture, something that could have worked. Peace only has a chance when two sides decide to give in a little to get something in return. Etienne Manac'h was not dreaming, or making anything up. He had direct confirmation that the North Vietnamese were willing to negotiate an end to the war. Who knows where those negotiations might have gone without such a strong denunciation? Perhaps, in the best of all possible worlds, it might have led to a reaffirmation of the Geneva Accord of 1954, a united Vietnam, and a mandate for an open and fair election. Probably not, but you never know. But because of domestic politics—the bitter rivalry between LBJ and RFK—the possibilities were scotched before they had a chance to develop.

And Lyndon Johnson was furious at me. When he read the *Times* article—which reported that I accompanied Kennedy to the meeting with Manac'h—the president exploded. "Who is John Dean?" he bellowed. "Fire him!"

I learned a couple of valuable lessons from that episode. First, do not always trust people on your own side—in this case, the administration for which I was working. Because of presidential politics, a State Department official went public with a sensitive diplomatic initiative before the initiative was ready to be revealed.

Second, make sure you have evidence of your own role in complex issues. If people are willing to subvert constructive work, and they are, you need to make sure they cannot lie about it as well. At that point in my career, I decided to keep copies of all memos and cables that I produced. If I was going to take risks for peace, which is what being a diplomat is all about, I needed to make sure that people with a stake in the status quo could not subvert my efforts without my being able to respond effectively.

More than one year later, in May 1968, as the election drew near, the peace talks got under way in Paris.

Some of the best people in the American foreign policy establishment—Averell Harriman, Cyrus Vance, Philip Habib, and, among the younger people, John Negroponte and Richard Holbrooke—worked around the clock to find ways to slow down and halt the war, and eventually find a formula by which North and South Vietnam could coexist. Because we had never had sustained negotiations, these talks were more exploratory than anything else. You might call them negotiations for negotiations. We did not feel we could formally offer to halt the bombing, because we had no assurances of how the North would respond—and we had not figured out how the South would participate in the talks as a separate party. At that stage, the South Vietnamese sat together with the Americans. Even when good things happened in the war, like the lull in fighting in July, we did not know what to make of it. We asked the North Vietnamese whether it was a signal of good intentions, but we never got a clear answer.

As is often the case with negotiations, we spent a lot of time shadow-boxing in Paris. We thought something important might be happening, but we did not know for sure.

In February 1968, Eugene McCarthy, an insurgent antiwar candidate, performed "better than expected" against President Johnson in the New Hampshire Democratic primary. Even though LBJ had won the primary—as a write-in candidate—the media interpreted McCarthy's showing as decisive proof that the president was finished. In a dramatic televised speech, Johnson dropped out of the race, telling the nation that he could not run for reelection while conducting the war. He devoted the remainder of his term to seeking a way out of the war. From that point on, the peace talks had the support of the administration. Johnson himself was reluctant to halt American bombing of North Vietnam, and did so only in the waning days of the campaign, when Vice President Hubert Humphrey was conducting a come-from-behind race for the White House.

But the Republican candidate for president, Richard Nixon, was maneuvering to subvert the peace talks. Behind the scenes, Nixon sent emissaries to South Vietnam with a simple message—Don't go too far in the Paris peace talks. You can get a better deal from a Nixon administration than from a Humphrey administration.

Nixon also told voters that he had a "secret plan" to get out of Vietnam with America's honor intact. The plan was really not a plan, just a scheme aimed at scaring the North Vietnamese into negotiating away everything they had fought for decades to achieve. The idea was to threaten to use such awesome force against the Viet Cong, not to mention neighboring countries like Cambodia and Laos, that the North Vietnamese would beg for peace. Henry Kissinger called it the "Madman" theory. Kissinger would pass the word, directly or through intermediaries, that Nixon was an irrational, trigger-happy leader, a madman with whom one could not reason. He-might-even–use-nuclear-weapons was the not-so-subtle subtext of the threat. Better to sue for peace now than face destruction later.

Nixon's aggressive approach and Ho's defiant response did not lend themselves to the kind of negotiations that had begun in Paris. Vietnam would be bogged down in a bloody war until 1975, when the Communists would take over almost all of Indochina and create some of the most repressive regimes anywhere.

When I left France in the autumn of 1969 after four years at the American Embassy, I nonetheless felt I had made a significant contribution to getting a dialogue started between North Vietnam and the United States regarding the future of Vietnam. But my determination to get real negotiations going in Paris between all concerned parties also got me in hot water. One day toward the end of 1968, in one of my conversations with Monsieur Manac'h, I asked quite innocently "Monsieur le Directeur, why don't you help us to extricate ourselves from this situation in Vietnam?" I alluded to my years in Indochina and the fact that the French had been unable to cope with the Vietnamese drive for unification and independence. Now the United States was more and more involved in the quagmire.

After that meeting, Monsieur Manac'h went to see the French foreign minister, Michel Debré, who was close to President De Gaulle, and reported that I had suggested that the French help the United States extricate itself from the Vietnam imbroglio. Later that same evening, Secretary of State Cyrus Vance got a phone call from Debré requesting a meeting. When confronted by Debré with the remarks I had made to Manac'h, Secretary Vance made it very clear that I was not authorized to put forward any ideas to the French authorities and that I had been speaking on my own. I laugh about this incident sometimes, wondering whether the idea of a "brokered solution" would not have been better than what actually happened.

Was there a difference between the Democrats and the Republicans in their approach to the Paris talks with North Vietnam? It was my impression that the first delegation to the Vietnam talks, led by Ambassador Harriman and Secretary Vance, was truly interested in finding a modus vivendi with North Vietnam. After the departure of the Harriman/Vance leadership following the Democrats' defeat at the polls, the Republican delegation to the Vietnam talks, led by Ambassador Henry Cabot Lodge, with the later involvement of Henry Kissinger, was less willing to negotiate with the North Vietnamese and more inclined toward unilateral action. The head of the North Vietnamese delegation, Le Duc Tho, rejected the 1973 Nobel Peace Prize on the grounds that peace was not yet established, but Dr. Kissinger accepted his half of the prize. Perhaps John Negroponte and Richard Holbrooke, who were both part of the American negotiating team for a longer period than I, can throw additional light on this important period of American diplomacy.

In 1970, with the prospects of an enduring peace growing doubtful, I was assigned to Central Vietnam as deputy to the American

Commander of Military Region 1 for CORDS (Civil Operations and Revolutionary[1] Development Support). We had responsibility for the five northernmost provinces of South Vietnam, where the most decisive battles for the independence of South Vietnam were taking place. My headquarters was in Danang. If South Vietnam could hold these regions, it might maintain its independence as a nation. But if the Viet Cong and North Vietnamese were to gain control over the area, the South would have little chance to prevail. As it was, the Viet Cong had already moved into all parts of South Vietnam, as well as Laos and Cambodia.

In my work with CORDS, I had 1,100 civilian advisors and military officers under my command. I started out as the Number Two in the region and then moved up. My mission was to help the South Vietnamese regime to govern and develop a society prosperous and secure enough to resist the North Vietnamese. We worked on a wide range of military, economic, and social issues, helping provide electricity, care of refugees, and security. And we confronted the Viet Cong.

I traveled by helicopter all over the five provinces under my jurisdiction, visiting and helping our advisors in the most remote villages and districts. My goal was to see the region as a whole, not as a series of individual battles. I sent my reports on what I saw, my conclusions on how the military, economic, and social situations evolved in Central Vietnam, to the Commander of U.S. forces in Saigon, which he would then incorporate into his overall assessment of how the war was going.

My service in Danang gave me an invaluable understanding of the American military, which in turn helped me to work with my military colleagues during the rest of my diplomatic career. Serving the U.S. military operation in Vietnam gave me insight and credibility that I could not have gotten any other way. I did not shirk when asked to go. That was my job. When I spoke up for peace later in my career, I could not be dismissed as a fuzzyheaded peacenik. I risked and almost lost my life on more than one occasion. More important, serving with the military gave me a deep, abiding respect for the military. You cannot serve your country without having that kind of understanding.

Soldiers and officers were trying to do a job under very difficult circumstances. Although they sometimes disagreed with

[1] Sometimes spelled out as "Rural" instead of "Revolutionary."

orders they received from politicians, they always did their best. Nobody enjoys war—especially not the military. When you have to write a letter—your husband died a heroic death under such and such circumstances—then you know what war is all about. I was responsible for 1,100 men and they were out in the boonies. My deputy, a full colonel, was killed, and writing a letter to his wife was a wrenching task.

The best way to win the respect of military people is to risk your life and survive to tell the tale. In 1970, I received reports that American tanks were surrounded in Quang Tri province in the northernmost section of South Vietnam. The tanks were returning to the province from Laos, where they had just completed a military operation. As soon as they crossed the border, they were taken by surprise when North Vietnamese troops began to pursue them. When tanks are surrounded and in danger of being wiped out, the instinct for survival impels soldiers to leave their vehicles and make a run for friendly lines, in hopes of saving their lives. And that is just what these soldiers did.

I happened to be in the safe area when the troops came running back. The American brigadier general there ordered the troops to return and bring back their tanks so that the enemy would not take them. The troops responded, in effect: "Up yours, general! You go get the tanks!" The general had failed a basic test of leadership. What he should have said was, "Go with me, men, and we'll take back our tanks." A good leader always shows the way into a dangerous mission. He doesn't just push dangerous tasks onto his soldiers.

At one point in April 1972, Quang Tri Province was completely overrun by the North Vietnamese. In the process, they had surrounded the provincial capital, where American advisers were hunkered down, awaiting rescue. To prevent our advisers being taken prisoner, I decided to fly with my assigned helicopter to Quang Tri City and retrieve as many Americans as I could. I was able to make three or four trips from Danang to Quang Tri City, and each time the helicopter would take seven or eight people out. On my last trip, as we were flying up with U.S. consul Fred Brown, we were shot down over Highway One, about 15 kilometers south of Quang Tri City. Fortunately the rifle shot hit the oil line of the helicopter and not the gas line, or I would not be here to tell the story, because the helicopter would then have exploded. Our helicopter dropped to the ground hard, like a sack of potatoes. Shaken up, we sent a "Mayday" distress call, which prompted another helicopter to fly in, under fire, to our rescue. It picked us up, lifted us out, and flew us to an installation near Hue.

I asked the U.S. military there whether the South Vietnamese could give us some tanks so that we could try to rescue the U.S. advisers for whom I was responsible, but this was no longer feasible. Roughly twenty-four hours later, U.S. Air Force General Hudson was flown to Danang, where he organized the extraction of the remaining fifty Americans, along with South Vietnamese who had been fighting the forces from the North, from the besieged Quang Tri City. After a certain amount of heavy bombing by U.S. planes to keep the enemy down, the helicopter pilots flew in. The entire operation was carried out at night while North Vietnamese tanks were attacking the installation. It was so hot that the pilots were flying in their underwear. The helicopters hovered over the extraction site just long enough for the people to climb aboard. We got everybody out who was supposed to leave. My staff and I were at the airfield, greeting the lucky survivors.

Quang Tri province fell to North Vietnam in April 1972. Commanding General Frederick Weyand, told me: "John you're not going back until the South Vietnamese take back the province," which they eventually did.

The best way to describe my time in Vietnam is to say that I was a loyal dissenter. During my time in the field, I saw countless visitors from the States who were trying to understand the American role in the war. Senator Frank Church and Representative Pete McCloskey came in 1972 and asked me what I thought about the Phoenix program, a CIA plan developed in 1967 that empowered the United States to kidnap, interrogate, and possibly assassinate Viet Cong. I told Church and McCloskey what I thought, trying not to defame the military or intelligence people who were struggling with a damned difficult job. Nonetheless, I clearly stated that the program violated the rules of international law and would tarnish America's good name. I was not happy with the trumped-up legal procedures. I had no problem with trying to root out potential VC, but I did have a problem using a phony legal approach to get rid of them. It was not a military operation. The question concerns how you fight a war. Are there not some rules you have to live by? Or does merely having enemies give you carte blanche to eliminate them as you see fit? I don't think so. This is an issue that will not go away. In the post–9/11 struggle against terrorism, the U.S. military set up prisons at Guantánamo Bay in Cuba to "process" prisoners as it saw fit. But if the United States is to promote the values of freedom and law, it needs to abide by the law. Not doing so reflects adversely on the country as a whole.

Most people I knew in Vietnam were not sycophants. Sometimes people just had different perspectives on what was happening. Some thought we were achieving our goals, while others thought the war was not going anywhere. Sure, some considered their own advancement more important than being truthful. But most people wanted to find the truth and express it, within the restraints of our operation. But it was hard to get a handle on the overall situation, and many were reluctant to extrapolate their own observations while contrary reports flowed in from other parts of the country.

One of the greatest horrors of war is that the burdens of death and suffering are shared so unequally. A few people in authority get to make the decisions, and then the vast majority of the people have to live with the consequences.

Every morning at 7 o'clock, I attended a briefing of generals at U.S. military headquarters in Danang. The commander would ask what was going on in the region and what we planned to do to improve the situation. To survive, to be useful, you have to know more than your superiors. So I had my colonel come to my residence at 6 o'clock to brief me on everything that had happened the previous day and night. He told me everything we'd learned, down to the names of the soldiers involved. The enemy overran this place, he would say. We lost that guy. This other guy was wounded. At 6:30 I'd get in a car and go to our secure headquarters.

Part of my job was to analyze every troop movement and record every casualty of war in the region. I was always impressed and moved by the care the American military showed for its soldiers.

If a kid from Arkansas had his legs shot off and a guy from New York was just killed, the military commanders cared. They saw it with their own eyes and received news of developments all over the country on a daily basis. They considered each soldier one of their own.

Sometimes, the Americans' concern for their own created a protective cocoon that distorted our view of the war. Americans got the best medical care and food. No costs were spared to feed and equip the American soldier or to care for him when injured or killed. Officers showed amazing compassion for the families of the war casualties. But the flip side of this extraordinary care for our own was, at times, the anonymity of the average Vietnamese soldier or family. In caring for our own, we too often lost sight of the horrors experienced by both North and South Vietnamese in their own land.

I remember walking past mountains of garbage in the predawn mist. As my car arrived at headquarters, its headlights revealed people atop garbage piled six feet high, searching for leftover scraps of hot dogs, hamburgers, buns, whatever they could find. The garbage came from the mess hall, and it was put there with the full understanding that scavengers would pick through it. That haunting image stays with me to this day—human beings picking over garbage to survive.

The American military cocoon also warped our understanding of events in the field. Officials at headquarters often interpreted what was going on differently from the guys on the ground. We told our soldiers that we were fighting for a great cause, that the Viet Cong were nasty and the South Vietnamese military were making progress. Often we knew that was not the case. What Clausewitz called the "fog of war"—the confusing madness that takes place on real battlefields, so different from the lines and arrows written on military maps—was often deliberately created by the rhetoric we had to use to keep our guys focused on their dangerous jobs.

But that was not the worst of it. There was an altogether different level of unreality in Washington. We plied Washington with masses of information about what was happening in the field, but Washington lacked the well-rounded understanding it needed to make smart decisions. Most politicians don't usually get too concerned with the complexities of policy and sometimes approach war—and other kinds of public policy—like a football game. They decide who has the white jerseys and who the red, and then adjust the facts to fit their ideas about the two sides. When we left scraps of food in piles of garbage for people to scavenge, some humanitarian impulses were at work there. But those impulses got lost when the "strategists" went to work in Washington.

The numbing of the human spirit that occurred in those circumstances took extreme forms, especially at some distance from the field. The United States used Agent Orange to defoliate the Ho Chi Minh Trail. We did not think much about the long-term consequences, which were severe. The chemicals seeped into the underground water supply and poisoned fish and food. New generations often arrived with birth defects. Napalm, too, had devastating effects. Who can ever forget the photo of the young Vietnamese girl as she ran screaming from the napalm bomb? The United States also laid mines all over Vietnam, and to this day, people get their legs blown off in the fields. This is particularly true in Cambodia.

In Vietnam I had a military adviser on my staff, a Marine captain who was involved in several cross-border operations into Laos. On one of these incursions he got caught on the Ho Chi Minh Trail when U.S planes were dropping defoliants onto the jungle. He became ill in Danang. When three years later I was appointed U.S. ambassador to Denmark, he was named my Marine attaché, having reached the rank of major. In 1989, when I participated in the global war games in Newport, Rhode Island, I came across my friend again. By that time he was a full colonel on the staff of the Naval War College. Shortly thereafter, he died of Agent Orange poisoning.

One of the more satisfying moments in Vietnam arose when I was able to protect one of Vietnam's great cultural treasures. In late 1971 the State Department advised me that President Nixon had ordered the U.S. military to protect the Cham Museum in Danang. The museum was one of a kind. French archeologists had built it in the late nineteenth and early twentieth centuries after discovering art objects in the ground in Central Vietnam and magnificent brick and stone monuments in the same area.

The objects the archeologists unearthed were in bronze, clay, silver, gold, and stone and dated from the fifth century to the fifteenth century when Cham kings ruled in Central Vietnam. Seafaring people who had come from the east by boat, probably from Polynesia, the Cham were carriers of Indian culture, both Hindu and Buddhist. They settled in the coastal plains of Central Vietnam and the Kingdom of Champa became a great rival to the Khmer Empire to the west. The great monument of Angkor Wat depicted in stone the wars between the Khmer and the Cham. They also depict in stone graceful, full-breasted Cham girls dancing before their king.

The French had approached the U.S. military in Vietnam in the late 1960s to help protect the Cham museum in Danang and the many temple ruins in Central Vietnam, but to no avail. In the early 1970s, the curator in Paris who had played a role in building up the Danang museum, Philippe Stern, wrote to President Nixon asking for U.S. protection of this priceless art heritage of Vietnam's past. President Nixon responded favorably and sent instructions to the American military in Saigon to protect the Cham museum. They, in turn, advised me of my new mission, that of protecting the Cham museum in Danang. I asked the South Vietnamese military to assign troops to live in the museum, and they occupied the building. When the United States withdrew from Vietnam in 1975, not a single piece of sculpture from the museum was missing. Unfortunately, soldiers and others ransacked temples in outlying districts. People saw ancient treasures and did not hesitate to steal pieces to sell to any willing buyers. By the turn of the twenty-first century, the museum in Danang had become Vietnam's leading tourist attraction.

In October 2005, the first Cham exhibit ever held outside of Vietnam was organized in Paris. Ministers from Vietnam and France attended the opening, to which I was also invited. The catalogue to this prestigious exhibit included on page 22 the following paragraph:

> Ambassador John Gunther Dean, who from 1970 to 1972 was deputy to the American commander of the 24th Corps based in Danang, remembers having received from the State Department the request sent directly by Philippe Stern to President Nixon to protect the museum in Danang and the

Cham monuments in the region. Thanks to the instructions sent by the White House in response to this initiative, the Cham Museum benefited from military protection which avoided looting during these troubled times. One of the American advisors working with the Vietnamese mayor of Danang, Carl Heffley, became enamored with Cham art and published in 1972 a brochure devoted to the museum's collection. At a time when Vietnam celebrates the 30th anniversary of its liberation, it is timely to recall the effort of those who did their best attempting to preserve this exceptional cultural patrimony during the terrible war years which have marked the history of Vietnam during the 20th century.

The Cham museum's guidebook makes the same point in six different languages. It is comforting to know that thirty years after the U.S. withdrawal from Vietnam, the Vietnamese and French remember at least one positive aspect of the American presence in Indochina.

From the beginning of my service with CORDS, I had the sinking feeling that the war could not be won militarily by the United States and South Vietnam. The people of South Vietnam were overwhelmed with fatigue and disillusioned. They had seen their fathers, their brothers, and their friends killed in both the war against the French and the war involving the Americans. In the United States we only think back to our own engagement in Vietnam. For the Vietnamese the war goes back far more than thirty years. Were they fighting to maintain the government of South Vietnam, which besides being inept was also dependent on outsiders for military assistance? No, they were fighting to keep North Vietnam from taking over South Vietnam. But in most people's eyes, Vietnam was one country. And the Viet Cong were all over South Vietnam anyway, and they were there to stay. The people in the north were tired too, but they were fighting with nationalist vision and energy.

In the final analysis, the Vietnamese people are pretty much the same as Americans or French or Salvadorans. The average man has a wife and family and just wants to live his life, bring home food, and educate his children. Whatever dangers the North

Vietnamese threatened, the average South Vietnamese felt caught in the middle.

No matter what Lyndon Johnson did, no matter what Richard Nixon did, the war was destined to go badly. The question that both presidents eventually had to ask was how to forge peace—and dignity—out of an unpopular and unwinnable war.

Before closing the chapter on Vietnam, I would like to dwell for a brief moment on how my service in Vietnam was perceived by my family. In the 1970s Vietnam had become an issue within American families. Often the younger generation held different views from their parents. When I went to Vietnam with the military in 1970, we were living in Cambridge, Massachusetts. Whenever anti-Vietnam War demonstrations or vigils were held in Cambridge, my children and wife always stood by me. When I left for Vietnam, my children said, "If my dad is involved, it can not be all bad," and they did not participate in demonstrations with their fellow students. I remain grateful to them for having had faith in me and allowing me to do the job asked of me by our country.

But service in Vietnam was not without risk. I corresponded with my wife, Martine, by sending her tapes. She replied by letter. In one tape that she has kept, I related what I had been doing for the previous few days when suddenly there came a loud bang on the tape. Somebody passing by my house, seeing the open window, had tried to throw a grenade into the bedroom where I was recording. Fortunately, the curtains had been drawn, and they stopped the grenade from reaching its target. Nothing personal, I believe, but it confirmed to me that some Vietnamese perceived Americans, however well intentioned, as foreign intruders and opposed their presence.

I doubt that I informed Martine until well after completing my tour of duty in Vietnam that I had been shot down in the helicopter in April 1972 near Quang Tri City while trying to rescue American advisors serving under my command. She would have worried even more than she already did about my being in wartime Vietnam. And she in turn kept bad news from me. When she broke her leg skiing, she did not want me to worry so that I could concentrate on my job and take care of my own security. When I landed in Boston at Logan Airport in the summer of 1972, after more than two years in Vietnam, Martine was at the airport with our three children, still in a wheelchair, recovering from her broken leg. More than fifty years after our marriage, I am still grateful to my wife and children that they always supported me in my determination to serve our country, wherever it might be.

5
War, Peace, Coup, Peace

Sometimes, just a hairline separates war and peace. Whether people fight or negotiate may depend on something as trivial as a speech, a shooting, a back-channel diplomatic initiative, a leader's weariness with war, or his desire to make a name for himself.

Usually, the difference between war and peace lies in the difference between fear and hope—and that difference often depends on people's ability to avoid simply reacting to the latest threat and instead to patiently put together the pieces of cooperation. Frightened people may act without thinking of long-term consequences. But with some hope that peace might work for them, people are able to show extraordinary courage. Most people don't need a guarantee of peace. But they do need hope.

When the State Department sent me to Laos in 1972, there was no real immediate reason to believe that a peace agreement could bridge the gulf between the two major warring parties. The Laotian Royal Army had been fighting the Pathet Lao, the rebel Communist insurgency, for more than ten years. The struggle was bitter and bloody. From a peacemaker's perspective, the two sides had little common ground. Their ideological rhetoric seemed certain to prevent them from engaging in any constructive negotiations for peace.

The rhetoric of the government of Prince Souvanna Phouma stressed the importance of maintaining the legitimacy of the royal government that nearly all nations of the world recognized. Above all, Prince Souvanna Phouma, a well-educated French-trained engineer, was eager to find a way out of being a mere pawn in the anticommunist struggle pursued by the United States in Indochina.

The Pathet Lao claimed that the Geneva Accords of 1954 had recognized them as a legitimate opposition group and that the royal government did not defend the interest of the "little people." The Pathet Lao also criticized the Royal Lao military and its ties to American policy in Indochina that it believed threatened the ability of Laos ever to have peace with neighbors like Cambodia and Vietnam. Only changing the composition of the ruling government, they claimed, could give Laos the second chance it needed to establish prosperity at home and security abroad.

Even the relationship that might seem to create the possibilities of a dialogue—the blood ties of the head of the government, Prince Souvanna Phouma, and the head of the resistance, Prince Souphanouvong—seemed only to poison the situation.

To begin to understand Laos, one must go to Vientiane, the administrative capital of the nation. When I first served in Laos in the 1950s, Vientiane had but few paved streets. The number of private cars could be counted in the dozens, surely less than a hundred. Walking down the street was like walking in a movie set in some dreamlike village. The city's most notable monument was the That Luong, a gracious old Buddhist religious shrine whose gilded tower is visible from far away. Vientiane had not changed much over the intervening sixteen years, except that there were many more cars.

The streets had a hushed feeling, with sounds of gongs, chants, and whispered voices. Buddhist monks would walk down the street, followed by their acolytes. Europeans would sit in small restaurants, talking quietly. Small shops sold fish, rice, perfume, salt, flowers, clothes, and wine. The greatest movement occurred on the Mekong River, which defines Laos at its western border. The Mekong served as the superhighway of Laos, transporting people from town to town, goods to market, missionaries from Europe and America—and war from surrounding nations like Vietnam and Cambodia. Most Laotians lived in small villages snuggled along the river.

The economic life of Laos was abundantly simple. The waters of the Mekong were filled with fish, the trees heavy with fruit. Rice farmers needed to tend their fields only four or five months a year to yield a harvest big enough to last the year. Laos seemed far indeed from the ideological worlds of the two superpowers—the American ideals of constant, individualist, capitalist striving, and the Communist ideals of collective struggle to overcome the poverty and indignities of capitalism—but their clash would make all of Southeast Asia squares on their global chessboard.

Laotians had a more relaxed outlook on life, a Rousseauistic ideal of simple self-sufficiency that neither of the global ideologies considered modern. At the center of this simple life were the profound ideas of Buddhism, the national religion. With the exception of the tribal peoples living on the mountaintops, away from the Mekong valley, the Buddhist way of life was extant in every aspect of Laotian life. The soft, slow lives that would be taken for lassitude by Westerners were really part of the Buddhist emphasis on living in the moment. Unlike the dreams of grandeur held by many Westerners—the constant talk about competition and power—Laotians understood themselves to be small specks in a vast universe, but specks that contained within them whole universes. Gentle acts of kindness—modest acts like buying small animals to free them, a kind of manumission for the natural kingdom—shed grace on Buddhists. Understanding living in the moment lends itself to a great modesty, which can be misunderstood as resignation. "There's only so much that we can control," Laotians would say. "Some things cannot be helped."

Certainly geography cannot be helped. Laos lies in the middle of trouble in Southeast Asia. It is a pile of mountains and hills that fall down to the river alongside the villages where most people live. To understand Laos, take a territory the size of New York and Pennsylvania combined, squeeze it into a thousand-mile long salamander, and surround it with unstable or unreliable neighbors. Thailand and the Mekong River define Laos on the west, Cambodia on the south, Vietnam in the east, Burma in the northwest, and China on the rest of the northern border.

Colonial history made it difficult for Laos to stand up for itself. The fourteenth-century kingdom of Lan Xan included not only present-day Laos but also much of today's northern Thailand. But that kingdom became divided, and Laos has been overrun ever since. At the time the French took over Laos as a protectorate in 1893, the land was divided into several feudal fiefdoms. Japan restored

Laos's unity in World War II. After the war, France resumed control but in 1947 allowed wide latitude for self-rule under a constitutional monarchy. During the war, Thailand had annexed the Lao land west of the Mekong River. France made the return of all the land annexed by Thailand a condition for French support for Thailand becoming one of the founding members of the United Nations.

Laos has always been an insecure sandwich between Thailand and Vietnam. When the Viet Minh began what they considered to be a nationalistic war for independence from France, Laos was often used as a staging area for the rebels. One of the most prominent families in Laos epitomized the growing cleavages in the nation's politics and geography—Souvanna Phouma became the prime minister of Laos, while his half-brother, Souphanouvong, became the leader of a communist insurgency in Laos.

When I arrived in Laos in 1972, Ambassador G. MacMurtrie Godley asked me: "Do you take war or peace?"

The practice of foreign affairs often requires two approaches, force and diplomacy. Even when nations are at peace, the possibility of war requires that they prepare themselves militarily. At that time, however, we were very much at war against the insurgency in Laos. Being at war required daily decisions about where to drop bombs and move troops. Had I wished, I could have been part of the team that decided what targets to hit in air raids.

As much as I respect the military, in Laos I had no interest in that side of foreign affairs. My interest was in finding ways to get adversaries to talk to each other. I wanted to get all sides to the conflict to understand that their interests ultimately lay with finding a way to end the war, that even if they did not get everything they wanted, they would win if they got some of what they wanted.

So my answer to Mac Godley was automatic: "I'll take peace."

One of the most important Americans working with us in Laos was Brigadier General Jack Vessey. He was stationed at the base of Udorn in northern Thailand but came regularly to Vientiane to meet with the embassy. Jack was in charge of supporting the Royal Lao Armed Forces with military equipment, advice, and funds.

Vessey became a friend, and quite often we would discuss the American engagement in Vietnam, whether it was the right place, and the right time to oppose communist expansionism. He was a thoughtful man, with great respect for others, Americans and foreigners alike. He was interested in learning more about foreign cultures and what made the enemy tick. Jack had earned his lieutenant's commission on the landing beaches in Southern Italy and would end his career as a four-star general and chairman of the Joint Chiefs of Staff under President Reagan.

I once traveled with Vessey to the Plaines des Jarres in northern Laos to inspect friendly troops. Out of nowhere, we came under heavy artillery attack from Pathet Lao rebels. Without a moment's hesitation, we both jumped into a ditch and held on to each other for dear life, waiting for the attacks to end. The Plaines des Jarres was a wide valley that controlled entry to the highlands held by the Pathet Lao and the route to the coastal strips along the Mekong controlled by the Royal Lao Armed Forces.

The attack showed that the enemy forces had weapons supplied by the Chinese or the Vietnamese and were willing to fight. They were not going to be any pushover. Beating them was going to take a lot of arms, a lot of men, and a lot of time. And if we won the war, what would we have on our hands? An embittered enemy, still without a stake in the success of the government, alienated from the government and much of the population of the country. Losing was not an option, but outright victory did not look promising as an option either.

When I traveled with Vessey, we talked at length about the importance of the military conflict in Laos. We wondered if we were on the right track. Vessey was part of the military establishment but with an independent mind. He had the quality I admire most in public servants, whether military, diplomatic, or political: the willingness to ask the right questions. Are we doing the right thing? Are we doing it the right way? Both Vessey and I, and countless others caught in the conflict all over Southeast Asia, were supporting what our superiors ordered us to do, but we were also asking questions.

The most important question, in the geopolitical context of the Cold War, was whether Laos was a "domino." If Laos "fell" to the Communists, what would happen? Would nearby states—Vietnam, Cambodia, Thailand—and other countries in the region also go Communist? Vessey and I were both skeptical. Like Vessey, I believed that people have it in their power to shape their own futures. Nothing is automatic; no trends are absolute or immutable. The decision of people to do the hard work of peace can make a difference. Academics talk about the power that people have to affect their own fortunes. Even in the most difficult circumstances—the battlefield, concentration camps, being part of despised minorities—people have the capacity to decide and act on their own. Though such actions may be constrained, every courageous and right decision changes the overall context.

Deep in the core of my being, I believe that peace is always an option. I always favored a negotiated solution, not only in Laos but wherever conflict threatened to destroy people and communities. Peace requires hard work—grinding, complex, nerve-fraying, sometimes thankless work—but it is almost always possible.

In pursuing peace, you must prove yourself to the people responsible for war. I have been around war for most of my life and have always believed that most people who fight wars do not like them at all. When they launch out to wage war, they do so with great passion, but most would rather be serving the cause of peace. More than anyone else, those who fight them see the consequences of war—the suffering of villages and families, the havoc wreaked on industry and infrastructure, the destruction of environment and culture, and the utter sense of hopelessness that war brings. And though most military people hate war, they are dedicated to carrying out the orders of presidents and generals. They want to fight, and fight hard, because they want it all to end as soon as possible.

So if you're a man of peace, you need to prove to military men and women that you are every bit as tough and committed as they are to the values of the nation and the values of service. And the way to impress the military is to get up earlier than they do, work twice as hard as they do, put yourself in danger, and never waver.

Then they will listen to you.

Soon after I settled into my work in Laos, Prime Minister Souvanna Phouma invited me to come to his house to play bridge. Both Martine and I had known Souvanna Phouma, son of the former Viceroy of Laos, from our first posting in Laos sixteen years earlier. Two of Souvanna's children had attended a fashionable boarding school in France, and during the summer break his children spent their vacation at the country estate of Martine's family. In the 1950s and thereafter, travel from France to Laos was still a long and costly journey; hence young students did not go back to their native lands that often. We had known Souvanna Phouma's first wife, as well as his current wife in 1972.

Even in the fifties, I had found Souvanna Phouma to have a lot of common sense and leaning towards keeping Laos out of the U.S.-Communist confrontation. Our professional relationship benefited from those personal links we had established over the years. Contact between us was relaxed and friendly. That Souvanna by instinct and education inclined more toward the civilian sector than toward the military further compounded this affinity.

Prince Souvanna Phouma lived in a modern, Western-style house he had built for himself in Vientiane. It was not a residence provided by the government. While Souvanna Phouma's family hailed from the royal capital of Luang Prabang, where they lived in a royal manner, in Vientiane he had adopted a Western life style.

Martine and I went to Souvanna's house as friends. We played bridge every week or so. I was not a good bridge player, but it was a great way to catch up on gossip, get a sense of the political mood of the times, and show an openness to whatever dialogue was possible. We played until leaving was most politic: If Souvanna was winning and it was 1:00 a.m., we would leave at 1:15. We would stand up, yawn, and declare that we hated to end a wonderful evening but had to get up early for work the next day. If Souvanna was winning at 10:45 p.m., we would do the stand-and-stretch routine at about 11:00.

Souvanna knew that I was personally supportive of a negotiated settlement, even though that was not the position of the U.S. government. But when I saw him socially, I would always explain the official U.S. position on Laos and Indochina. It was important for the prime minister to understand both sides of the equation, and above all, that I would always support my government despite any contrary ideas I might have on how to prevail in Laos and Southeast Asia. If he also understood my personal position, he was likely to keep an open mind himself about his options as head of the government.

Mac Godley, my ambassador, was a big barrel of a man with a commanding presence that won the loyalty of many but also caused friction. He had a cocksure attitude about how to wage war and win the peace in Laos. Well known for his use of paramilitary activities in the Congo, he took a similar approach to the Laotian conflict. Godley believed that military action offered the only way to protect U.S. interests in Laos. He acted more like a general than an ambassador, coordinating activities throughout Laos and discounting overtures to negotiate an end to the war. Mac coordinated a wide range of anti-Communist forces in Laos, including some Americans and tens of thousands of Laotian and Thai guerrillas fighting against Pathet Lao and communist Vietnamese forces. By the end of his term as ambassador, Laos had 300,000 refugees in a country of three million people. One in ten Laotians was displaced by the war.

Mac Godley subscribed to the Nixon administration's commitment to bombing. He thought that bombing the enemy was going to win the war against the Communists. Godley had no problem whatsoever asking Prime Minister Souvanna Phouma to request a United States bombing attack on communist military positions in Laos.

Having been involved in Vietnam, when I heard a U.S. Air Force general make the case for heavy bombing of the enemy, I had my doubts. Ever since World War II, it had become an article of faith that massive bombing could "soften" the enemy's defenses. Throughout Indochina, the United States used air raids to cripple infrastructure, roads, and public facilities—to force a virtual shutdown of everyday life—but the raids did not achieve this objective. Proponents of air raids said it would achieve two goals. First, it would create an incentive for the enemy to come to the bargaining table. Second, it would provide better conditions for ground attacks and takeovers of strategic areas.

But for reasons that often puzzled American generals, life continued with little disruption after raids. After decades of war, Laotians and others learned how to anticipate the raids, protect themselves during raids, and return to normal activities afterwards. In many cases, bombing raids seemed to strengthen the enemy by bringing them together against a common foe, just as the British pulled together against the Nazi raids during World War II.

At the Embassy we had an officer whose principal duty was to select targets for bombing by the U.S. Air Force. For this he needed up-to-date information on Pathet Lao troop movements as well as the latest intelligence on where Royal Lao Armed Forces were facing trouble from the enemy. This officer worked closely with Ambassador Godley, who took a personal interest in selecting targets. To demonstrate the different approaches to the problems of Laos, I would like to jump ahead a few months and relate how I was "officially reprimanded" by the State Department for advising Prince Souvanna Phouma against asking for a U.S. Air Force bombing strike against Pathet Lao forces.

By the summer of 1973, a bombing halt had been agreed in Laos. The United States no longer employed U.S. aircraft to bomb enemy positions in Laos, unless for a specific reason, such as the prime minister's personally requesting such a strike. When I went to see Souvanna Phouma in the summer of 1973 on a negotiations issue, he informed me that the Royal Lao forces had been driven off a hill and replaced by Pathet Lao troops. Souvanna asked me whether he should ask for a U.S. air strike on that hill, which would probably kill most of the Pathet Lao military there. This in turn could permit the Royal Army to retake the hill. "What do you recommend, John?"

I replied that his government was in the midst of diplomatic negotiations with the Pathet Lao, that prospects for a negotiated settlement were promising and, if the United States were to respond favorably to the prime minister's request, the Pathet Lao would interpret this as the Royal government's willingness to undermine the entire negotiation. Furthermore, I added, a couple of weeks later the Pathet Lao would most likely retake the same hill, if they were really determined to hold that position. Hence, in my opinion, I would not jeopardize the prospects for a successful negotiation that might put an end to the war by asking the intervention of the U.S Air Force.

When I reported this conversation to Washington, pretty much as I have here, I received an official reprimand. I was told that I should not have made the decision myself but should have told the prime minister that I would ask for official guidance from Washington. That this would have taken at least twenty-four hours was of no importance to our folks back home. In their view, it was not up to the man on the spot to take that decision but merely to be the messenger conveying the question to higher authorities back home.

When I later discussed the matter with Souvanna Phouma after the Lao had reached a negotiated settlement to their differences, he reminded me of the "good advice" I had given him, which had maintained the proper atmosphere for both Lao sides to bring the negotiations to fruition. In Washington, not all people saw it the same way. Nonetheless, the "official reprimand" did not stop the president from appointing me ambassador to Cambodia five months later.

The question in Indochina was one of how to contain communism. I have always believed that a coalition government is good enough to prevent communism from holding sway over whole societies. As long as there is something to balance the communists, the interests of the United States would be protected. As long as a society contains a variety of functioning institutions, such as courts, an army, schools, hospitals, occasional elections, and basic legal and political freedoms, democratic values have a reasonable chance to prevail. When the Communists are forced to compete in a battle of ideas, they can be contained.

Mac Godley disagreed. He was part of the Cold War generation, which applied the bitter lessons of appeasement from World War II. Mac, like many others, equated negotiations with giving in to the other side. Chamberlain's ill-fated agreement with Hitler loomed over diplomacy all over the world. Give in to the opposition, and you're a sucker. Delay standing up for yourself, and you find yourself in a weaker position over time.

The Pathet Lao in 1971 sent a delegation headed by Phoumi Vongvichit to Vientiane to negotiate an end to the war and the eventual creation of a coalition government. Pheng Pongsavan, the head of the Laotian National Assembly, negotiated for the government. I would go to see my friend Pheng Pongsavan nearly every night and ask how the discussions had gone. I would take notes. When these sessions ended, I would meet with Dick Howland, the head of the U.S. embassy's political section. We would review all of the negotiating points—who made what offers and asked what questions, and how the other side responded—and then type up summaries of the day's work and send them to Washington. These talks took place three or four times a week. The work at the office ended for us around midnight.

The Lao negotiators believed that they could put an end to the fighting. But Ambassador Godley really believed that a coalition government was not desirable.

"John, this is not going to lead anywhere. The real thing is we have to beat the Communists," Godley told me. He believed in the Dulles doctrine: You're either with us or against us.

Then a political development changed everything. President Nixon nominated Mac Godley to serve as assistant secretary of state for Far Eastern affairs. But the Senate rejected his nomination, largely because of his record in Laos. He later served as U.S ambassador to Lebanon.

Mac's departure left me in charge of the U.S. embassy in Laos as chargé d'affaires. It was the first time I would be in charge of a large operation. I had usually worked for someone else, and now I was in charge,

The importance of the new position hit me immediately. Taking over was exciting in a way. But more than that, I felt a sense of responsibility. When you're in charge, it's a lot more difficult than being the Number Two, Three, or Four person in the embassy. Being the top political officer is a lot different than being a top deputy. I did not feel any more pressure, and I always thought I had the support I needed from the embassy staff. In some ways, life was easier as the top person, because when I issued requests and orders, people acted, whether or not they might wonder if they were doing the right thing. And I spoke with much greater purpose and confidence. For my entire career, I had implemented other people's agendas. Though I was free to say what was on my mind, I always understood myself to be an advisor and implementer rather than the policy maker. Now when I ordered something done, it was done.

I wanted to act. I believed that Laos had suffered enough and that the Laotian Army wasn't bringing the war any nearer to an end. There was a certain weariness of war. And both sides had to come up with a solution that would save the country and save face for both sides. That's what I hoped a coalition government would do.

Everyone worried about another faction's getting the upper hand. The answer, though, was not to return to the battlefield but to try even harder at the negotiating table. Both sides had to work hard to understand and bargain over all the details of their political, social, and economic disputes. I believed that if they worked out principles suitable for guiding a coalition government and wrestled over the details of implementation, all parties could bring an end to the war and give the Laotians a coalition government.

I enjoyed incredible latitude in working with the government side and in giving my views on the progress of the negotiations between the opposing sides. The Nixon administration, previously adamant about gaining military victories before negotiating an end to the war, left me alone for most of my time as acting ambassador. Nonetheless, I was only an unofficial adviser to the negotiations, not a party directly involved in the negotiations.

At the time, the Nixon administration followed a strict policy of linkage. Peace could not come to Laos unless it also came to Vietnam and Cambodia, and peace was not conceivable without some sort of military victory. It was an all-or-nothing approach that got in the way of give-and-take negotiations.

There was no likelihood that I would convince President Nixon to "de-link" Laos from Vietnam and Cambodia. So what I did was to treat Laos as a separate question and focus on protecting American interests there. I decided the best way to do that was to help bring peace to Laos.

I sent regular updates to Washington describing Laotian efforts to end the war. But I did not always seek advance consultation for my advice to the Royal government's negotiator, Pheng Pongsavan. Stopping talks to write a cable to Washington would have been impossible. So I had to trust that I understood American interests and would be able to persuade everyone in Washington that in Vientiane we were pursuing American interests in Indochina.

The negotiations were strictly between the two opposing Lao parties: the Royal government and the Pathet Lao. All I could do was "kibitz" and find out in the evening from the government side the status of the negotiation seeking a definitive agreement between Pheng Ponssavan and Phoumi Vongvichit. I could then give my views to Pheng whether the government had given away too much, how easily the compromises could be carried out, and most importantly, what the impact of an internal Lao agreement on the rest of Indochina and on the U.S.-communist confrontation would be. Though the United States was not a party to the negotiations, both sides' negotiators were aware that I was personally favorably disposed to their reaching an agreement. This may have encouraged both sides to search for compromise solutions.

Other foreign powers represented in Vientiane shared my approach to the Lao negotiations. The French ambassador, my good friend André Ross, and Russian ambassador Andrej Vdovine both supported my efforts in their direct contacts with both Lao parties. I was also under the impression that both the Chinese communist chargé and the North Vietnamese ambassador were not opposed to the advice I was dispensing in my nocturnal meetings.

A coup d'état might have ruined everything.

In August 1973, a former military officer in the Royal Lao Air Force attempted to take over the government and end the peace negotiations with the Pathet Lao. I received a phone call at the embassy from one of the American advisors to the airport authority. In a panic, he exclaimed: "Hey, they came in and they're getting ready to take over the planes!" The coup plotters were pilots, and they planned to bomb strategic targets.

General Thao Ma was a former Lao Air Force general who had long been outside the mainstream of Souvanna's government. He had been living in Thailand, while consulting other former members of the Laotian military and various exile political elites. After months of planning, the general decided to cross the Mekong River, take over the Vientiane airport, and from there take control of other strategic sites. Ultimately his plan was to oust Souvanna and create a new military government. The general's forces succeeded in briefly taking over the government's radio station in Vientiane, from which they announced that a new government was in charge in Laos.

The coup plotters were rightist Lao officers who wanted to overthrow what they considered to be a wishy-washy government. Undoubtedly they got both direct and tacit support from the Thai government and from some Americans. They took off from a base in neighboring Thailand. Taking a passive approach to the plotters, some American officials said, in effect, "This is not a bad thing." Negotiations between the two Lao parties were in high gear, and many Laotians and foreigners opposed the neutralist solution toward which the negotiations were heading.

General Thao Ma and his gang took complete control of the airport and the control tower. From there, they planned to use small planes given to the Royal Lao Army by the United States to take over the capital and from there the rest of the country. And they might have succeeded.

When I got the news of the coup attempt on the morning of August 20, 1973, my first action was to provide for the safety of Prime Minister Souvanna Phouma. I found him a safe house in town, where he could elude capture by the coup plotters. I also asked American Marines to protect the house in Vientiane of the lead negotiator for the Pathet Lao, Phoumi Vongvichit. They ringed the house and controlled the entry and exit to the Pathet Lao house. I was afraid other people might be coming by foot, either to arrest him, kill him, or force him to leave town, thereby ending the negotiations for a settlement.

Then I had my driver take me to the airport. I did not try very hard to get other Americans in the American mission—more than 600—to go with me to confront the plotters, because I feared that some might have refused. Many felt that it was not their jobs to take sides in an internal Lao dispute but to observe events and file reports to Washington.

When you take on something like this you do not think about the dangers. You act. I wish I could say I had had a plan or done a quick analysis of the possible costs and benefits of different options. But I did not. I just moved. The American advisor in charge of the Vientiane airport was on the payroll of the Agency for International Development, but I never knew what his real job was. Anyway, he was a good friend, very capable, and later wrote up the events that had taken place at the airport.

My driver was shaking in his boots as he drove me to the airport. I was not sure what to expect once I got there. I was just going to see what I could do to protect the legal government of Laos. Many of the U.S. embassy's 680 people were on hand at the airport. They were nowhere near the runway or the control tower but rather were watching from the distance, like spectators, to see what was going to happen.

I took a bullhorn to the tower and shouted—in French, our common working language—"Listen, you guys, I'm paying all of your salaries here. My orders from Washington are to support and protect the legal government of Souvanna Phouma. What you are trying to do is against this policy. Get your asses back across the river. I'm against this coup."

A large detachment of the Royal Lao Army was sitting on the side, in the bushes, waiting to see who was going to win this standoff. Among them were some high-ranking Lao military who were known to be close to their American advisors. They were going with whoever won. They waited.

I repeated my challenge to hundreds of people standing near the airport tarmac: "Everyone here, Lao or American, you are going against the orders I have to support the existing Royal Lao government." The way I saw it, I was acting according to my instructions. When one is in a crisis situation, he or she doesn't have time to phone home for instructions. When I took the position in Laos, I was told directly that my job was to support U.S. interests and the Laotian government. In no way did a coup advance either's interests.

From a distance, I could see that the government's armed forces were not moving, either to support me or to support the rebels. Meanwhile, the propellers were turning on the small planes that the plotters planned to use for their raids. I had my driver move onto the tarmac and block the runway, thereby making it difficult for the planes to take off. My driver was scared and so was I. Stubbornly, probably because I had no other possible moves, I stayed in the car.

General Thao Ma, the coup leader, tried to fly off in the airplane he had requisitioned, while trying to avoid hitting my car.

As he took off, he veered to the right. Unable to lift his plane up, he crashed it at the side of the tarmac.

I took the bullhorn again. "OK, guys it's over. Go back where you came from."

The plotters finally departed, crossing the Mekong River by boat back to Thailand.

After the whole episode was over, I went to the house of the Pathet Lao negotiator, Phoumi Vongvichit, and we had some fizzy drinks. The negotiations were back on. Then I went to see Souvanna Phouma, who by that time was back in his own house. A few days later, in front of all the foreign ambassadors and chiefs of mission accredited to Laos, Souvanna Phouma thanked me publicly for the firm support the United States had given to the legal authorities of Laos. The newspapers around the world gave accurate coverage to the foiled coup. Among the American print media reporting on the event were lengthy articles in *Time* Magazine, *Newsweek*, and the *New York Times*.

None of the coup plotters were punished for their plot. And there were no consequences for the people in Thailand who had given the coup at least tacit approval.

In March 1974, when I appeared before the Senate Committee on Foreign Relations for confirmation as ambassador to Cambodia, the Senate hearing turned largely to questions by some senior U.S. senators about my intervention at the Vientiane airport on August 20, 1973, to foil rightist Lao General Thao Ma's efforts to overthrow the legal and internationally recognized government of Prime Minister Souvanna Phouma. The questions asked by some senators turned on the following: Did John G. Dean have the right as chargé d'affaires to intervene in the coup attempt against the legal government of Souvanna Phouma, thereby foiling the coup, or should he have confined himself to reporting such events? In the precise language of the senator from New York, Jacob Javits: "In your opinion, [Mr. Dean,] which is the more important consideration [in deciding whether to intervene or not:] legitimacy or control?"

My answer on that day was "legitimacy." In the case of Thao Ma's coup, there is no doubt that certain elements in the U.S. government had sympathy for the rebellious Lao general's effort to overthrow "neutralist" Souvanna Phouma. I defended my action in foiling the usurpers by pointing out that supporting the "legitimate" government of Souvanna Phouma was the policy Washington had asked me to carry out in Vientiane.

With the defeat of the coup, the two sides were free to negotiate an end to the war. The protocol of September 14, 1973, produced a coalition government, with members of the Vientiane government controlling the Finance, Defense, and Interior departments and the Pathet Lao controlling Foreign Affairs. Under the agreement, the two sides would also collaborate on a consultative council, which would guide the nation toward elections. All foreign troops were to leave the country within two months, and both sides would station troops in the major cities to assure their neutrality.

The Laos agreement did not solve all problems in the country. In fact, when the governments of South Vietnam and Cambodia fell in 1975, the communists also took over the Laotian government, and Souvanna Phouma was removed. (He died a natural death in Laos in 1984 and is buried in his native city of Luang Prabang.) One could say that this represented a failure of the peace process. But I look at the issue from a larger perspective. None of the brutal violence that accompanied the ending of the Vietnamese and Cambodian wars came to Laos. When the communists took over Laos, too many people lost their political liberties and property, and that was wrong. Some leaders from the royal government felt compelled to go into exile and some were sent into "reeducation" camps. But in a part of the world that had experienced little besides violence and political repression for over thirty-five years, the result in Laos was the least bad option. And I remain proud of the imperfect peace we made in Laos, all these years later.

In 2005, the communist government of Laos received a $1.5 billion loan from the World Bank to build an electric power–generating dam in Laos. Does this mean that Laos today is again accepted as an active participating member of the world community? I hope so.

6
From Shangri-La to Hell

When Richard Nixon appointed me ambassador to Cambodia in March 1974, Washington was consumed with an event that the president called " "a third-rate burglary."

The Watergate scandal was anything but a simple burglary. Nixon's reelection committee, with the help of the White House, set out to eavesdrop on the Democratic National Committee. They got caught doing so on June 17, 1972. Then they tried to cover up the crime. They got caught doing that over the next two years, by the *Washington Post* and congressional committees and by assorted people inside and outside the administration who unraveled the conspiracy like a suspense novel.

People sometimes forget that President Nixon's motivation for Watergate began with foreign policy. He was infuriated when the *New York Times* published the Pentagon Papers, an in-house study of U.S. involvement in Vietnam, and wanted to get dirt on the leakers. He also wanted to get dirt on antiwar protesters and other political enemies. And with growing public opposition to the war—as well as complications in the war itself—he authorized secretly bombing Cambodia in 1969.

No secret to the Cambodians, the bombings were somehow kept secret from the American public and from Congress. Perhaps that secrecy itself was grounds for a constitutional crisis.

In July 1974, the House Judiciary Committee approved three articles of impeachment focused on the Watergate break-in, cover-up, and related abuses of power. In the spring of 1974, Nixon's presidency was in mortal danger. By August, when the Supreme Court ordered him to release tapes that implicated him in the cover-up almost from the beginning, he resigned rather than face certain impeachment. His successor, Gerald Ford, had become vice president when Spiro Agnew resigned the office after pleading no contest to charges of taking bribes.

The fate of Cambodia would be decided in the last six months of the Nixon presidency and the first eight months of the Ford presidency.

In foreign affairs, continuity between Nixon and Ford would come in the person of Henry Kissinger. Under Ford, Dr. Kissinger continued to serve as both national security advisor and secretary of state, wielding unparalleled power over foreign policy—including Cambodia.

I received conflicting signals as I prepared to assume my new post. I met Kissinger at the State Department, and he defined my role narrowly. "John, you're going out there to be ambassador," he said. "You size up the military situation and take control of it. I'll take care of the diplomatic side."

That sounded backwards to me. A diplomat is supposed to take care of the military side of things? No. Diplomats are supposed to bring friends and foes together to find ways to live side by side. Diplomats exist to negotiate, to seek nonmilitary solutions to problems.

When I left Laos, I stopped in Bangkok and asked Tom Enders for advice about my new assignment in Cambodia. Enders had been chargé d'affaires in Cambodia before taking up ambassadorial assignments around the world. Everyone assumed that I would try to do in Cambodia what I had done in Laos—bring people together to negotiate an end to the war. We had a chance to try. Enders thought it was a good idea and said he had told Kissinger that we should have tried to end the war in Cambodia in 1973.

Tom understood that we had reached a critical moment in Cambodia. "Time is against a military solution," he said. "The more time passes, the more authority you lose. We have to find a way to end the war in Cambodia before we lose the ability to get all the parties to the table."

I came to the country with a reputation for making peace. People in the Khmer government thought the United States had a chance to help end the war in Cambodia the way we had helped in Laos. I went everywhere and talked to everyone. I have a lot of energy, and I am by nature an optimist, and I think some of it rubbed off on people. Maybe that wasn't a good thing. Maybe it got people's hopes up too much. Maybe it made people think that an outsider could save the day when the reality was that Cambodians themselves had to be determined to save the day.

The Cambodians wanted me to broker an agreement. When I made a courtesy call on Prime Minister Long Boret, he asked me to repeat my feat in Laos and bring about reconciliation in Cambodia."

Some people started to call me "King of the Khmers." It was a double-edged comment. I mostly took it as a compliment for my willingness to try to hold the country together. But I flinched when I heard it. I knew that my role was limited—and I knew that generals and other members of the government would resent my playing too large a role. But if I had been sent to Cambodia to broker a deal, I had to work as hard as possible to succeed.

The American people had two real choices. On one extreme, the doves said we should just get out no matter the cost and disruption, and they lost out. On the other extreme, the hawks said we should stay until we achieved total victory.

Was there a middle ground? In Vietnam, the middle ground was handing over the war to South Vietnam. That meant training their soldiers, helping with intelligence, providing weaponry and funding—but getting our boys out. It was, in essence, a return to Lyndon Johnson's 1964 election year statement that he did not want "to send American boys nine or ten thousand miles away from home to do what Asian boys ought to be doing for themselves."

I had misgivings about Vietnamization, as the policy came to be called under Richard Nixon. But I knew that simply passing off the war to Cambodians did not make sense. The problems in Cambodia stemmed mostly from outside forces fighting each other inside the country, dragging different factions into their battles. The result was chaos.

The problems started when the Viet Cong took over sections of eastern Cambodia from which to launch attacks on South Vietnam. The VC moved down the Ho Chi Minh Trail with soldiers and weaponry for attacks. The United States, in turn, bombed these "sanctuaries." But rather than taking out the sanctuaries, the bombing had the effect of driving the VC forces further into the country. Both sides of the U.S.-VC struggle had supporters in Cambodia. In addition, China and the Soviet Union worked behind the scenes to support the VC-allied Khmer Rouge.

The whole mess was framed in Cold War rhetoric. It was the communists against the noncommunists. These labels did not always mean much to the Cambodians, but they meant everything to the United States, China, and the Soviet Union. And when these superpowers decided that Cambodia was part of a great testing ground—which would cause the dominos to fall decisively one way or the other—it was harder to convince everyone to sit at a table and negotiate a truce.

One more impediment to peace in Cambodia was the idea of linkage. Under the Nixon Doctrine, the United States was committed to preventing communism from extending its control beyond existing strongholds. It was in essence a call for freezing the current balance of power, at least for the time being. Under linkage, the destinies of Vietnam and Cambodia were connected. If Cambodia were to end its war with a coalition government, elements in South Vietnam might be willing to make compromises with North Vietnam. And that, in turn, would create the possibility of communist dominance over all of Indochina one day.

I always thought the linkage idea was flawed. For diplomacy to work, you have to do two things—expand the range of issues people deal with and isolate the issues into workable components. You need many issues on the table in the beginning to have an understanding of the cards that you can play. Sometimes, you can make connections between issues that might not be obvious right away—like the connection between infrastructure and military bases or the connection between agricultural subsidies and drug trafficking. But once you have all the cards on the table, you need to do what's possible. That usually requires accepting something less than a comprehensive solution. Always, you need flexibility to expand and contract the issues under discussion. The major question you have to ask is, what might work?

By insisting on linkage, Kissinger demanded that we solve too many problems at once and at the same time cut us off from making arrangements that might work.

I first got to know Cambodia in the 1950s, during the early years of Prince Sihanouk's reign. In those days, Sihanouk could call Cambodia "an oasis of peace." You could say that Cambodia was primitive, that its people were unambitious and its economy undeveloped. Cambodia has its own internal divisions—educated and uneducated, Cambodian, Chinese, and Vietnamese, businessmen and unskilled workers, Buddhists and Roman Catholics. Real poverty and want seemed to exist side by side with real happiness and peace.

What was Cambodia like before warfare spilled over from Vietnam? It was a peaceful country, bounded on the west by Thailand, on the east by Vietnam, on the north by Laos, and on the south by the Gulf of Siam. In the sixth century, the Khmer built up an extensive empire, which retained power until the fourteenth century. That period is best remembered for the famous temple of Angkor Wat, which marked the highest attainment of Khmer classical art. Attacked from the northwest by the Thai and from the east by the Vietnamese, the border of the Khmer empire gradually receded.

Becoming a French protectorate in 1863 probably saved Cambodia from extinction. From 1887 until World War II, Cambodia was part of French Indochina. Complete independence came to Cambodia in 1955. In the march from French protectorate to independent nation, Prince (later King) Norodom Sihanouk had played a key role. As for the economy, the growing of rice on numerous small landholdings sufficed for most Cambodians to make a modest living. French planters had introduced large rubber plantations and built a few latex plants. In the mind of most visitors, Cambodians were gentle people with the famous smile of the Angkor Wat sculptures transferred to the faces of the Cambodian population.

And Norodom Sihanouk not only led his nation to independence from France but also maintained the country's neutrality—a major feat considering past struggles with China, Thailand, and Vietnam.

In our younger days, I had had fun with Sihanouk. We went to nightclubs together. On a couple of occasions, he sang to Martine and me. With other young diplomats we watched movies together at his palace—even saw some of his own movies, which he admitted were not always a success. We ate and drank, told stories, and reveled in the beauty and energy of the country. He even settled down. Sihanouk had many wives, and some say he had thirty children. When he said he was the father of his country, he wasn't kidding. But he achieved stability with his final wife, Monique.

Sihanouk's story as ruler began in 1941 when the Vichy French rulers of Indochina—under the watchful eye of Japan, which held sway over Asia during World War II—selected him to succeed Sisowath Monireth as king of Cambodia. The selection was a calculated effort to keep Cambodia in servility. Sihanouk was only eighteen years old and already had a reputation as a playboy. Surely he could be kept under the control of the French when French interests were at stake. Sihanouk would soon step down as king and become the prince—a shrewd move that would exemplify the spirit of Machiavelli's *Prince*. As prince, Sihanouk took on the more substantive role of prime minister and political spirit of the nation and in 1955 used his command over Cambodia's political machinery to win the nation's last election until 1993.

Sihanouk's consolidation of power left opposition groups on the periphery—and may have contributed to the intensity of the guerrilla war against his regime. Over the years, Sihanouk would move in and out of alliances with different factions in Cambodia. He was loyal to the French, but when the Japanese removed France, Sihanouk joined the forces of independence—only to chafe when his rival Son Ngoc Thanh became prime minister. In later years, he would work alternately with and against France, the United States, China, Vietnam, and the Khmer Rouge. His ultimate goal was neutrality, a value difficult to sustain in the war-torn region.

Whatever his faults, Sihanouk was a person full of life, the kind of person you can almost always talk with. And that's what I wanted to do when I became ambassador in 1974. But since the coup of 1970, Sihanouk had lived in Beijing, outside the real action in Cambodia. After Lon Nol overthrew Sihanouk in the coup, Sihanouk threw his support to the opposition Khmer Rouge. His support gave the communists the cover they needed to stake a claim to legitimacy. People remembered Sihanouk's gentle and carefree ways, and they assumed that the Khmer Rouge could not be all bad. But they were.

If the Khmer Rouge were to win, everyone assumed that Sihanouk would come back and take the throne once more in Phnom Penh. He would be a unifying figure, though he would not necessarily exercise any power. The new rulers would not want him to be at the controls, balancing off this group against that one, determining who controlled the bureaucracy and the spoils of government. But his very presence might bring the country together.

Sihanouk was not always easy to read. In an August 12, 1973, interview with the *New York Times Magazine*, he displayed his playful and defiant ways, laughing about his past life as a playboy with many wives, a jazz band, and B movies. But it was all to make a point, and that point was that the United States had committed unspeakable crimes against Cambodia and betrayed his trust. "When a man suffers as I suffer for his country, on which B-52s carry out daily bombing raids, do you really think he can regret the soft easy life of jazz bands?" Sihanouk reserved his greatest vitriol for Lon Nol, but also expressed little confidence in his allies in the Khmer Rouge: "I understand very well that when I shall no longer be useful to them, they'll spit me out like a cherry pit. But what does that matter? . . . Aren't they fighting against my enemies?" In the interview, Sihanouk offered America a simple bargain: Abandon Lon Nol and we'll talk.

The X factor in the Cambodia conflict was whether Sihanouk might play a useful role in a settlement. When I came up for confirmation before the Senate, John Sparkman of Alabama—one of the more conservative members of Congress—encouraged me to get the exiled prince involved. But with Nixon and Kissinger wary and preoccupied—and committed to linking the fates of Vietnam and Cambodia—that would not be easy.

I wrote a detailed memo to the State Department suggesting how we should approach Sihanouk. We needed to be sensitive to his pride and vanity but more important, we had to take responsibility for our own actions in Cambodia.

"Whoever has the first substantive contact with Sihanouk must be prepared to listen silently to a lengthy and violent diatribe about

American wrongdoings in Indochina," I wrote. "I wish to remind the Department that Sihanouk has a paranoiac obsession with the CIA, which he holds responsible for much of what has happened to him. . . . In talking with Sihanouk, we must imply that perhaps we made a mistake in the past but have now seen the light, and that is why we are coming to him. We should stress that if the Prince comes back to Phnom Penh with the Khmer Republic's army, navy, air force, Buddhist clergy, and governmental administration intact, he would be cast in the position of arbitrator with a real power base from which to operate."

Who could approach Sihanouk? Any number of people could. Our own envoy to China, George H. W. Bush, might be a good person to start, as would Chinese statesman Chou Enlai. Chou was Sihanouk's host in China—the two saw each other on a regular basis—and had also developed a working relationship with Nixon and Kissinger. Another possibility was Etienne Manac'h, the longtime French diplomat who had known Sihanouk since the 1950s. Or we could prevail on Secretary-General Kurt Waldheim of the United Nations to get involved. And what about the Soviets, with whom we had just embarked on a new relationship of détente? They had expressed concern for China's dominance in the region and support for a "Lao-type solution." The Soviets had no real entrée to the Khmer Rouge, but they did have entrée to Saigon, which had contacts with Sihanouk.

Eventually, we made some attempts to approach Sihanouk. Kissinger talked to the Chinese, and they said no. Waldheim was cautious. Bush and his deputy called on Sihanouk and got the cold shoulder. But you have to ask the right way. We took so long to seek out Sihanouk's help, and asked in such a halting and halfhearted way, that his refusal was almost automatic.

My boss on all Cambodian matters was Henry Kissinger, who continued as secretary of state in the new Ford administration. I have always liked and admired Kissinger. Like me a refugee from Nazi Germany, Henry was not only brilliant but he also worked hard. The story is told that when as a student at Harvard he asked a professor for advice on understanding politics, he was given a long list of books to read—kind of a joke, an Ivy League hazing. But Henry went back to his dorm and read every one of the books.

It's that kind of driving ambition that made him such a formidable figure in American politics for a generation.

Kissinger's theory of international politics—that the peace can be kept when there is a stable balance of power among nations—helped him break down barriers that had straitjacketed American politics for three decades. To create an effective bulwark against the communist bloc, he reached out to them. He masterminded a state of détente with the Soviet Union, under which the two superpowers recognized that though they were foes they could find ways to cooperate and defuse tensions. He arranged Richard Nixon's historic 1972 trip to China, which the United States had continuously refused to recognize since Mao's 1949 revolution.

But Kissinger was also trapped. In the 1968 presidential campaign, Richard Nixon had said he had a "secret plan" to end the Vietnam War. That plan was really not a plan but a pose. The idea was to convey to North Vietnam that an unreasonable Nixon was capable of using nuclear weaponry if the war did not end on terms acceptable to South Vietnam. Kissinger had the assignment of passing the word that Nixon was adamant, uncompromising, about the war. The message was simple: You just can't talk sense to the man. Better to give in than risk annihilation.

As I understand it, that approach had the effect of stifling efforts to find diplomatic solutions to the war.

When I settled into the U.S. Embassy in Phnom Penh, I got right to work to organize negotiations to end the war. I traveled around the country and talked to U.S. military and intelligence officers about the war's progress. What I learned was twofold. First, the Khmer Rouge were making substantial progress in their war against the government of Lon Nol. The guerrillas took over about two-thirds of the country, mostly in the countryside. Lon Nol's government still controlled the cities—which meant most of the population—but those on his side were weary of war and aware of corruption in the government. With every passing day, the Khmer Rouge gained more territory and military strength.

Prince Sisowath Sirik Matak told me in May 1974 that Cambodians were losing the will to fight. As I stated in a telegram to Washington: "It is questionable whether the Khmer people are willing to continue this struggle much longer. Sirik Matak said frankly that war weariness has set in and that if the Cambodian conflict is to be resolved through other than military means, this alternative route should be explored sooner rather than later."

Sirik Matak himself adopted a dependent attitude toward the United States. The Cambodian government, he said, does not have the power or authority to solve its civil war on its own. The United States has a moral obligation—and a political imperative—to end the war peacefully and soon—before the KR take power by force. Lon Nol expressed the same need for the United States to take the initiative. In a conversation with me that September, Lon Nol went so far as to say that he would leave power to make an agreement possible. I cabled to Washington: "Since time is not on the side of the government we support, it is incumbent on us to arrange for an end to the conflict within the time frame allowed us."

The second thing I learned was that the Khmer Rouge were a brutal, murderous band who would create a bloody reign of terror if they were allowed to win the war and take over the country. Contrary to the media's naive depiction of the Khmer Rouge as agrarian reformers, they were vengeful and violent. They had no internal checks against committing unspeakable violence against anyone who opposed them.

In my opinion, the logical third part of this syllogism was that we should therefore sit down at the table with the Khmer Rouge and negotiate a ceasefire—with the prospect of a coalition government that included all sides in the conflict.

The sooner, the better. Time was not on our side.

To some people, sitting down with murderous thugs like the Khmer Rouge might seem like the ultimate betrayal of human values—and hopelessly naive as well. How can we even talk to a band of murderers? If we agree on anything, how can we trust them to keep their promises? They should be punished, not rewarded with seats in a coalition government.

But that kind of thinking gets things backwards. I do not need to negotiate to get along with my friends. It's my enemy that requires a special effort. Most diplomatic challenges are so complex—with so many people and issues at stake—that you can always find things to trade. You feel insecure in cities? OK, we'll protect you this way.

You want support for farmers? OK, we'll provide programs to get seed and equipment to the hinterland. You're concerned about the rights of minorities? We'll provide open trials with appeals processes. You want protection from foreign traders? We'll make access to the market more difficult. And so on.

I want to negotiate with the adversary. We worked with Stalin, didn't we? To save people from the devil you work with the devil. But you have to fortify yourself so you can hold your own with the adversary. If you sit down with the devil, you must figure out a way to cut off his hoofs.

Negotiating is not just a means to make exchanges and compromises. It's also a way to get the other side invested in something you care about. If the other side's interests are embedded in a system that you can accept, the other side isn't so dangerous anymore.

I had all kinds of ideas about how to coordinate talks that might lead to a Cambodian protocol such as we had achieved in Laos. I would want everyone at the table. I wanted the three superpowers involved, as well as neighbors like Thailand. I wanted to find ways to protect the territorial integrity of Cambodia—to prevent encroachments like those from North Vietnam and Thailand. But at the same time I wanted to bring foreign investors and travelers to Cambodia. If possible, I wanted to get Norodom Sihanouk—once a friend of America, now a bitter enemy living in Peking—to come back and play a role in a transitional government.

This last point shows how hard diplomacy can be. I thought involving Sihanouk—the most revered figure in Cambodia, a person who could win the trust of both sides in the conflict—could make peace possible. But getting authority from Washington to contact him took months—and was ultimately unsuccessful. Kissinger was not enthusiastic about using my old friend Etienne Manac'h as a go-between. After Valéry Giscard d'Estaing took over as French president, I thought Kissinger might approve the idea, but his heart was never in negotiating with the Khmer Rouge. I thought Chou Enlai was another possible interlocutor, but perhaps Kissinger did not want to distract him from his own game of global chess with China and the Soviet Union.

Lon Nol, once an ally of Norodom Sihanouk, had become the president of Cambodia when he participated in the military coup of

April 13, 1970. Sihanouk was in France at the time getting a medical checkup. Lon Nol was a strong ally of the United States and, by extension, of South Vietnam, and the U.S. government immediately recognized him as the legitimate leader of Cambodia.

What prompted Lon Nol to overthrow Sihanouk? Was it opposition to Sihanouk's policy of nonalignment? Personal ambition? A desire to reform Cambodia's society and bring Cambodia into the twentieth century? Breaking ties with Cambodia's former colonial masters? Fear of encroaching Marxism emanating from China and North Vietnam? Whatever the reason, Lon Nol and his plotters were adamantly opposed to Sihanouk, who never forgave them for what he considered treason. It is also undoubtedly true that a number of foreign countries at the time looked with favor upon Lon Nol's efforts to overthrow Sihanouk. In the forefront of these was the United States, which saw in Lon Nol and his group staunch opponents to communism and an opportunity for opposing expansion of this doctrine into Southeast Asia. These foreign countries preferred an untested Lon Nol to the wishy-washy neutralism of Prince Sihanouk.

In the long run, though, Lon Nol's ascension shattered Cambodia's vaunted neutrality. Once in power, Lon Nol had to pursue actively a policy in conformity with those who paid the bills, notably, the United States. From 1970 onward, he harmonized his policies with those of American anticommunist efforts. But as the war dragged on in Vietnam, and with a neutralist solution in Laos achieved in 1973, Lon Nol and his team grew increasingly aware of the need to find a way out of the war in Cambodia, and the need to talk with the Khmer opposition.

The performance of the Cambodian government complicated our hopes of doing anything—supporting Lon Nol or ushering in a new era of neutralism and peace. The government had become ineffective and corrupt. The economy was a shambles. The military was losing the war. Most important, the people had lost their will for a long drawn-out battle. There are only so many years of warfare to which you can subject a people. At some point, you cannot drag them along anymore. You have to find a way to end the misery and build something new.

Since taking over in 1970, Lon Nol had been weakened by age, a stroke, and war weariness. The once erect, proud military leader had become an old man with a crippled left side, walking with difficulty but nonetheless maintaining a dignified demeanor. Even more than from his personal frailties, his government suffered from ineptitude and corruption. The corruption included all the usual petty crimes of governments—stealing war materials to sell on the black market, providing special favors to friends and family, and the like. The logic of corruption merged with the logic of fear. The presidential palace was bombed by government pilots, who then switched over to the Khmer Rouge; the government logically ringed the palace with soldiers armed with 33-mm guns to shoot down any aircraft hovering near the palace. Because those soldiers got bonuses any time they shot at something, they often shot at friendly planes, which then shot back. This would have been comical if it were not so disastrous.

Lon Nol himself often acted out of fear. When President Nixon invited him to the States for medical treatment, he refused out of fear that the Nixon administration was employing a ruse to get him out of the way. Rise by coup, fall by coup.

The Cambodian army was not bad. Soldiers worked hard and were pleased to earn a living. Most officers were professional, and to the extent they were honest, enjoyed the support of their men. I always found it easy to talk with them and work with them. Naturally, when you are financing the whole war and propping up the regime, you expect your clients to listen and cooperate. The problem was that everything around them was failing.

The Khmer Rouge were a determined enemy. Their movement began in 1966, when some officers of the Royal Army deserted and took to the countryside. They didn't like Sihanouk because they considered him too mercurial to protect the neutrality of Cambodia and too closely linked to the rich, who had no social conscience. The Khmer Rouge gained strength with the American bombings of Viet Cong sanctuaries in Cambodia in 1969. Sihanouk did not like the bombings but did not protest publicly.

By the early 1970s, the Khmer Rouge had no trouble supplying their army and moving about the countryside. They obtained arms and other materials from the North Vietnamese, the Chinese, and the Russians. Young people thronged into the Khmer Rouge, especially from the tribal areas. A few older people, educated in France, also participated in the movement.

The Khmer Rouge posed a difficult problem. On the one hand, we knew they were murderous thugs. We received regular reports about K.R. atrocities. Our sources had contacts who reported firsthand on the attitudes and actions of the leadership.

We took journalists to sites where there was evidence of torture, starvation, and mass killings. The evidence was very strong that they were a violent bunch. But people had a hard time believing that they would continue to be so brutal once they got into power. My view was that they would become more brutal once all the checks on their power were removed.

But even members of the Lon Nol government entertained fantasies about the K.R. reforming itself. Even Long Boret, the prime minister, thought he would survive in a new regime because he shared school ties with some of the Khmer Rouge leaders. The gentleness of the Cambodian people blinded them to how ungentle some of their countrymen were.

Diplomacy is the sum of countless actions and inactions, recognitions and slights, assaults and reconciliations. Over time, the way people interact creates a pattern. Sometimes, regardless of people's real interests, no matter how clear the pattern, opportunities for something positive to happen disappear forever.

That's what happened with Norodom Sihanouk: So much chaos occurred in Cambodia after he became king in 1941. So many real opportunities were missed. So many injuries could not, or would not, be forgiven.

Since 1970, when the military group led by Lon Nol deposed him, Sihanouk had been living in Peking. Why Sihanouk was deposed, who was behind the coup, is one of those topics for eternal debate. But this defender of Cambodian neutrality was suddenly out, and a government loyal to the United States was in. In exile, Sihanouk displayed his characteristic mix of elitism and populism, grace and petulance, accessibility, and remoteness.

I always got along well with Sihanouk. I thought he was the glue that held Cambodia together. He loved the Cambodian people, and they loved him back. For longer than anyone would have predicted, he maintained Cambodia's neutrality while awful wars and dirty tricks raged nearby. Named king precisely because he was considered pliable, he was flexible with a purpose. He nimbly played off factions against one another, brought them together again, and then rose above them for the goal of a united and neutral Cambodia.

The final months of my life in Cambodia were desperate. Unless some sort of "controlled solution" could be negotiated, the Khmer Rouge would win a bloody war and impose a bloody new regime.

I cabled Washington regularly with proposals for initiating peace talks that would lead to what I called a "controlled situation." I tried to explain all the benefits of peace beyond peace itself. The Soviets would look favorably on a controlled solution—good for detente. The Chinese would accept it too—good for the triangulation that Kissinger was trying to achieve. It would also make it easier to get peace in Vietnam. It could clear America's name with an increasingly critical world community.

Then there was the reality of Congress. Since the Watergate scandal broke, forcing Nixon to resign in August 1974, most representatives and senators on Capitol Hill had been reluctant to vote for more U.S. aid to Cambodia. Nixon had failed to bring about a lasting peace on his own terms in Southeast Asia. Congress was determined to take a dramatic new approach. The congressional appetite for foreign ventures also soured with revelations of abuses by some American civilians and military in Southeast Asia.

I tried to use Congress's failure to vote funds for Cambodia as an argument for expedited peace talks. I was trying to tell Ford and Kissinger: "You're right to be upset. But that's the reality. Let's work as effectively as we can within that reality."

In a memo on November 11, 1974, I wrote: "Unless it is believed that someone, somehow can make the U.S. Congress see the light as regards the level of resources needed to keep this country afloat, it becomes even more imperative that a major effort be undertaken to achieve some forward motion on the negotiating front. It seems to me essential that we at least get some kind of talks started before available or anticipated resources fall below the critical level. We cannot wait until the ammunition depot is visibly depleted or until runaway inflation has destroyed public confidence in the currency to move this conflict toward a resolution. If we can get some talks started, perhaps it will be easier to get Congress to give us the resources to preserve this side as at least a temporary going concern so that it will have the option of offering the other side a compromise."

But the most important reason for our urgent pleas to Washington—always—was that war was brutal and the unchecked advance of the Khmer Rouge could produce a human disaster. "If no solution is found, then we must be prepared for an uncontrolled dénouement to the Khmer drama," I wrote in early 1975. "Under [these] circumstances, a bloodbath cannot be ruled out."

President Ford made increasingly desperate pleas to Congress to provide economic and military aid to save South Vietnam and Cambodia from the communists. In February, for example, and very much encouraged by the U.S. mission in Phnom Penh, President Ford asked Congress for $222 million in aid. "This is a moral question which must be faced squarely," Ford said. "Are we to deliberately abandon a small country in the midst of its life and death struggle? Is the United States, which so far has consistently stood by its friends through the most difficult of times, now to condemn, in effect, a small Asian nation totally dependent upon us?"

I grew more and more desperate as time passed. "We concluded [in June 1974] that a political solution must be found to the Cambodian dilemma as soon as possible. Everything we said in this assessment seven months ago remains as valid today as it was when we wrote it last year," I wrote in January 1975. "We are heading towards a debacle unless a political solution can be found rapidly, putting an end to the conflict."

At one point I raised the specter of resigning in protest. But as I stated in a strongly worded February 4 memo, "Such an act might be misinterpreted as a desire on my part to get out.... However, I want to register my profound disagreement with what appears to be the department's reasoning, i.e., that we will be in a better position for negotiations some months from now or that developments will have occurred in the U.S. or in Cambodia which will shed a kinder light on our five-year effort in Cambodia."

The war continued to go badly, but I wanted to keep trying to get a peaceful solution. In one February 14 memo, I argued against quitting: "[A] last-minute extraction of the American official mission from Phnom Penh is, in my opinion, contrary to the long-standing American tradition of living up to our responsibilities and would be unworthy of the efforts both American and Khmer people have made in Cambodia in the last ten years. We have little time left. Let's use it to obtain an orderly settlement here."

In February 1975, I learned that the Khmer Rouge said they would negotiate an end to the war if eight officials of Lon Nol's government were to resign. I thought that might be worth exploring. We needed to get off the battlefields and seated around a negotiating table. I mentioned this to Sydney Schanberg of the *New York Times*. I thought I was speaking off the record, but he published my remarks. Some in Washington thought I was making too many public statements rather than just implementing U.S. policy. Maybe so, but things were getting desperate.

I was starting to annoy the decision makers in Washington. Lawrence Eagleburger sent me a bug-off memo on February 27: "As a friend I want to give you my very personal reactions to your latest messages on how to proceed with negotiations," he said. "In utterly frank terms, these messages are seen here as confirmation that your interest in negotiation has now become an obsession. I must tell you that such cables are increasingly counterproductive."

Around this time, I ordered embassy staff to evacuate their spouses and children, and they all went to Thailand. Cambodia had simply become too dangerous for people who did not have work assignments. We wanted to bring the families back when possible but did not hold out too much hope. The Embassy became a much quieter place. We continued to observe the authorized maximum limit of 200 embassy staff members that Congress mandated be in the country at any given time. Family members were exempt from this limit. Not having family nearby took away the life of the place, but we also thereby gained the opportunity to concentrate on the crisis.

Kissinger's view—and therefore, the administration's view—was that peace talks would work only if Lon Nol's government enjoyed a military advantage. Kissinger did not want to negotiate if the Khmer Rouge held most of the chips. But waiting for Lon Nol and his adherents to gain an advantage was futile. Absent a miracle—congressional approval of major new funding, a turnaround in the fighting spirit of the government forces—it simply was not going to happen.

What could I do? I may not have been winning with my appeals for action, but shutting up would not help either. All I could do was fight for what I believed, marshaling as many arguments with as much evidence as possible. I am not a quitter. I tried every angle, hoping that someone somewhere would agree with my logic. Until a war is over, there is always a chance to win the peace.

Over time, it seemed that my role in Phnom Penh was to provide updates on the Khmer Rouge's inevitable march to victory so that Washington would know the best time for us to flee the country.

And the updates were grim. The Khmer Rouge had a stranglehold on the Mekong River. The Khmer Rouge had taken a string of villages on the way to Phnom Penh. The Khmer Rouge staged regular guerrilla attacks on the capital. The Khmer Rouge ambushed a government railway, cutting off the country's last link to the outside world. The Khmer Rouge had punctured the wall of soldiers that the government assembled on the outskirts of Phnom Penh. The Khmer Rouge were in rocket range of the Phnom Penh airport. The Khmer Rouge were adding recruits to their ranks, and military supplies from foreign sources kept on coming.

What is the best way to end a bad war?

That's not a question any world power wants to ask. But it is essential, because every great power loses at some point. France and Britain, Portugal and Spain, all lost empires. The United States did not develop a colonial system like these nations, but we did exert great sway over every corner of the globe. Maintaining control over everything—the Philippines, the Panama Canal, client states in Latin America and Asia—simply did not make sense. It is also costly to maintain a global military. We need to make sure that we do not sink so many resources into losing causes that we are short on money and equipment when emergencies arise.

As a nation, we also need to do the right thing. Sometimes, other nations and their people need and want us. Other times, they don't. We have to have the wisdom to tell the difference and act accordingly.

The French established a good model for leaving when they are no longer wanted. After Dien Bien Phu in 1954, they chose to leave Indochina. The French supported the Geneva Convention of 1954, which granted independence to Vietnam, Laos, and Cambodia. The French made sure that their people had the chance to leave honorably.

Most important, the French reconsidered their colonial system. It took several more years for France to leave Algeria, but leaders like Charles De Gaulle began to understand that sometimes the national interest of France meant letting go. The French national interest did not involve dominating unwilling colonies, but in protecting the real vital interests of the country—defense of the nation, participation in international affairs as a respected power, development of an equitable society. De Gaulle was the embodiment of nationalism in France. For him to let go of colonial ambitions was a powerful acknowledgment that power over someone else does not always give you power to control your own destiny.

If we had found a way to settle for part of the cake, and if we had met our responsibility to protect the people we were allied with, we would have been better off. We might not have been able to bask in victory, with pliable allies wherever we wanted them; but we would have avoided wholesale death and destruction. Just taking care of business required extraordinary efforts—and hard moral choices and risks.

Richard Armitage was among the bravest during America's last days in Cambodia. He coordinated the movement of huge barges, carrying food, ammunition, and other equipment down the Mekong River from Saigon to Phnom Penh. He had the idea of armoring the sides of the barges; but metallic armor was no good when the Khmer Rouge dropped missiles from above into the barges. When you drop missiles from above, the explosion can be catastrophic because of the ammo on board.

What could we do? General Jack Palmer suggested using "lazy dog" grenades. I had never heard of them before. Palmer explained that the grenades would explode six or seven feet off the ground, wiping out people standing up to launch the missiles. But the lazy dogs might be in violation of the Geneva Convention on warfare. I could have asked Washington what to do, but thought I would get a runaround. I decided that I should exercise the authority the president gave me to coordinate all U.S. activities in Cambodia and gave the go-ahead to use the lazy dogs. But they did not help much. The Khmer Rouge steadily tightened their grip on the Mekong River. Soon, we had to abandon river cargo.

So we went to Plan C. Inspired by the Berlin airlifts, six to eight DC-6s bearing food and military supplies from Thailand landed in Phnom Penh every day. We took the goods and distributed them—often by helicopter—to cities and other places under the control of the Lon Nol government.

If we could not win the war in Cambodia, the very least we could do was to exit with grace and dignity, helping as many people as possible escape the brutality of the incoming regime. In late 1974, we began planning an evacuation that we called "Operation Eagle Pull."

Getting out was going to be a delicate matter. We had to do things gradually, because a big, ostentatious effort would attract the fire of the enemy. And we had to wait until the last possible moment, when we knew we had no chance to prevail, as our departure would undermine the morale of the Khmer people and military personnel.

I told Washington that we should leave Phnom Penh with a series of helicopter runs to neighboring Thailand, where airplanes could be ready to carry Cambodians, Americans, and other foreigners to safety. In a series of messages, I told the U.S military in Hawaii (CINCPAC) and in Washington (State and Defense) that I was not going out by fixed-wing aircraft, because that would be easy for everyone to see, and we would not get safely to the airport several miles from the Embassy. The primary goal was safety. If we tried to drive people to the airport to get them out of Phnom Penh, we could be attacked by the Khmer Rouge—or even by embittered Cambodians who felt the United States had betrayed them and left them to face the Khmer Rouge alone.

I also thought that when we left, we should leave open the possibility of returning. If we could somehow get peace talks going to agree on a new government, we would be back. That was an extreme long shot, but I don't believe in giving up while hope remains.

High officials in the administration debated my approach. Defense Secretary James Schlesinger told Henry Kissinger I was grandstanding, looking for a way to make a conspicuous exit. He said my approach was "loony." When Kissinger told Phil Habib about Schlesinger's comments, Habib bristled, recalling a conversation he and I had had. "Our airplanes are under fire," I had told him. "They lost another airplane at Phnom Penh airport last night. The Cambodian military had a few people killed there two miles from the airport. Phil, if you want to save lives, do it this way." Phil responded, "John, you've got your hand on the throttle. You do it your way."

Kissinger told Habib that Schlesinger was playing the old Washington game, setting himself up to dodge blame if the operation failed. "If anything goes wrong, it's our fault," Kissinger said. If everything worked well, no one would remember Schlesinger's advice or condescending statements.

What *were* loony were Washington's cables wondering whether I should stay behind in Cambodia after the exit. I wouldn't have been able to accomplish anything. I had asked for support to negotiate a year earlier. This was not the time to negotiate. At the beginning of 1975, a negotiated solution would still have been viable, but not at this late stage.

As I had said a hundred times, the aftermath of a Khmer Rouge victory was likely to be bloody. Nothing anchored the Khmer Rouge. Nothing checked their behavior. They were going to round up officials and sympathizers of the Lon Nol regime and either kill them or hold them hostage. Without some kind of force to keep the guerrillas in line, they would be violent and indiscriminate. Did the United States really want its ambassador held hostage, humiliating the United States before the world?

The few Americans who stayed behind—like Sydney Schanberg, the brilliant *New York Times* reporter, disguised themselves as French so they could stay alive and get out of Cambodia. Obviously, I could not do that.

I wanted to give safe passage to all who wanted to leave and who felt their lives were in danger. We had a difference of views with Washington over whom we at Embassy Phnom Penh were responsible for. Obviously, all official and nonofficial Americans were eligible for evacuation. In reply to a query about which Cambodians we should take out, Washington suggested Cambodians in the government, Cambodian military closely linked to the United States, and all well-educated Cambodians who Washington felt (and rightly so) would be targeted by the Khmer Rouge once they came to power. Our mission took exception to that cable, pointing out that anyone would be in danger that had been working for Americans, Cambodians, or third country nationals, whether illiterate or holding a PhD.

Our team agreed that we would take everybody who wanted to go and whose life could be endangered when the Khmer Rouge came to power. We took gardeners, houseboys, Koreans working for our mission, Cambodian generals and ministers, and educated Cambodians. One of them, a Cambodian atomic scientist still in Phnom Penh, later went to work for the French Atomic Energy Commission outside Paris. I also sent helicopters into the provinces to bring back some members of the International Red Cross. Sixteen of them came back to Phnom Penh by U.S. helicopters.

I went to see the Archbishop of Phnom Penh at the beginning of the year. He believed that all clergy, nuns, and monks, regardless of nationality, would be safe. Some of the young French priests were not particularly supportive in their sermons of the American role in Cambodia. By the end of March 1975, I pleaded with the Archbishop to permit all Cambodian priests, nuns, and monks whose lives might be in danger to leave with our planes for Thailand to await developments. After a great deal of pleading, I was able to take out some forty nuns and monks on the DC-8s to Thailand.

No one who asked was refused evacuation. I thanked God that some people had changed their minds at the end and agreed to leave Phnom Penh.

Lon Nol resigned as president on April 1, left Cambodia for Thailand, and ended up in Hawaii. I took out the former head of the Cambodian Senate, Sokom Khoi, who had taken over as chief of state when Lon Nol left for Hawaii. Sokom Khoi was an honorable man, honest and willing to find a compromise settlement. He never had a chance to try his hand at negotiations. His family came out with us, and he stayed in Bangkok for a while before settling in America. Wherever these elderly Cambodians went was exile, and they always missed their homeland. But better alive than falling victim to Khmer Rouge death squads.

The day we left Phnom Penh, April 12, 1975, I sent word to Sirik Matak, Sihanouk's uncle, who had played a major role in the Lon Nol government, that the United States would help him to leave the country if he so chose. He responded with a letter that chills me still:

> Dear Excellency and Friend,
> I thank you sincerely for your letter and for your offer to transport me towards freedom. I cannot, alas, leave in such a cowardly fashion. As for you, and in particular for your great country, I never believed for a moment that you would have this sentiment of abandoning a people which has chosen liberty. You have refused us your protection, and we can do nothing about it.
> You leave, and my wish is that you and your country will find happiness under the sky. But, mark it well, that if I should die here on the spot and in my country that I love, it is too bad because we are all born and must die one day. I have only committed this mistake of believing in you the Americans.
> Please accept, Excellency and dear friend, my faithful and friendly sentiments.
> Sirik Matak

He did not survive.

A dozen Marine CH-53 helicopters took off from the USS *Okinawa* in the Gulf of Thailand and landed on the soccer field near the Embassy. Then we took the filled 'copters back to the American warship, from where we flew to an American base in Thailand.

The American Embassy in Phnom Penh was a three-story whitewashed building surrounded by a high wall and screens designed to intercept missiles. When I had arrived, it buzzed with activity. We had 200 embassy staff and their families. Other countries had representatives in town, and we saw them regularly. We also saw businessmen, workers from NGOs, a steady stream of politicians, and even tourists.

In the final days in April 1975, we were just a shell of an operation. We worked frantically to save Cambodia, but deep down we doubted that there was a will in Washington to engage the enemy in negotiations. So all we could do was to keep trying, and to arrange for as dignified an exodus as possible.

Those final days were chaotic. We wanted to be fair about how we left, so we set the same rules for everyone. Each person could take one bag on the helicopter and plane. We worked frantically, burning documents and destroying files that contained secret information. We did our best to pack personal belongings, books, rugs, and ornaments to ship out, but most everything remained behind.

The physical strain was intense. I had lost twenty pounds since arriving in Phnom Penh and got snappish at the end of long days when everything I tried to save the situation failed. My deputy Robert Keeley—one of the great figures in modern diplomacy— had to leave for a while to treat a bleeding ulcer, but he was back for the exit. Another embassy official had a heart attack and was sent back to Washington to take a desk job. One of our men, the head of the AID Economic Assistance Mission, Thomas Olmsted, collapsed and died of pancreatitis.

Together with the French, the United States had the last functioning foreign mission in Phnom Penh, so there was no one left with whom to commiserate and plan except journalists.

On Friday, April 11, I understand President Ford contacted Norodom Sihanouk in China and asked him to go to Cambodia to save his country. He said no.

The next day, the United States left Cambodia.

We had set up a procedure whereby key Cambodian leaders were told to send an assistant or a secretary to the U.S. Embassy at 6:00 a.m. every day to find out the situation and the decision taken by us regarding taking people to safety. This system worked rather well until the fateful day of April 12, 1975, when we decided to leave Phnom Penh by helicopter. At 7:00 a.m., we sent our people to the hotels and houses where embassy staff, journalists, and others were sleeping. They pounded on the doors. "Get up! We're leaving! Call anyone you want to call, get anyone you want to get! Go to the Embassy right away! Bring only one bag! No one gets more than one bag!"

People moved fast. They had known for weeks that this day would come soon. As our Marines ringed the Embassy, protecting the area from enemy fire, other soldiers guided people to the helicopters. The helicopters came, one after another, to a soccer field near the Embassy. Some people fussed and pressed to take more than one bag. Most accepted the rules without comment.

I wanted to be the last American out of the country. It is important for the person in charge to see that everyone else is taken care of before he leaves. Finally, at 10:30, after thirty-five helicopter trips, it was time for me to go.

Somehow I had to demonstrate the dignity of the American mission in carrying out the task assigned to us. All of us at the embassy cared about our country, and we cared about our mission in Cambodia. We had to do something to show that we were going out with a sense of patriotism.

Waiting to be called to move to the extraction site, I sat in my office fully aware of the meaning of the moment for our country. I read the letter from Sirik Matak, which had arrived about forty-five minutes earlier. Looking out the window, I saw the Marines taking people to the helicopters and to safety. I watched the embassy personnel exerting themselves to do all they could to help those who had thrown in their fate with us. Many had worked all night long preparing the letters, drafted by Bob Keeley, to be delivered in the early hours of April 12, offering to take people to safety. Nobody was turned down for evacuation, including at the last moment, Sydney Schanberg's Cambodian staffer, who worked for the *New York Times*. We took out foreign nationals for whom we had responsibility, and even if we had no responsibility. We took the Cambodian girlfriends of some of our Cambodian bachelor staff members. I asked our resident military and the Marines in charge of the evacuation to take out anybody who wanted to go with us.

At one point, I took a pair of scissors and cut the American flag and the ambassadorial flag off the poles in back of my desk in the ambassador's office. I was trying to figure out a way of giving some form of protection to the symbols of our country and to the people whom I represented in Cambodia. Tears were rolling off my cheeks. I was alone. I took the two flags and put them over my arm. I got some plastic so they would not get wet. On our way to the helicopters, I stopped at my residence where the American flag was flying and struck the colors. I put this third flag with the other two and walked to the waiting helicopters with the American flags over my arm.

Pictures of me grimly carrying the flags ran on the front pages of newspapers and magazines across the world. Some said it was a picture of American defeat. Some said it was a picture of American patriotism. It was both.

From Phnom Penh I flew to the USS *Okinawa*. President Ford called to thank me and my embassy staff for our orderly evacuation. Then it was on to Thailand, where I was reunited with my wife. I hunkered down at the American Embassy in Bangkok for three weeks and wrote reports about what had happened and what the prospects were for the final days of the American-backed regime.

The Cambodian experience was a wrenching one for all of us who served there. Whether secretaries or generals, ambassadors or clerks, we stayed in contact for a long time.

While in Bangkok, all those who had served together in Cambodia—Americans and Cambodians—got together one last time on a pleasure cruise boat on the river to say goodbye. As the leader of the team of 200 people, I was asked to speak. I thanked them for what they had done and for the valiant service they had rendered our country. I closed my remarks on that occasion with a quotation from Shakespeare's *Hamlet*, Act 1, Scene 3. It is Polonius addressing his son Laertes:

This, above all: to thine own self be true,
And it must follow, as the night the day,
Thou canst not then be false to any man.
Farewell; my blessing season this in thee!

This quotation became the leitmotif for the rest of my years in the Foreign Service.

Four months later, on August 14, 1975, President Ford sent me a most gratifying letter, saying, "I want to commend you and your staff for your valiant leadership and service in the successful evacuation of Americans from Phnom Penh." He further wrote: "In reviewing the events surrounding our last few tragic months in Indochina, I can look with pride at your selflessness and devotion, which are so appropriately in keeping with American sacrifices of the last decade. You were given one of the most difficult assignments in the history of the Foreign Service and carried it out with distinction."

Vietnam fell on April 30, 1975. The American exit from Saigon did not go as well as ours. That was no fault of Ambassador Graham Martin. His job was harder than ours. We had the luxury of planning our exit for weeks. He had a lot more people to evacuate. We had more DC-8s to do the job during the weeks and months before the evacuation. Perhaps more important, there was something more devastating about the American loss in Vietnam. Cambodia was always understood to be a "side show." Vietnam was the main event. When Graham and his brave colleagues left Saigon, they bore the unfair brunt of all the U.S. failures in the region.

Five days after we left, Phnom Penh fell to the Khmer Rouge. Government officials expressed defiance, but their defeat was inevitable. Long Boret agreed to step down—no surrender or democratic elections.

It did not take long for the Khmer Rouge to unleash the full ferocity of their new power.

One of the victims of the early executions was, unsurprisingly, Prince Sirik Matak. He had taken refuge in the French Embassy. The Khmer Rouge surrounded the Embassy and vowed to cut off all supplies unless all Cambodian citizens left the building. Sirik Matak marched out proudly, defiant against the KR. They shot him in a public execution near the Grand Hotel in the center of Phnom Penh.

Long Boret had stayed in Cambodia, thinking that he could have some kind of dialogue with the Khmer Rouge. When he realized that that was impossible, he raced to the airport with his family in a Jeep to try to get out of the country. When they arrived at the airport, they got on a helicopter with some military officers. One officer brutally shoved him off the helicopter. The 'copter took off. The Khmer Rouge captured Long Boret and his family and killed them all.

The Cambodian Bishop of Phnom Penh had also decided to stay. He was a shepherd of God and did not want to leave his flock behind. The Khmer Rouge shot him as soon as they could catch him.

In the next five years, the Khmer Rouge would kill more than one and a half million Cambodians, the worst genocide since Nazi Germany. The K.R. emptied the cities, forcing young and old to take long marches to the countryside; soldiers shot those who straggled or otherwise irritated them and forced the survivors to continue marching over dead bodies. The K.R. especially targeted anyone with any ties to the previous government, Vietnamese, or intellectuals. God help anyone wearing glasses.

The genocide took place mostly out of view of the rest of the world, which was too weary to watch anyway. But when journalists and human rights activists pieced together the real story, many people just shrugged. Leftists often made excuses along the lines of not being able to make an omelet without breaking eggs. Conservatives huffed about how the genocide just confirmed their own suspicions about leftists in general. A few hardy souls desperately spoke out and sought an international solution.

We knew before we left that Cambodia faced a major crisis of survival in the early days of a Khmer Rouge regime. Quite apart from their brutality, the K.R. had no ability to run an economy or get food to the people who needed it. I lobbied for weeks before our evacuation that we should develop an emergency humanitarian program to prevent Cambodians from starving.

No one knew that the Khmer Rouge would empty Phnom Penh and other cities, forcing the healthy and frail alike to march mile after mile under inhuman conditions. But that's what happened. It probably would have happened whether or not we had embraced a humanitarian mission. But I don't know that for sure.

After leaving Phnom Penh, I stepped up efforts to convince Washington to meet its moral responsibility to care for refugees and feed people displaced by the war. My attitude was that if we needed to work with the Khmer Rouge, so be it. "We are on the verge of a human catastrophe unless we move rapidly to avert it," I wrote from Bangkok on April 13. Only the United States had the capacity to bring in 600 to 1,000 tons of food a day. "To the extent that the U.S. government can still contribute to an orderly solution to resolve the Khmer tragedy, I think we should leave no stone unturned."

But Washington said no. On April 16, I got a telegram from the State department: "We do not repeat not wish to establish contact with the Khmer Rouge. You should therefore make no repeat no effort to get in touch with the Khmer Rouge. We maintain relations with the GKR and you continue to be accredited to that government. When it is no longer a government we shall consider what our policy toward its successor shall be and how we shall deal with it."

Losing does not come easily to Americans. The failure of American policy in Southeast Asia prompted a generation of confusion driven by ideologues on both the right and left—and, perhaps more important, by the enduring innocence of the American people.

In his classic work *Democracy in America*, Alexis de Tocqueville noted that a lack of history and an "equality of conditions" shaped every aspect of life in the United States: America lacks the historic roots found everywhere else in the world. If you make it in the States, it's because of what you do now—not what some ancestor did on the same land three centuries earlier. Everyone has a chance. That's what amazed me so much about the Midwest when I moved there as a boy. Everything was so open and accepting. That is probably one reason why immigrants continue to flock to the United States year after year.

And we are forever young. We think we can do anything, just like an adolescent. We idealize ourselves and the objects of our affection. And when we fail, we have a hard time understanding it. And we also have a hard time understanding the depth of other people's tragedies.

America failed in Southeast Asia and still has not reckoned with that failure. We make our treks to the magnificent Vietnam Memorial in Washington and mourn our 55,000 dead. We make every effort to track down POWs and MIAs, even when there's no real evidence that any remain. We debate, in emotional and moralistic turns, who lost Vietnam. Too often it's a black-and-white proposition. Liberals say we lost because we never belonged there, that it was the military-industrial-capitalist-colonial mission that brought us there. Conservatives say we lost because we didn't give the military the authority to do whatever it took to win the war.

But it is not that simple. We lost because we blindly followed the Cold War ideology of the 1950s. We attributed great strategic value to a backwards, faraway land. Once there, we fooled ourselves about the motivations and resolve of the enemy—sometimes not respecting them at all, sometimes thinking too well of them. We lied to ourselves about the war's progress. We stubbornly refused to find a way out of the conflict. We extended the conflict into neighboring countries and undermined the fragile fabric of their societies. We bent our own democratic institutions to save face.

We made mistakes—lots of them.

Everyone fails at some point. The British failed in India. The French failed in Indochina. The British, French, and Portuguese failed in Africa. The Spanish and Portuguese failed in South America. Yet in historic terms, most of these "failed efforts" nevertheless had a profound impact on the development and culture of the areas where the foreign initiatives had taken place. Everyone has to learn how to deal with the consequences of failed efforts, even those made with the best of intentions.

I would not be true to myself if I did not end this chapter on a few words regarding my personal relationship with Dr. Kissinger. We differed on a number of foreign policy issues, especially on American policy towards Cambodia. But as a career American Foreign Service officer, I also recognize the great contributions Dr. Kissinger made to U.S. foreign policy by establishing a new relationship with mainland China and exploring détente with the Soviet Union. It is therefore with respect and gratitude that I would like to close this chapter by citing Dr. Kissinger's letter to me as he left public office in early 1977. The letter dated, January 18, 1977, was sent to the American Embassy in Copenhagen, where I had been appointed ambassador by the Ford administration. Following is the text of his letter:

> I did not want to leave office without telling you personally of my appreciation and admiration for your contribution to our foreign policy over the past few years. You have served with honor and integrity, and I will especially remember the dignity with which you conducted yourself during the difficult days of our withdrawal from Cambodia. You can take pride in the service you have rendered your country, and I wish you all the best for the future.

1. John Gunther Dean meets with Modibo Keita, first president of Mali in 1960. On the table is a letter from the U.S. secretary of state designating Dean chargé d'affaires *en pied*.

2. Dean's wife, Martine, greets the wife of Sylvanus Olympio, the first president of the Togo Republic, in the capital, Lomé, in 1960.

3. Dean (at left) accompanies Senator Robert Kennedy when the senator visited Paris in late January 1967. In the course of his visit, Senator Kennedy received via the French Foreign Office the "peace sign" from North Vietnam, which implied that if the United States stopped the bombing of North Vietnam, it could have "direct talks with Hanoi" about the future of Vietnam-U.S. relations.

4. Dean and Prime Minister Souvanna Phouma celebrate at the latter's house after Dean helped to put down a coup d'état against the legal government of Laos in September 1973.

5. Dean greets the king of Laos at the king's palace in Luang Prabang in 1973.

6. Dean meets with Secretary Kissinger at the State Department in 1974, after Dean was named U.S. ambassador to Cambodia following his return from Laos.

7. Dean presents his credentials as U.S. ambassador to Cambodia to President Lon Nol on April 3, 1974, in Phnom Penh.

8. Ambassador Dean carries the American flag from the U.S. Embassy in Cambodia as he arrives at the Utapao air base in Thailand following evacuation by helicopter from Phnom Penh on April 12, 1975. The photo ran on newspaper front pages around the world. Shown here is the cover of the April 21, 1975, issue of *Newsweek*.

9. President Ford chats with Ambassador Dean, Queen Margrethe II of Denmark, and Vice President Rockefeller at the White House in 1976, during the Danish Queen's state visit to the United States on the occasion of America's bicentennial.

10. Ambassador to Lebanon John Gunther Dean meets with Secretary of State Cyrus Vance in 1980.

11. Ambassador Dean visits a school in northern Lebanon in 1980.

12. Ambassador Dean visits a monastery in 1980 accompanied by his wife Martine (at left) and Amine Gemayel (at right), a future president of Lebanon.

13. Ambassador Dean meets with King Bhumibol of Thailand at the king's palace office in Bangkok in 1982.

14. Secretary of State George Shultz congratulates new Ambassador to India Dean in 1985.

15. Prime Minister of India Rajiv Gandhi visits President Ronald Reagan at the White House during a visit to Washington, accompanied by Ambassador Dean (center) on October 20, 1987.

John — Great seeing you again. Keep up the great work there in India. Geo Bush

16. Vice President George H. W. Bush receives Ambassador Dean in his office in Washington in 1987 and inscribes the photo of their meeting: "Keep up the great work there in India."

17. Ambassador Dean pays his respects to Mother Teresa in Calcutta, India, in 1988.

18. Rosalynn and former president Jimmy Carter receive John Gunther Dean in April 2007 at the Carter Center in Atlanta, which houses Dean's documents and oral history.

7
The Crucible of Lebanon

On a warm evening in the late summer of 1980, I had one of the most unsettling experiences of my life.

I was the target of an assassination attempt by terrorists using automatic rifles and antitank weapons that had been made in the United States and shipped to Israel. Weapons financed and given by the United States to Israel were used in an attempt to kill an American diplomat!

On August 27, 1980, my wife and I were riding in a car from our residence overlooking the city of Beirut to the American University of Beirut, where we were to have dinner with the university's president. It was a beautiful evening, about 6:45 p.m., still light outside. Our daughter, Catherine, and her fiancé, William Curtis, rode in the first car of a three-car caravan. We were in the second car, making a left turn onto the rue de Damascus. We didn't notice a white limousine on the side of the road, but our bodyguards later told us they did and were immediately suspicious.

Suddenly rapid rifle fire, aimed at my car, erupted from above. On the right side of the car was a hill, from which the attackers shot at the cars. The firepower from two light antitank weapons (LAWS)—bazookas, essentially—was powerful enough to penetrate the car. Investigators later concluded that the assassins were using the bazookas in an attempt to knock the roof off the car so they could then shoot directly at their target—me—before any of our security detail could respond.

The bullets from the rifle fire also hit the lead car, where Catherine and William were traveling. Their tires were hit and blown out, causing the car to come to a sudden stop. Then the shots hit us—first the right side of the car, then the ground. My wife Martine threw her body over mine and shouted: "Down!"

The car had Plexiglas windows—bulletproof for most attacks, but not always against this kind of fire. For some reason, probably the angle of the strike, the bullets did not penetrate the car, but did hit the tires. Fortunately, the car was equipped with automatically inflatable tires designed for just this kind of emergency. All told, our motorcade took twenty-one bullets and two missiles, which bounced off the rear fender.

As my driver sped away—the security people were given strict instructions to protect the ambassador at all costs, no matter what happened to anyone else—the missiles fired from the LAWS landed on the ground. We looked through the back window and saw what looked like a spectacular fireworks display.

The lead car was destroyed. Catherine, William, the driver, and the security man had gotten out, under fire, and run to safety in the third car.

As all this was happening, one of the security men in the third car sprayed the hills where the shooting originated. He emptied his 20-round repeating rifle. The attackers fled, leaving behind their weapons and the spent shells from the attack.

In a matter of minutes, our car was back at the Embassy. As soon as we got there, the car collapsed. It was almost as if it had stayed together long enough to get us back to safety and then fallen apart from exhaustion.

It was not the first attack on an American diplomat in Lebanon. In 1976, Ambassador Francis E. Meloy, economic counselor Robert O. Waring, and a chauffeur were kidnapped and murdered on their way from West Beirut to East Beirut to meet with the new president of Lebanon. They were traveling through one of the more disputed parts of town when their car was stopped. Meloy and Waring were shot and left at a nearby site. Some time later Yasir Arafat, leader of the Palestine Liberation Organization (PLO), helped us to recover the bodies of these two American diplomats. Until today nobody knows who committed the crime, but most observers absolve the main PLO from responsibility for the murder.

Being the target of an assassination attempt was a horrible experience. Catherine was shaken up. Almost a quarter-century later, she still gets rattled when she thinks about the attack. But what rattles me is the aftermath of the event.

After the attempt on my life, I worked the telephone for three weeks, trying to find out from Washington what had happened.

Meanwhile, the newspapers were filled with sensational stories about the attack. Some Lebanese newspapers reported that the government of Lebanon did not exclude the possible involvement of the Israeli intelligence service, Mossad. Other newspapers claimed that Christians with close ties to Israel had done it. Whether it was Lebanese surrogates or Israeli agents themselves, the media concluded that all the evidence pointed to the Israelis being behind the attack.

I could not, however, get a prompt answer from my own government as to who tried to kill me. "Hey fellas, I've just been nearly killed," I said when I called the State Department. "Can you find out what happened?" No matter how hard I tried, I could not get a straight answer from the State Department about what the U.S. government had discovered in its investigations. I got all kinds of nice letters from the president and others, saying, in effect, "John, are we ever relieved that you're alive!" But nothing else. I was simply told to resume my duties as ambassador. That was not so easy when I learned what the Lebanese intelligence agency found out.

Lebanese intelligence personnel quickly combed the area of the attack and found the weapons and ammunition left behind by the attackers. And when I sent the numbers of the individual weapons used to Washington, I learned that I had been attacked with American-made weapons that had been shipped to the Israeli government. The information was precise. It gave the name of the ship, the date the ship sailed for Israel, and the numbers of the light antitank weapons in the shipment, which included the two missiles used against my car in Beirut.

Every piece of weaponry in the world is tagged with numbers that identify where it was made and who made it. These numbers showed, without any doubt, that the weapons had been sent from the United States to Israel, which in turn shipped them to a Lebanese Christian militia ally. I know as surely as I know anything that Mossad, the Israeli intelligence agency, was somehow involved in the attack. Undoubtedly using a proxy, our ally Israel had tried to kill me.

Scurrilous attacks on me in the Israeli Knesset and the Israeli press just prior to the assassination attempt indicate that the Israeli authorities were unhappy with the activist role I played in Lebanon, defending Lebanese sovereignty and maintaining an active relationship with the PLO—the very policies I was given to pursue by the president of the United States. The venomous talk in the Israeli Knesset by the right-wing parties portrayed me as a tool of the Palestinians. Because I was willing, even eager, to talk with all factions in Lebanon's civil war, I was suspected of being anti-Israeli.

How did the situation in the Middle East reach a point where a diplomatic representative of the United States, Israel's greatest champion and supporter in the world, could come under attack by Israel? And how did the situation reach the point where the U.S. government would not work actively to determine the truth behind an assassination attempt on one of its own?

Early speculation was that Palestinians made the attack. But that could not be. The attack took place in an area outside of the Palestinians' control. To carry out an attack like that, you need to be in control of the area. The attack did not just happen because someone saw a last-minute opportunity to make a hit. It was planned; and it required easy movement along the route that my car traveled. Lebanese rightists with close links to Mossad occupied that area.

In the days before the attack on me, the Israelis had launched preventive strikes against Palestinian targets in Lebanon. I condemned the attacks, and so did the State Department, but some people said I was too rough in my statements about the Israelis. As before, I was accused of being too "activist," not friendly enough to Israel, and too friendly to the Palestinians.

What was the political landscape like during my years as the American ambassador to Lebanon? Lebanon then, as now, was a mosaic of eighteen different religions, with each religious group often subdivided into rightists, leftists, and moderates. These same subgroups were pro- or anti-Syrian, pro- or anti-Israeli, pro- or anti-Iranian, pro- or anti-British, pro- or anti-French, pro- or anti-Turkish, pro- or anti-Saudi, pro- or anti- Iraqi, and pro- or anti-American.

Many groups had their own militias. For example, the extreme rightist Christians came together under the banner of the "Guardians of the Cedars." Other Christian rightists fought under Bashir Gemayel's Phalangist command. The more free-enterprise Christians under the leadership of Camille Chamoun fought the more socialist-oriented Lebanese. The Shia of the South had empathy and support from the Shia in Iran. The Sunni establishment felt at home with the Turks, Egyptians, and Saudis. The more secular Baasists of Lebanon worked with Ba'athists in Syria and Iraq. The Druze under the leadership of Walid Jumblatt and Talal Arslan had links with their fellow Druze in Israel, Syria, and Jordan, or wherever they might be.

Was it a fragmented landscape? Yes. Though they were all Lebanese, the trouble was that they identified themselves more often in those days according to their religious affiliation and less with fellow Lebanese with whom they shared the same nationality. The Lebanese of Armenian or Kurdish descent had bad memories from their days under Ottoman rule. And then there were the Palestinians, who had fled from the fighting in Palestine when the Israeli state was established in 1948. Many of these Palestinians had lost everything and were housed in camps in Lebanon.

My task was to encourage all Lebanese to band together as Lebanese to protect their homeland, within their internationally recognized borders, against all who have designs on their land, water, sovereignty, and independence. Elias Sarkis, then president of Lebanon, encouraged me to pursue these policies, which were the very instructions President Carter had given and which President Reagan later renewed.

Today, more than twenty-five years later, a younger generation of Lebanese, regardless of religion, show signs of thinking in national, even nationalistic, terms. If so, then the new Lebanese generation has learned a lesson from their history and decades of suffering.

In diplomacy, one quickly learns that everything is connected with everything else. The job of foreign policy is to determine how to reach out to all factions and to understand how they relate to each other. When a president or ambassador understands the full range of factions and issues in a place, he or she can start to identify people's common interests and negotiate their differences.

I experienced the interconnectedness of everything when I worked in Southeast Asia. Vietnam, Laos, and Cambodia were separate nations with unique cultures and histories, but everything that happened in one place could affect what happened elsewhere in the region, as we saw in the tragic example of Cambodia.

This interconnectedness is particularly applicable to the Middle East, the cradle of three great religious traditions—Judaism, Christianity, and Islam. It is the home of Arabs, Kurds, Persians, and Mongols. Since the end of the Holocaust and World War II, it has been the home of the state of Israel. Because of the circumstances surrounding Israel's creation by the United Nations in 1948—after Great Britain had removed itself from the region as a colonial power—and its survival since the ensuing war of independence, the interests of other important groups in the region have at times been forgotten, neglected, or trampled. The resentment of those groups— most notably the Palestinians—has generated two multilateral wars (the June 1967 War and the October War of 1973) and further eruptions of bilateral conflict with Lebanon and the Palestinians. The 1967 war resulted in Israel's occupation of Palestinian territory, which has generated periodic outbreaks of guerrilla war and the interventions by not only the United States and its allies but also the Soviet Union, Syria, Libya, Saudi Arabia, and Iran. Add to this volatile mix the politics of oil and the struggle over control of Jerusalem, a city holy to all three religions.

Everything is connected to everything.

These Middle East conflicts spilled over into Lebanon, which was linked in one way or another to all these issues. The way I saw it, the only approach to the many festering problems and resentments in the country to which I was assigned was to talk to everyone in the country. The job of a diplomat is to see the whole country and everyone in it—get out of the Embassy, travel all over, try to understand people on their own terms, and report back to higher-ups in Washington and colleagues in the area about the possibilities and obstacles to peace.

Not long before the attack on my car, PLO leader Arafat stated that the PLO would no longer work for the elimination of Israel, would accept its right to exist, and would not engage in terrorist activities against Israel. Good news, right? But Israeli officials were not just wary; they were downright hostile. They called his move a danger to peace. They cited the PLO's Fatah faction, which had recently considered a new resolution condemning Israel. But when asked about the resolution, Arafat said the resolution had been put forth by a splinter group in Fatah and never passed.

You cannot always know what people's real intentions are, so the job of diplomacy is not to reject possibilities for peace but to build on them. Suppose Arafat was being completely cynical and dishonest. Suppose he was only duping the West in order to reduce Israel's preparedness. Wouldn't it be better to say, in effect, "We welcome this endorsement of our right to exist, and we're even more pleased that Arafat understands why peace is better for his people as well as ours"? When Nikita Khrushchev sent President John Kennedy two letters during the Cuban Missile Crisis, Kennedy publicly responded to the conciliatory letter and ignored the threatening letter. He boxed in Khrushchev. Why not pull a Kennedy? Or why not pull a Reagan? When negotiating with the Soviet Union, Ronald Reagan quoted an old Russian saying: "Trust, but verify."

I want to talk with everyone when I'm on assignment in a country. I want to do everything I can to bring people together, to get them talking and cooperating on economic development, technology, education, culture, sports, and all the rest. When I arrived in Lebanon, I went to the Soviet ambassador, Alexander Soldatov, and said: "Let's keep our rivalry out of the Middle East. We won't take shots at you, and you don't take shots at us. This mess is complicated enough without us bringing our rivalry into it." Unfortunately the State Department did not encourage my efforts to have a constructive dialogue with the Soviet ambassador to Lebanon at this stage of the Cold War.

I was always looking for ways to demonstrate that people on opposite sides of conflicts could get along. In Lebanon, I organized a movie outing among all the political factions inside the country as well as the key international players with a presence in the country—Christians, Muslims, and Jews, rightists, leftists, and centrists, Americans, Russians, and Syrians. Though such an approach won't save the world by itself, it could improve—infinitesimally—the chances for people to get together to make peace.

Over my term in Lebanon, I gradually developed a close working relationship with the Palestinian Liberation Organization. My contacts with the PLO, authorized by the government in Washington, demonstrated how the engagement of all factions could produce positive results.

At first, I was authorized to communicate with the PLO only about my own security. If I wanted to travel all over Lebanon, I needed to get assurances from different factions that they would not attack me. So I told PLO officials where I wanted to travel in territory that they controlled. They made sure that I was safe when I was in PLO territory.

When I had a problem of an American tourist, a government employee, or an American resident of Lebanon being detained anywhere in Lebanon, I would first ask the Lebanese intelligence chief, Johnny Abdo, for help. But I would also ask the Palestinian authorities in Lebanon for assistance. On a number of occasions the PLO helped me to get Americans released, either in the Bekaa Valley or in the south of Lebanon. Gradually this security link with the PLO expanded into a channel for exchanging information on other subjects. Using a secure telephone, Assistant Secretary Harold Saunders or his deputy, Morris Draper, passed me messages from the Department of State and asked me to convey them to the PLO. Replies received from the PLO leaders were then conveyed to Washington through the same secure telephone link. It was clear from these contacts that even more than twenty-five years ago American authorities considered the PLO a valid interlocutor for discussing ways of finding a nonmilitary solution to the Israeli-Palestinian conflict.

On November 4, 1979, Iranian militants stormed the United States Embassy in Tehran and took American officials and their family members hostage. The hostage crisis would cripple U.S. foreign policy for more than a year and devastate the Carter administration. President Jimmy Carter and Secretary of State Cyrus Vance worked overtime to negotiate the release of the hostages. Other Americans were doing their best to ensure that no hostages would be released before the presidential election in early November; and they were in fact released only as Ronald Reagan was being inaugurated in January 1980. Once Carter had lost the election to him, Ronald Reagan vowed to take a more aggressive approach to restore American supremacy in world politics.

Whatever one may say about President Carter, he was one of the most honorable men to sit in the Oval Office. He read everything submitted to him—often many pages—but like many highly intelligent, thoughtful people, he was reluctant to make decisions. I remember once being in Washington and meeting with President Carter to urge him to intervene with the Israelis regarding Lebanon. He agreed to take action. Back at the State Department about one hour later, I received a call from an aide saying that the president would delay any action for a while but that I would hear from him on the issue. I never did. Nonetheless, I remained an admirer of Jimmy Carter for, among other qualities, his consistent and fair approach to the problems of the Middle East.

Soon after arriving for my mission in Lebanon, I had asked my superiors whether I could make discreet contact with the PLO. The answer was yes. Then, after the U.S. Embassy in Tehran was invaded, an interlocutor in Washington asked me whether we might be able to use my PLO contacts to get some Americans out of Tehran. I worked on that issue with a number of Palestinians—Walid Khalidi, Basil Aql, Abu Jihad, and Abu Walid. (The Israeli secret police would later murder Abu Jihad in Tunisia.) I asked Abu Walid whether he could do anything to get hostages out of Iran.

He and Arafat went to Tehran and negotiated the release of thirteen American hostages on November 17, 1979. Under orders from Ayatollah Ruhollah Khomeini, the captors released only blacks and women, a seeming propaganda move to create divisions among the Americans—saying, in effect, "We recognize the difference between Americans who are the oppressed and Americans who are the oppressors." Even though the move may have been cynical, it meant freedom for thirteen Americans. It was progress in a terrible stalemate. It could also have been the beginning of a new relationship with the PLO. With some luck, it could have helped to produce an earlier end to the hostage crisis. You never know. That's why you talk and talk and talk and talk. The PLO's role was not acknowledged in the newspapers, but it was real.

Later, our contacts with the PLO helped us rescue an ally from a mob in Beirut.

One evening I got word from a friend, Assad Nasser, chairman of Middle East Airlines, that the Saudi and Kuwaiti ambassadors to Lebanon had been shot down over the Christian part of Lebanon. The Saudi ambassador was in pain, with a bullet lodged in his leg and had been taken to one of the private hospitals in the Christian heartland. My friend Assad Nasser told me that I should go and see him.

I said: "Who said I should go and see him?"

"I am telling you that," said the Middle East Airlines chairman.

I said: "Why?"

He said: "Because the Saudis look to the United Sates whenever they have a problem; you are supposed to help them out."

I said: "Wait a second. It's 9:00 p.m."

He said: "Yes, 9:00 p.m., but Saudis expect service all year round and twenty-four hours a day."

I asked: "Does that mean I have to get my entire convoy going and we have to cross over from West Beirut to East Beirut and go up to the hospital in the hills?"

He replied: "Yes. That's what you've got to do, I tell you. It's good advice."

I said: "I will take it."

I got my security team together, the convoy of three cars with bodyguards ready to drive at night from West Beirut into East Beirut and into the hills often manned by Christian militiamen. Driving at night between these two areas was not without risk. I told my wife that I was going to visit my Saudi colleague and she pointed out to me the danger of being on the road at that time of night.

When I got to the hospital, I saw Lieutenant General Ali Shaher, ambassador of Saudi Arabia, lying in a bed under a religious image. He was a very tall man. He said: "John, please get me to the American hospital. It's not that I am not getting good medical care here, but I am in pain. I want to go where I am completely at ease and my family can visit me. I want to go to the American hospital in West Beirut."

I answered: "Ok. It's now after 10:00 in the evening, so tomorrow morning at 10:00 we will have the motorcade take you to the American University Hospital in West Beirut." I went back to the residence in West Beirut that I used in case I was stuck in the city, as was the case that night. I must have gotten there about 11:30 p.m. and proceeded to make arrangements to have the Saudi ambassador moved by motorcade and ambulance at 10:00 a.m. the next day to the American University Hospital. The transfer went smoothly. Ali Shaher got a nice room at the American Hospital, his family visited him, and he received great medical attention.

One of the great figures at the time was Danny Chamoun, the son of Camille Chamoun, former president of Lebanon and leader of the Christian, free-enterprise political elements in Lebanon. Danny Chamoun had the idea to visit the Saudi ambassador at the American Hospital. Like his father, Danny had a relationship with the Saudis, but was that enough to risk his life by crossing over from Christian-held East Beirut to the more international West Beirut, where enemies of Danny could easily try to kill him? When it was known that Danny Chamoun was at the American Hospital, elements hostile to him gathered around the hospital and started shooting out its windows. Who made up the mob trying to storm the American University Hospital? Mostly Lebanese who opposed the Phalange and Chamounists—people who were more influenced by leftist propaganda, who believed that the Syrian model had some value for Lebanon, dissatisfied Moslems, and Palestinians who saw in Chamoun "a friend of Israel."

By late afternoon, a couple of thousand demonstrators had surrounded the hospital, and the worst was to be feared. By about 8:00 p.m., I was informed by one of my valiant men: "It is absolutely essential that you come immediately to the American Hospital. They are shooting up the hospital. There is going to be nothing left. They are going to take it by storm to capture Danny Chamoun. The crowd is made up of Palestinians, Syrians, Muslims, Christians, and crazies who are absolutely determined to destroy the American Hospital. The Saudi ambassador's life is in danger. He needs you badly. This time, he is calling for you."

I replied: "Okay, fellows, let's get the motorcade ready and go!"

We entered through the large garage door of the hospital. As it opened, the guard who opened it was shot and killed by one of the snipers in the crowd. Once inside the hospital, I rushed to Ali Shaher's room. There he was with his wife and daughter. He said: "Listen, this crowd is crazy. You've got to help stop this madness."

I replied: "What shall I do?"

He said: "Go and call Crown Prince Fahd of Saudi Arabia, and tell him to contact Arafat and President Assad of Syria and tell them to stop this shooting. Otherwise, this thing is going to get out of hand and everything will go up in flames."

I got in my car in the garage and as the garage door opened for the drive to the Embassy, rifle shots killed two Lebanese security people protecting the garage door! My entering and leaving the American Hospital had resulted in the killing of three people. Once I was out of the hospital, the road to the Embassy was safe. My car picked up a bullet, as usual, but as the limousine was armored, I was used to that kind of harassment.

By the time I reached the Embassy it must have been 9:00 p.m., and I asked for the communicators to come to the office. I never realized how easy it was to communicate with the world from the American Embassy. The communicators came within ten minutes. I said: "I would like to talk to Crown Prince Fahd in Saudi Arabia." It was as if I had asked to speak with my aunt in New Jersey. The communicators did not ask me to give them the telephone number. They took it in their stride.

Within two to five minutes, I had the Lord Chamberlain of the Crown Prince of Saudi Arabia on the line. I identified myself. He said: "What can I do for you?"

I replied: "I have a message from Ambassador Lieutenant General Ali Shaher in Beirut who asked me to transmit it to Crown Prince Fahd."

"Yes, Prince Fahd is standing right next to me. What is the message?"

"Tell him that they are shooting up the American Hospital in Beirut, where Ambassador Shaher is recovering from a flesh wound in his leg. Please call President Hafez El-Assad and Arafat and tell them to stop the mob from attacking the hospital. If there are no interventions from above, the hospital will be destroyed, many innocent lives will be lost, and the confrontation in the Middle East will get much worse. Ali Shaher and his family fear for their lives."

The Lord Chamberlain said: "Yes sir, I will transmit the message."

We then left the Embassy and drove back to the American Hospital. In the process, we picked up a couple of stray bullets as we entered the garage. Nobody was killed this time, but the situation was out of hand. The mobs were shooting all over the place. It was about 10:00 p.m. I asked one of my security guards who had a walkie-talkie to call my wife. "Tell her that I am not coming home tonight. I am spending my night at the American Hospital, near the room of the Saudi ambassador so he will be reassured." Then, I told Ambassador Shaher that I had conveyed his message to the Crown Prince and that I was taking a room near his.

By one a.m., silence descended on the entire area of the American Hospital of Beirut. There was hardly any air-conditioning left. It was hot outside, and there were no windows left in many parts of the building. The crowds had dispersed. Next day, I went to see Ambassador Ali Shaher in his room and then returned to my office. My security guards informed my wife that I was back at the office and not to worry about me.

Ambassador Shaher had the bullet removed from his leg. After his release from the hospital, he gave me a small, intimate reception and thanked me for my assistance. After he returned to Saudi Arabia, Ali Shaher became minister for information for the next ten years and then one of the advisers to King Fahd. From this episode, I came away with a feeling of respect for the role of the Saudis in the Near East, and a better understanding of the U.S. relationship with Saudi leadership. If the Saudis want to play a role, they certainly have the power to do so. If nothing else, this episode proved that we were better off because we knew people from all factions and nations who could help us out. That's what diplomacy is all about.

But why all this fuss about Lebanon? Is it really so critical to peace in the Middle East? Lebanon has no oil, though it does have water, both from its mountains and from its rivers. Above all Lebanon has proven over centuries that different religions—Christians,

Moslems, and Jews—could live together and prosper, and with a certain amount of individual freedom. The Lebanese have sent their sons and daughters around the world, where they have succeeded well. Many kept a link with the country of their origin. They have helped to develop economies in South America and Africa. Their skills are in demand in the Arab world. Lebanon has truly been a bridge between the Mediterranean world and the Arab hinterland. The events of the 1970s and 1980s have also borne out that Lebanon is part of the Near East and that the creation of a separate Christian homeland—"Maroonistan"—is nothing but an unrealistic dream. Israeli Zionism is no longer an example for the great majority of Christians in Lebanon.

While working with the Palestinians was an important part of my job in Beirut, my primary mission remained helping the legal government of Lebanon to cope with the civil war, maintain the Lebanese economy on an even keel, and have foreign powers respect the sovereignty and independence of Lebanon within its internationally recognized borders. In my daily activities, I often went to the presidential palace or the prime minister's office to discuss the problems of the day. President Elias Sarkis was an intelligent, honest, tolerant, middle–of–the–road leader. Prior to becoming president, he had been governor of the Central Bank of Lebanon.

One of the goals Sarkis had set for himself was to defend the value of the Lebanese pound. He believed, and rightly so, that such a policy was essential for the government to prevent inflation and economic hardship while the country was torn apart politically by civil strife. He had set for himself the goal that the exchange rate of the Lebanese pound to the U.S. dollar be the same when he left office as when he became president. The exchange rate then was three Lebanese pounds to one U.S. dollar. When he left office in 1982, the rate indeed remained the same. Shortly after his departure, the exchange rate soared to 3,000 Lebanese pounds to one U.S. dollar. When Rafic Hariri became prime minister in 1992, he succeeded in cutting the rate in half—to 1,500 pounds to one U.S. dollar, where it is today.

In the defense of the Lebanese currency I was able to be of assistance to the Lebanese president and the governor of the Lebanese Central Bank, Michel Khoury, the son of Lebanon's first president after independence. One day I was persuaded to accept the power of countersignature over the foreign exchange reserves of the Central Bank of Lebanon, which were held in Switzerland. To the best of my knowledge, the reserves at that time were still several billion dollars. The bank's governor, Khoury, said he was afraid that, in these unsettled times, some gangsters could come and hold a gun to his head saying, "sign this paper," thereby releasing millions of dollars to a thug in Zurich or Bern. By requiring two signatures, all releases from the reserves of the National Bank of Lebanon needed my countersignature. As long as I was ambassador in Beirut, this situation prevailed. When I left, I suggested that my American colleague in Switzerland be given the signature. The answer was "No, when you leave, the arrangement ends." I honestly believe this arrangement was a sign of the confidence the Lebanese government had in the policy I pursued in Lebanon on behalf of my government. During my time in Beirut, most of the Lebanese government and people felt that the United States was trying to be even-handed on problems dealing with Lebanon.

But I confess this was not always easy. The Israeli press and government criticized me publicly for being "pro-Palestinian" and "anti-Israeli," especially on occasions when I publicly condemned Israeli bombing of Lebanon. The number of times that I pleaded with Washington to speak up publicly against Israeli violations of Lebanon's land borders, airspace, or territorial waters was legendary in the State Department. Today, years later, when the Israelis violate Lebanon's sovereignty, nobody speaks up to criticize this violation of law.

But I was equally firm when Syrian troops or intelligence officers would tell me that I could not travel to certain parts of Lebanon under their control. I always made clear that only the president of Lebanon could tell me where I could not go by car or foot. This matter came to a head several times and, without exception, the Syrians authorized my three-car motorcade to proceed wherever I wanted to go.

Perhaps what was held against me the most by the Israelis was that I weaned away the Phalangist military and political militia leader Bashir Gemayel from his complete dependence on Israel. Prior to my arrival in Beirut, the Israelis provided arms, money, and advisors for Bashir's Phalange militia. The Israeli military sent a helicopter about once a month to Lebanon to bring Bashir Gemayel to Israel for meetings with Israeli political or military leaders. Bashir had no alternative but to go to these meetings if he wanted weapons and money to maintain his militia.

I was able to meet with Bashir Gemayel in 1979. On that occasion I explained to him that in my opinion he should not have such intimate links with Israel because such a bond appeared to be resented by many Christians and Muslims in Lebanon. I suggested to Bashir that the United States could provide arms and money for the Phalange, because I felt all Lebanese at the time could be seen working with the United States but not with the Israelis or, for that matter, too closely with the Syrians.

A word about Bashir Gemayel himself. He was more of a Lebanese nationalist than many other Maronite personalities. He enjoyed broader support than any other Christian militia leader. Even some Muslims could identify with his opposition to Syrians, Palestinians, and Israelis. But the United States had to pursue an even-handed policy in Lebanon, and above all on the Israel-Palestine Jerusalem imbroglio. I would like to believe that as long as I was the U.S. ambassador to Lebanon—1978–1981—this was the case.

On the Palestinian issue, one cannot factor out Lebanon. One of my few differences with Philip Habib—one of the great diplomats and peacemakers in modern American history—is that you cannot separate Lebanon from the central issues of the Middle East. That is not to say that Lebanon is the one key—the situation is too complex for that—but you do have to engage the Lebanese factions and untangle the antagonisms to achieve peace in the Middle East.

In the final analysis, the question is simple: How can we work together? These people have been living together for centuries. They revere the same holy land. They marry one another. Their languages have the same Semitic roots. Why can't they find a way to work together? Certainly, the Israelis have a lot to offer the Arabs and the Palestinians, such as their sophisticated educational systems.

And they are all victims of some kind of injustice. How infinitely sad it would be if the victims of injustice were themselves to act unjustly—violently, undemocratically—because they were too scared to talk and embrace their mutual fragility.

I am of Jewish descent. My family also suffered during the Holocaust that contributed to the creation of the state of Israel. Jews have been discriminated against for millennia and ought to have a home. I believe that among the Israelis are many good people, and they deserved to have a nation with secure borders. But I fear that Israel will not exist in fifty or sixty years if we do not all find a way to integrate Israel into the region. Violence never made us more capable of living together.

King Abdullah of Saudi Arabia, then crown prince, offered peace to the Israelis on the basis of the 1967 borders and recognition of Israel by all Arab states. This proposal appears to be a realistic approach to finding a way to prevent more decades of conflict in the Near East.

8
Asian Tiger

When I arrived in Bangkok in October 1981 to take up my post as the American ambassador, it was not the first time I set foot on Thai soil. Twenty-eight years earlier, in 1953, I had been sent to Bangkok from Saigon, where I was posted to reroute the transportation of petroleum products to Laos. Prior to 1945, international oil companies in French Indochina working in Vietnam trucked petroleum products to Laos by road from Vietnam. Laos was 100 percent dependent on Vietnam for its petroleum needs. My mission in 1953 was to get American oil companies to send petroleum products to Laos via Thailand. For this purpose I also worked with the Thai government–owned trucking company to haul the oil drums from Bangkok by road to Nong Khai, a small town in northern Thailand. From there the drums were loaded on barges to be shipped across the Mekong River to a village in Laos near the capital, Vientiane, from which the petroleum products were distributed throughout Laos. Thus, as far back as the 1950s, oil played a role in orienting Laos toward Thailand and away from Vietnam. In 1953, when my wife and I were in Bangkok, the great development boom had not yet taken place. Thailand then was the way tourist posters described it, a peaceful, beautiful, largely agricultural country with graceful people and smiling faces.

My second time in Thailand was in the early 1970s, when I was chargé d'affaires in Laos. I needed to consult with my American colleagues in Bangkok to obtain material support for our embassy as well as concrete help for the policies we were carrying out in Laos. Nearly everything the embassy needed in Laos came from or via Thailand. Bangkok was to Vientiane in those days like Kansas City compared to Wichita.

Thai civilian and military officials knew me for the role I played in supporting the neutralist Lao prime minister Souvanna Phouma, putting down a coup d'état against him that had originated in Thailand. The Thai authorities at the time did not share or approve my actions and policies. Then as today, the Thais saw Laos moving in the Thai sphere of influence, not as a nonaligned nation or one with close links to communist China. As I was responsible for bringing about the reconciliation between the Royal Lao government and the Marxist Pathet Lao, the Thai press in 1973 would have preferred a more anticommunist American diplomat in Vientiane.

Hence, when I arrived in Bangkok with my wife in 1981 as the U.S. ambassador, the Thais were probably wondering what line I would pursue there. In fact, most of my time in Thailand from 1981 to 1985 was devoted to strengthening bilateral U.S.-Thai relations, including already close military links. The United States had usually sent very able ambassadors to Thailand, among them Wild Bill Donovan of OSS and CIA fame. All of my predecessors and successors did their best to make Thailand a true ally of the United States. And toward that end, we maintained one of the largest embassies around the world in Thailand. Some 680 Americans worked for the U.S. government in Bangkok and in consulates in Thailand during my tenure. Coordinating their activities turned out to be one of the most difficult tasks I faced. Nonetheless, when I ask my wife which country she liked the most among the many postings I had, she usually mentions Thailand. Thais are nice people, and even if they have to do something unpleasant, they do it with a smile. It goes down easier that way. And when it comes to tolerance, the Buddhist Thai may have an edge over most Westerners.

In the 1980s, the United States still had considerable influence in Thailand. The ambassador's personal influence, role, and ability to succeed in his mission depended largely on the amount of support he received from U.S. departments and agencies involved in international affairs. If the ambassador wanted to get things done, he needed to have an open, trusting relationship with the various elements represented on his staff. If I succeeded in my assignment to Bangkok, much of the credit goes to the strong support I received from my country team. In this connection, attention is called to President Reagan's letter to the ambassador dated October 1, 1981, which restates the ambassador's direct responsibility to the president for all U.S. activities within the country of his or her accreditation.

In the early 1980s, the U.S. priority in Thailand was to find a mutually acceptable way for the Thais to give us access to certain Thai naval and air facilities in line with America's global responsibilities. When the United States helped the Thais in modernizing and developing their country, they reciprocated by giving us the requested access.

As long as the Cold War dominated the international scene, Thailand had no problem lining up with the United States. The two countries and governments cooperated closely in supporting the Khmer anticommunist resistance in opposing the Vietnamese-supported Phnom Penh government in Cambodia. Opposing communist expansionism in Asia was not only the policy of Thailand at the time but also that of the other ASEAN members.

At its heart, politics is about making tough choices. Easy choices, anyone can make. Choices that do not hurt someone, anyone can make. Starting in 1981, my time as ambassador to Thailand exposed me to some of the more difficult issues of any of my stints in the Foreign Service.

This included drugs. Under President Ronald Reagan, the United States was committed to a global war on drugs. Reagan committed unprecedented funds to interdicting drugs at the U.S. borders. He and his wife, Nancy, used their powers of persuasion to create a new antidrug culture in the United States. Reagan also committed American agencies abroad to disrupt the production of drugs overseas.

A U.S. embassy in any country may be an umbrella for dozens of different agencies and interests, from the Army, Navy, Air Force, or Marines to cabinet departments like Treasury, Agriculture, Commerce, Labor, you name it. Coordination can be difficult in an embassy overseas, where we all live together and have to get along with each other. Most staff members do not always know what others are doing. Most officials in an embassy also work for someone outside the embassy, back in Washington.

As ambassador, I had the authority—memorably first outlined by President John F. Kennedy—to manage these different interests.

For that the ambassador must know what is going on in every section of the embassy. A knowledgeable ambassador can balance and integrate these interests so that the United States speaks with one voice in the host country. But at the end of the day, the different U.S. agencies and departments are often at odds with each other. Sometimes the best you can do is acknowledge a fundamental conflict and simply make sure that all sides get some of what they want.

So it was with the problem of drugs.

In Bangkok two American agencies not only battled within the embassy but also did so all over the country. Both had allies in the government of Thailand and worked closely together with their Thai counterparts. When they located a factory in northeast Burma on the other side of the border, it could happen—and it actually did—that there was a competition to get to the factory first. It was like cops and moonshiners racing to get to the still first. The idea was to close the heroin factory or at least make it inoperative. The competition became so keen that the two groups, both made up of American and Thai professionals, would literally fight each other. The two sides and their allies would be shooting at each other and commit other forms of violence to prevent the other side from getting there first.

I recall a case where the target was a heroin refinery run by outlaws. One American-Thai group was flying near the destination to overrun the factory. Another American-Thai group was driving to the site by jeep and hoped to capture the chemists working at the factory. It got so bad that the two American-Thai teams literally bombed each other. The problem was the absence of coordination between the two offices in Bangkok. When the operation was completed successfully, and since I had not been informed ahead of time, I asked that the employees involved be recalled.

Sometimes there's not much you can do. And sometimes you have to accept the deals that others made long before you ever got there. Well after I had left Bangkok, two Thai officials were denied a visa by the State Department because they were alleged to have protected some high-ranking individuals involved in the drug trade. Sounds like the right thing to do, right? It sends a strong message: "You can do in your country what you like, but we don't have to condone it by letting you into our country." But this view created problems. The two Thai officials in question had taken certain actions at our request. After some confidential discussions, the two got their visas for the United States and their reputations in Thailand did not suffer from the publicity they had received in the media.

Sex is another one of those topics that produce a full range of attitudes, all of them uncompromisingly right in the eyes of their holders. In Thailand, as in many poor countries of the world, the exploitation of girls and women in prostitution has been going on for centuries. Poor girls from the faraway regions of Thailand would come to Bangkok to earn enough money through prostitution to build a dowry for themselves. With money, or a new sewing machine, they would then return to their homes to establish a family and live a normal life. Poverty could make these girls sell their bodies in a strange city, far from home, so that they could live a better life once back home with their savings.

It is amazing to consider how much our attitudes about sex have changed in the last generation or two. Until 1932, for example, Thailand allowed polygamy. After it was banned, it was kept alive in a new form. Men of means often kept a *mia noi*, or minor wife—in Western terms, a mistress. The minor wife had no legal standing, but the children born of that relationship had inheritance rights equal to those of children born to the official wife.

Or consider prostitution, which exists everywhere, legally in some jurisdictions (including, the Netherlands and the state of Nevada). Prostitution existed legally in France, a Catholic country, until 1947. Bordellos followed the French armed forces around the world. Prostitution exists—will always exist—because of an eternal demand for anonymous, uncommitted sex. As long as girls and women are poor and desperate, someone will meet that demand.

There was not much I could do about that in Thailand, except to support efforts to provide girls and women with access to education, health care, real jobs, and housing. This I did, working closely with many Thai organizations devoted to improving the fate and condition of these women.

What I did speak out against as ambassador was the involvement of minors in sexual activities. I could act when American citizens were involved. As president of the American High School of Bangkok, I had to act to protect a fourteen-year-old girl from a predatory (if consensual) relationship with a sixty-year-old man who had taken a fancy to this young lady. The girl's father worked at the U.S. Embassy. Every afternoon after school, a large black limousine waited to take her to the home of the man in question. He lavished her with jewelry and gold. I asked my deputy to take care of the situation. He talked to officials in Washington and had the girl's father transferred to another post. The entire family left Bangkok within a month.

The most constructive thing I could do, long term, was to help the country develop alternatives for its economy. I could promote education for young girls and their families. I could promote enterprises that would provide other opportunities. I could contribute to cultural events that lifted up people's sights rather than degrading them and their victims. I could also lend assistance to church and civil rights organizations—both Thai and foreign—in Thailand, seeking to root out prostitution rings and rescue girls from pimps. And I could cooperate with journalists who wanted to shine their lights on the problem.

But it was not my job to shut down the brothels or change the customs or inclinations of people around the world. My job was not made any easier when I was reminded by my Thai friends that the American military had greatly contributed to making Bangkok the sex capital of Asia. As long as American military were involved in Vietnam—roughly from the mid-sixties to 1975—GIs could relax from their dangerous duty in Vietnam by getting leave to spend a few days in fun-loving Bangkok. What do soldiers who face death in a foxhole do when on holiday? They look for attractive female company. And Bangkok had many lovely hostesses to cater to the needs of lonely bachelors. Thus, there is no doubt that the United States contributed to making Bangkok "sin city."

Many people in America know Thailand as Siam, the country depicted in the Broadway musical *The King and I*. But for most, their knowledge is often confined to what Hollywood has shown on TV or at the movies. Reality is quite different.

Thailand is a nation about four times the size of New York State. During my time there, Thailand was surrounded on three sides by danger. In the south, border skirmishes took place from time to time with Malaysia. On the southeastern border, Thai forces battled Vietnamese troops who occupied Cambodia. And on the northern and northeastern borders was Laos, a country populated by the same people who live in northern Thailand and speak a language closely related to the Thai language. Thailand is a land of contrasts—the bustle of the big city and the ancient quiet of the countryside, where about 85 percent of the population lives. Thailand's rural base gives the country its serenity and stability. Agriculture, notably rice growing, remains the main activity on the fertile soil of Thailand. With the exposure to the West, Thais now grow crops such as asparagus and mangoes for export.

But the cities give Thailand its economic power and the dynamism that attracts tourists and businesses from all over the world. More than 60 percent of the people work in rural industries—farming, fishing, and forestry—but they produce only about one-quarter of the nation's gross domestic product.

With a population of about fifty million, Thailand was the eighteenth largest nation in the world when I served there. The population itself is about 85 percent Thai, 14 percent Chinese.

What makes Thailand a marvel is its ability to steer a steady course through turmoil. Since 1932, when a military coup restricted the powers of the royal family, the nation has accepted an arrangement whereby the military holds the nation together and the king uses his prestige to limit the military's excesses. That has been an amazing trick for the king, since there have been thirteen coups and attempted coups during that period.

Thailand was lucky to have someone like General Prem Tinsulanonda as prime minister for eight and a half years. No political leader had ever lasted that long in Thailand. Constant turnover created instability for Thailand's economy, military, and social life. Prem was an ideal leader because he had experience both as a military and a political leader, so he understood and respected both worlds. Prem was commander of the Thai army before the king named him prime minister. Maybe even more important, he was a bachelor, so he never had any family members needing jobs or wives who wanted jewelry or big houses and lavish vacations. He was a modest servant of the king. As ambassador to Thailand,

Morton Abramowitz had supported Prem's efforts to remain in office when challenged by some Thai politicians. When I arrived, Prem had been prime minister for about two years. He was skilled at working with all factions in Thailand.

Another enduring figure in Thai politics over the years was Thanat Khoman, who served as foreign minister for fourteen years. During my time as ambassador in Bangkok, Thanat was deputy prime minister. He did as much to shape Thailand's political landscape as almost anyone and was actually present at the creation of ASEAN. A fervent nationalist, Thanat did not always work well with the United States, and over time, became increasingly critical. Concerned that America would undermine the integrity of Asia as a region, he wanted Asians to work together and not rely on a superpower for leadership.

Thanat was a great practitioner of Thailand's penchant for playing foreign nations off against one another. The Thais had a long history of independence—the only Southeast Asian nation not to be colonized—and they protected their independence by this practice. Thailand's diplomatic relations with France since Louis XIV had balanced British influence in Malaysia and Burma. In the late nineteenth century, the Thais began to modernize their country by bringing in advisers from small countries. The Thais called on Denmark to help with security issues. Belgium advised them on legal matters. Later the United States provided foreign-policy advisors for decades.

During World War II, Thailand acquiesced in the Japanese occupation—a strategy of survival and flexibility known as "bending bamboo." In 1948, the U.S. ambassador to Thailand retroactively made Thailand an "honorary neutral" during the war in recognition of the Free Thai who fought with the Allies. Recruited and trained by the OSS, this elite group would play key roles in Thai politics in the next generation—and enabled the United States to maintain a close relationship with Thailand, from the king to the political establishment to the military and intelligence services. Thailand became our closest ally in Southeast Asia. The U.S. diplomatic mission became huge, with representatives of every agency of the U.S. government.

After the Vietnam War, many Thais favored balancing the U.S. superpower with Japan in the matter of economic development.

The Japanese became a major presence in the auto industry, television and other consumer goods, and tourism through investments and production. When the People's Republic of China emerged as a power, Thailand invited the European Union to develop closer economic relations.

I worked with Prem and Thanat on the critical issue of military bases. The war in Indochina had ended in 1975, when Communists overran the governments of South Vietnam and Cambodia and then took over the government of Laos. Even though the United States had a hard time acknowledging defeat, the job of American foreign policy was to rebuild our reputation and relationships after losing those wars.

Thailand was Ground Zero of the post-Vietnam rebuilding process. We had to move decisively, but with some subtlety too.

My top priority in Thailand was to insure that the United States had a secure base for military operations. We had used Thai bases throughout the Vietnam War, but those bases had reverted to Thai control after the war. And no one in Asia was thrilled about the United States staying in the neighborhood.

Our military wanted to use the base of Udapao, which had been a huge air base for B-52 bombers during the Vietnam War. It had a superb runway and warehouse. After the end of the war in 1975, we could not use Udapao. The Thais—like many other nations— had adopted a cool policy toward access to former U.S. bases. Reagan's people asked me to negotiate for the use of Udapao for American aircraft flying from Japan westward and as a place to stock spare military parts.

After some negotiations with Prime Minister Prem, we came up with an agreement. The United States would modernize Udapao's fueling facilities for aircraft, a significant investment. The Thais would fly their own flag over the base, symbolizing that they were in charge. The new refueling system would permit any aircraft to be refueled within an hour. In return, the United States would enjoy the right to use Udapao when it needed a base of military operations. We also got permission to stock spare parts and equipment needed for the revision of aircraft.

The administration's commitment to planning ahead paid off. Udapao played a major role as a base for U.S. aircraft in the Persian Gulf War of 1990–91.

The U.S. administration also wanted to work closely with Thailand's armed forces. Ever since the coup d'état of 1932, the military had played a critical role in the governance of Thailand. Together with the king, the generals provided the stability that kept the country free from foreign domination. Americans trained Thai officers and enlisted personnel for the Air Force, Navy, and Army. We also helped to modernize the Thai Navy with ships built in Tacoma, Washington. These vessels were equipped with advanced technology, including certain missiles.

Working with the Thai military also meant working on economic development. The Thai army and Public Works Ministry built roads into the isolated rural areas of Thailand so that dissatisfied elements—farmers, mostly—could get products to the market. By building roads, we helped make it possible to bring schools, television, health clinics, and other basic services to the hinterlands.

In a century when democracy and totalitarian dictatorship warred with each other for control of world politics, Thailand provided an object lesson in the sway of ancient tradition in a developing nation—specifically, the enduring importance of royal power.

The king and queen of Thailand did more to maintain the peace—and the legitimacy of government—than any other figures in the nation. Wherever they went, they found people who adored them and revered their authority. And the royal couple returned the affection and respect to everyone in the nation—from warring political factions to humble farm workers. The king made it a practice to appear in public with all factions of Thailand, giving them the recognition they craved but also softening their hard edges by their submission to him.

When public crises were not resolved quickly with a minimum of conflict and bloodshed, the king could use his influence to bring the two sides together. Like the pope, the king had an uncanny understanding of the power of symbolism and mass media. Years after my tour in Thailand, in 1992, the king brought together the prime minister and military leaders after soldiers fired into crowds calling for greater democracy. At the meeting—which was televised—the two sides approached the king on hands and knees and acceded to his command that they work out a governing coalition acceptable to both sides.

When he felt an issue needed to be raised in the public's consciousness—like AIDS or pollution—the king spoke out. While kings wade into ordinary policy problems rarely, rightly fearing that they will lose their mystique if they become just another complainer, King Bhumibol knew how to speak out "as a citizen" when the nation was stuck in a logjam and needed a push to get out.

No one could have predicted the rare influence that King Bhumibol Adulyadej would hold over his people when he assumed the throne in 1946 under tragic circumstances.

Born in Cambridge, Massachusetts—his father was a medical student at Harvard University, his mother a student at Simmons College in Boston—Bhumibol rose to the throne under difficult circumstances. Before Bhumibol ascended, the king of Thailand was his brother, the twenty-year-old Ananda Mahidol. But on June 9, 1946, Ananda was found dead in his chambers with a bullet in his head. The circumstances of the young king's death have never been fully explained, creating an awkward scenario for the new king.

Bhumibol ended a centuries-old tradition of polygamy and took only one wife. He has stayed by her side his whole life. I am not a big believer in the slogan "the personal is the political," but the idea applies to the king of Thailand. In his life with Queen Sirikit and their three children, Bhumibol found the energy and identity that has helped to hold a restless nation together.

Most of the members of the royal family have contributed to Thailand's national work. When I was in Thailand, the king's mother, known as "The Prince's Mother," was still extremely active, flying all around the country, in spite of her advanced age, and dispensing assistance, such as medicine, blankets, and clothing, to the hill tribes. She was a wonderful old lady, an excellent role model for the Thai elite.

Over time, Bhumibol would become the longest serving king in Thai history. The ruler he would overtake, in 1988, was King Mongkut, the nineteenth-century monarch made famous to Western cultures by the *The King and I*. Mongkut was, in fact, Bhumibol's great grandfather. Like Mongkut, Bhumibol is a man of great reverence but with a keen interest in science and progress. It is hard to explain to Americans the unique personal power of the king. On the one hand, he was an exalted figure. No one in Thailand would dare to criticize the king or the queen. On the other hand, he was humble, modest, and serene.

I developed a close working relationship with King Bhumibol. His interest in the people led him to visit the countryside with his wife on a regular basis to meet ordinary Thais. He would ask them humbly what they needed to make life better. Traveling in the provinces offered the royal couple one of their greatest means of influence. They initiated hundreds upon hundreds of public works around the nation and personally tracked the progress of these projects. Rather than developing their ideas for projects by appointing blue-ribbon commissions and commissioning master plans, the king and queen discovered many ideas through their travels among the people.

Surrounded by as many as fifty aides, the king would meet his people and hear their requests. "What can I get you?" he would ask a villager.

"I need water," would be the response. In three weeks, there would be a water pump in the village.

"What can I do for you?" he would ask.

People would line up for hours to meet the king and queen, and when they got to the front of the line they would kneel before them, tears of joy in their eyes. "I need someone to fix my teeth. We all need a dentist." Indeed, on some of their trips the king and queen brought along a dentist, who would care for hundreds of people in one visit. The king also encouraged doctors to spend time "up country" to provide care for people living in areas without clinics or hospitals.

Bhumibol was gently strategic in his visits to the countryside, using the people's requests not only to answer immediate needs but also to highlight large-scale policy initiatives. On one of his visits he announced the funding of a fertility clinic. On another occasion he announced a grant for an alternative fuels factory. Another time he gave money for a milk-pasteurizing plant.

The king was always concerned with the self-sufficiency of people in the hinterlands. He undertook many projects to gently move farmers and foresters from destructive practices—so-called "slash and burn" cultivation—toward more sustainable practices that not only protect the land but also produce higher yields.

Because of the drug epidemic in Thailand, the king worked hard to shift the agricultural economy from poppies to food. That is a tough trick, because the profit margins for drugs are so much higher than they are for all other crops. But Bhumibol understood that the farmer at the bottom of the system did not make much money from drugs. The guy who grows poppies does not get much money. It is the middlemen who make the most profit. If you go after the refineries and markets, you have a chance to break down the system, and then the farmer will use the incentives you offer to switch to legitimate crops. To some extent, these efforts have been a success. You can buy Thai produce in Europe in the middle of the winter, such as asparagus and all kinds of fruit.

When I was in Thailand, the AIDS scourge was just starting to afflict Thailand. The king announced initiatives for hospices and clinics that would care for victims of the disease. His embrace of this issue took away some of its social stigma.

At my meetings with the king at the royal residence we would talk regularly about political and military affairs. "Give me bulldozers," he would say. "F-16s are another matter. I might need them, but I need the bulldozers more." Bhumibol understood that communism would succeed only when people lacked the means of making their own living. "You have to give people a chance to make a living," he told me. "Don't just give us the ships we need to defend ourselves. Help us build ships rather than getting them from foreign countries."

When the history books are written, they may conclude that refugees best symbolized the violence and destruction along with the mobility and opportunity of the twentieth century. Just in the last fifty years, the United Nations estimates, more than fifty million people have been forced out of their homes. As a refugee from Nazi Germany, I had a personal commitment to make sure that the wandering groups of our time found a safe and secure place to settle—just as I did.

My embassy staff in Bangkok worked more on Cambodian refugees than on any other issue. Cambodians fled a genocide that killed more than one and a half million out of a population of only seven million. Those who could get away deserved whatever refuge other nations could provide. Since Thailand borders Cambodia, the American embassy worked with other governments and nongovernmental organizations from across the world to provide the refugees roofing, food, medicine, and schooling. Ad hoc refugee centers became little towns. Women and children went about their daily rounds, but often the men did not know what to do. Some carved small wooden artifacts, while others enlisted in the anticommunist resistance in Cambodia.

In 1979, hundreds of thousands of Cambodians fled to Thailand, a crisis that had occupied my predecessor, Ambassador Mort Abramowitz, for two years. In 1979 Vietnam invaded Cambodia, evicting the Khmer Rouge, who had not only murdered their own people but had also attacked Vietnam. A new government of KR dissidents then took over Phnom Penh. Thailand's eastern border was defenseless against the flow of Cambodian refugees and attacks from remnants of Pol Pot's forces. Some of the Cambodians in the refugee camps—with the support of Thai and American organizations—joined the armed struggle against the new regime in their country.

As the refugee camps swelled, the only hope was resettlement in other countries. Hundreds of thousands of Cambodians and some Vietnamese moved to the Americas, Europe, Australia, and, to a lesser extent, other parts of Asia. Many of these refugees became homeless and in need of help because of the political, military, and strategic struggles between ideological rivals. Most of the refugees just wanted to find a place to live in peace and raise families that would live better lives than they had during half a century of warfare in Southeast Asia.

The whole situation—the refugees, the camps along the Thai-Khmer border, Vietnam's growing power—affected U.S. relations with Thailand. The Thais needed us, and we needed the Thais more than ever. They set up a special unit on the border to prevent Cambodians from slipping into Thailand. Nations that received refugees set up good processing systems. But the camps were a no man's land, with Thai troops stationed on the western side, NGOs working within the camps, and Cambodian troops blocking reentry into the country.

Another unfortunate legacy of the Vietnam War was the emotional and often cynical efforts by some Americans to track down servicemen missing in action. Groups organized by people like Ross Perot or retired GIs believed that Laos, Cambodia, and Vietnam still held prisoners of war, and they were determined to get them out.

A certain Mrs. Chapman, whose husband had flown Air America planes in Laos, came to see me in Bangkok. I had met her years before in Laos when I had to give her the bad news that the airplane her husband was piloting had crashed. Since the plane was carrying ammunition, it had also exploded. There was no way there could have been any survivors. Years later, in Bangkok, Mrs. Chapman came with a group of other family members who had lost loved ones in the war. She told me: "Mr. Ambassador, I am sure that my husband is still alive and he is held prisoner in Laos." Since the time of her husband's death, some unscrupulous bounty hunters in the United States had convinced her that he was not dead. These so-called patriots were nothing more than conmen who profited by raising the hopes of stateside victims of the war.

I asked Mrs. Chapman to excuse herself from the group to talk with me. "Mrs. Chapman," I said. "You know me. I was the one who gave you the bad news that your husband had been flying a plane with ammunition and that it had exploded."

She broke down in tears. "You know, these people who talk with me give me hope and I live on hope," she said. "They said maybe he is still alive and I believed it." She left my office, perhaps better informed. But I don't think I made a friend by being truthful.

Other people—often former military—came to Thailand with the sole purpose of searching for MIAs or POWs in Laos. They brought sophisticated communications equipment into Laos. A backup group in Thailand stayed in touch with them as they searched the Laotian jungles.

Having served in Laos twice and having been involved in the Vietnam War, I knew about the few soldiers who went AWOL, found a local woman, and stayed behind. Some of those men became homesick or ill, walked out of the jungle, turned themselves in, and asked to be repatriated. On the whole, the U.S. military dealt fairly and humanely with them.

But I do not believe any Americans were held prisoner in Laos. I do believe that a number of servicemen were still missing in action. American agencies continued searching for MIAs. I supported that effort fully. But the private groups looking for POWs in Laos in the 1980s had arrangements to get paid for the bones they brought back. They came out with bones, but not the bones of American GIs.

One group of American adventurers got into trouble with the Lao Army. An American and a Lao who came with the group were wounded as they tried to escape capture for entering Lao territory without authorization, and they radioed for help. They did not contact the U.S. Embassy directly, but an American came and told me. "Mr. Ambassador, this gentleman and his party are in serious trouble. They are surrounded. They need to be extracted from there." I did what I could to enable their departure from Laos.

When the rescued Americans got to Bangkok, I told my consul general to get the Americans medical attention and seats on a plane back to the United States. He came back later and said, "I don't think we should do that." The Americans, it seems, had some high-level advocates back in the States who supported these cynical ventures.

Since our own consul general was reluctant to act, I went to the prime minister to suggest that Thai authorities curtail the intruders' visas, forcing them out of Thailand. That they did. But it was a shame that the situation had arisen in the first place and that these frauds had such support in America.

These private groups attempted to get me involved as a middleman. The manager of an American bank in Bangkok came to me one Friday afternoon with an envelope containing $50,000 in cash. "John, I have been asked to give this envelope to you because you would support efforts to recoup the remains of Americans killed in action," he said. "These Americans are infiltrating Laos and are bringing back remains for the families back home. Please give them this money when they return with the remains."

I was angry. "These guys come back from Laos with chicken bones. I don't want to be involved in this transaction. I don't want this money in a government safe over the weekend. Please take it back." That was the end of that story.

There are occasions when any embassy is asked to do favors, often for well-connected people. But when those favors deal with illicit activities like drugs, it pays to tread warily. Every once in a while, Thai authorities arrested a "mule," someone who would bring heroin from Bangkok to the West by plane. Mules got paid from $3,000 to $4,000, not bad pay for a day's work unless you consider that they often got caught in the act. At the same time, a number of users and dealers were nabbed by various Thai and international efforts to interdict drugs. We always requested stiff sentences in these cases, and the sentences could be twenty or thirty years. I got a number of requests from U.S. senators or high-ranking administration officials for the liberation of prisoners who had well-placed connections back home. Usually, I was asked to request royal pardons for the offenders.

Once, an American who had worked at the embassy got caught with drugs in his shipping crates as he was returning home to the United States. Was he responsible for hiding the drugs? Did somebody else place them there to frame him? He was convicted and thrown into jail. I received a personal note from a high American official asking me to seek a royal pardon.

At first it was not too hard to ask for a pardon when high-ranking Americans asked for it. But soon, requests came in from representatives, senators, generals, admirals. It was too much. I could not keep asking the king for these favors. It was an affront to the Thais' effort to confront the awful scourge of drugs. And what about the Americans in Thai prisons who did not have those connections? The problem was how to protect American citizens and at the same time be fair to the other Americans in prison.

Once, while on vacation in France, I met a distinguished Frenchman. "Mr. Ambassador, I made a terrible mistake," he said. "Many years ago I married a much younger wife who was part of the hippie generation and deeply into drugs. A couple of years ago, she took our three children to Thailand, and all of them are now deeply into the drug culture. They have all been arrested in Thailand and are serving long-term sentences in Thai jails. Can you do something? I am willing to pay any amount of money to get them out."

I told him I would see what I could do. Back in Thailand, I told my French counterpart, Jean Soulier, about the request. "That's the last thing you want," he told me. "Don't ever get involved in this sordid case. There is a story around in some countries that the Thai judges are corrupt. Most of them are not. They are just applying the law. If you offer them money, you will be accused of corrupting them."

Instead of asking for pardons from the king, Soulier said, why not negotiate a prisoner exchange treaty? After a convicted person serves a year in the local jail, he or she could return home to serve the rest of the sentence. The Thais would accept the proposal because it would not undermine antidrug efforts and would rid the country of lawbreakers. We took the idea to the king, who approved. Both the United States and France signed the pact with Thailand that year.

That took care of the royal pardon problem, ending the insider dealing and allowing the Thais to be even-handed with all offenders. With the end of the Cold War in 1989, and the gradual reassertion of mainland (communist) China's traditional role in Asia, Thailand appeared less openly aligned and more in tune with the other ASEAN countries. Nonetheless, by the 1990s U.S.-Thai cooperation had been so close for such a long time that much goodwill remained toward the United States in Thailand.

Mainland China's rise as a major economic and cultural center did, however, have an impact on Thailand. By the late 1990s some countries in Southeast Asia believed that several power centers, not the United States alone, would determine things around the world. Thai businessmen of Chinese ethnic extraction began to invest in mainland China and no longer looked exclusively to Taiwan for business ventures. Such Thais took renewed pride in Chinese traditions and culture. This phenomenon also occurred in the other countries of Southeast Asia with citizens of Chinese extraction.

Southern Thailand has five million Muslims and a common border with predominantly Muslim Malaysia. In the past, Buddhist tolerance had enabled all citizens to live more or less harmoniously together. Southern (Muslim) Thailand needed economic development, as did rural (Buddhist) northeast Thailand. Both received the same treatment. Might religion become an issue for Thailand in the twenty-first century? Thailand has always adjusted to reality and will likely continue to do so in the future. But recent fighting and killing in Southern Thailand bodes ill. By the 1990s the political landscape had changed. Early in the decade, the Paris Peace

Conference on Cambodia had settled on a coalition government for that country, Cambodia was no longer a bilateral issue between the United States and Thailand. Cambodia, Laos, and Vietnam had joined ASEAN. As Thailand was no longer a "front-line state" in the Cold War nor in Southeast Asia, U.S.-Thai relations evolved.

Perhaps King Bhumibol had had a point when he suggested to me in the early 1980s that U.S. military assistance should give greater emphasis to providing bulldozers rather than advanced aircraft to the Thai Armed Forces. Bulldozers, materials for building bridges and erecting schools and hospitals, he argued, would improve the infrastructure and thereby facilitate life for the upcountry rural population. This in turn would do more to unite the nation than would sophisticated arms for the Thai military. Was not the potential enemy from within (poverty, unemployment, social inequalities) just as threatening to the nation's survival as a potential foreign military foe?

The United States and Thailand built a mutually beneficial relationship when the world's political situation pitted the United States against the communist world. Rather than overreliance on military cooperation, in this changing political atmosphere education, trade, finance, science, and agriculture would become the more valuable way to nurture a friendship dating back to 1833.

9
Fatal Embraces

The beginning of any term as ambassador is full of ceremony and high hopes. Before dealing with the hard work of diplomacy—war and insurgency, drugs and arms, religious strife and economic development—the new ambassador gets to bask in the glow of hope.

When India's chief of protocol came to the residence to take me to the Presidential Palace to present my credentials, twelve Indian lancers dressed in colorful costumes and mounted on beautifully groomed horses accompanied him. After reviewing a detachment of Indian troops in modern battle dress, I walked up the huge stone staircase at the palace to meet the president of India. At every step of this very broad staircase, Indian lancers, with their staves and small flags, saluted. At the summit, the president stood in front of the silver throne formerly used by the British Viceroy.

When President Reagan appointed me ambassador to India, I got a nice send-off from the administration. "You will find him an 'active' ambassador,'" Vice President George Bush had written to Prime Minister Rajiv Gandhi to introduce me. "We believe that there are unparalleled opportunities to strengthen relations between India and the United States and that an ambassador like John is what is needed to take fullest advantage of them."

I was not the type to sit in the Embassy reading cables and hosting parties. I needed to get out, see the whole country, talk with every group, and bring people together when there were conflicts. My activism always irritated some people—whether I was trying to find a "controlled solution" in Cambodia, working with the PLO in Lebanon, or mediating the conflicts among Americans in Thailand. But Bush—whom I had known when I served as ambassador to

Cambodia and he served as envoy to China—seemed to approve. So did Ronald Reagan.

When the president and vice president approve of your activist approach to diplomacy, what can go wrong?

The challenge I had faced in New Delhi was how to be activist without becoming too much of an advocate for one side. I had to deal with parties that were at odds with each other—Hindus and Muslims, fundamentalists and secularists, corporations and government bureaucrats, castes and modernizers, the central government and regional administrations.

Dealing with any issue in India also required taking on complex foreign policy conflicts. India's everyday life turns often on lethal foreign conflicts with Pakistan and Afghanistan and, by extension, other nations involved in the centuries-old Middle East conflicts. Anytime something big happens in a nearby country—a coup attempt in Pakistan, the sale of arms to guerrillas in Afghanistan, Iraq's occupation of Kuwait, insurgencies in Israel's occupied territories—life in India is affected.

Over my whole career, I had always gotten involved not only with the host country but with all countries having a direct impact on the host country's interests and those of the United States. Laos, Vietnam, and Cambodia all required hard work with each of the three as well as with France, China, and the Soviet Union. Thailand required addressing Laos and Burma. Lebanon required dealing with Israel, Syria, Jordan, Saudi Arabia, the PLO, and others. No nation is an island anymore, and diplomats cannot define their work too narrowly. As long as they coordinate their activities with Washington, activism offers the best approach to finding solutions to complex problems. And so I expected to spend a lot of time dealing with Pakistan and Afghanistan during my term as ambassador.

One of India's concerns during this period was Pakistan's effort to obtain the nuclear bomb. India was not the only country that feared Pakistan's nuclear ambitions. Israel and its American friends openly worried about any Muslim nation getting the bomb.

The crisis in Afghanistan also riveted the attention of both India and Pakistan. For seven years, the Soviet Union had been fighting a civil war there. When the Soviets invaded Afghanistan in 1979, no one expected the country to put up much of a fight. But a growing movement of Muslim insurgents had fought the Soviets with amazing effectiveness—newspapers called the war in Afghanistan "the Soviet Vietnam." The insurgent mujahidin had received arms from the United States and Pakistan, and money from Saudi Arabia. By the time I took up my post in New Delhi in 1985, the insurgents were making progress. By 1988 Soviet leader Mikhail Gorbachev announced a six-month timetable for leaving Afghanistan, with a new government to take over in Kabul.

But behind the headlines lurked dangerous problems. For one, the anti-Soviet resistance movement in Afghanistan was deeply involved in drug trafficking. Pakistanis, including Pakistani military, helped to export the Afghan production.

Over time, the anti-Soviet resistance became an Islamic fundamentalist movement, developing an organization and tactics that would eventuate in the horror of September 11, 2001. For reasons that I struggled to understand, the United States and its Pakistani allies were throwing their support behind the most fundamentalist elements in Afghanistan. These fundamentalists had no tolerance or respect for democracy or basic human rights.

However complicated India's relations with other nations, its internal relations were perhaps even more complex. Jawaharlal Nehru, the leader of its independence movement and first of a three-generation political dynasty, once called India "a geographical and economic entity, a cultural unity amidst diversity, a bundle of contradictions held together by strong but invisible threads." As such, India poses the essential test of modernity: How to bring together people from different backgrounds so that they see common interests but also have the freedom to express themselves freely and pursue their unique interests.

India is the biggest and most complex democracy in the world. A nation roughly the size of Western Europe, its population in the 1980s was about 700 million, second only to China's one billion. In 2008 it had more than 1.1 billion people.

Like America, India manages its diversity within a federal system. The nation is not ruled from the top down; rather, power is dispersed among twenty-five states and seven territories. The states exercise extraordinary power over culture, language, and religion.

The states' administrative systems are designed to meet local needs and traditions.

India's diversity extends to religion as well. Hinduism is the country's most prominent religion. But India also has a sizable Muslim community. Other religious traditions include Buddhism, Jainism, Sikhism, Christianity, and even a few Jews.

Indira Gandhi used to say that only she and her Congress Party could unite this vast and complex nation. Mrs. Gandhi was a powerful force in all she did—whether she was confronting Pakistan, developing the nation's nuclear capacity, building heavy industry, cutting deals with the Soviet Union, or leading the worldwide "nonaligned" movement.

But Indira Gandhi's powerful presence could also weaken Indian democracy. While she helped to tamp down ethnic and religious divisions, she did not end them. And by pushing them to the side, she created a pressure-cooker effect that was bound to explode one day. But her vision of Indian independence and development also had an impact on India's foreign policy.

It was not Indira Gandhi's doing that India ended up relying nearly exclusively on Russian weapons for the Indian armed forces. Rather, U.S. policy makers, including Henry Kissinger, decided during the 1971 Bangladesh War of Independence that the United States sided with Pakistan and was unwilling to provide the spare parts and ammunition India requested for the American equipment it had bought since independence in 1948. After the Bangladesh war, India no longer bought American weapons. During that war, the United States sent an American aircraft carrier off Calcutta, an action India had interpreted as an unfriendly act. Henceforth—in Indian eyes—the United States was no longer a reliable friend. The Soviet Union became India's principal provider of modern weapons.

Starting in the 1970s, Indian opposition groups grew bolder and more creative and persistent in opposing Indira Gandhi's rule. Opposition to Indira and her Congress Party grew steadily over the years. Her program of sterilization in the late 1970s and resulting riots throughout the country led her to invoke a state of emergency in 1975. In 1977, she ended emergency rule, ran for reelection, and lost. By 1980 she had mounted a comeback, but she never regained the authority or love that had marked her early career. In June 1984, in an effort to calm the unrest in the province of Punjab, Indira Gandhi ordered troops to take over a temple and clear the building of Sikh rebels. This action led to a new wave of riots and religious strikes. That October, Gandhi's Sikh bodyguards avenged the attack on the temple by assassinating her.

Rajiv Gandhi was fiercely loyal to his mother and her legacy, but he was also a modern man. He understood that India needed to embrace new technologies and new freedoms to thrive. In a way, he anticipated the post–Cold War era while the Cold War was still under way. He had been a pilot for most of his young life and got involved in politics only after his brother Sanjay had died in a plane crash in 1980.

Just as India possesses the most diverse religious and social system in the world, it also possesses one of the world's complex economies. The fundamental nature of India's economy was set soon after independence, when Nehru decided that India should be autonomous and not depend on outside trade or assistance. For Nehru, the goal of economic independence meant adopting a system of centralized economic management. Using five-year plans reminiscent of the Soviet system, India guided manufacturing and other industries, created output goals, and determined the flow of resources across the subcontinent. The state directed resources away from agriculture and toward industry, turning India from an agriculturally self-sufficient nation into a net importer of agricultural commodities, a situation exacerbated by fast population growth.

High tariffs, a major policy of the period, sought to protect Indian producers from the flood of foreign consumer goods. India's tariff rates in 1985 were among the highest in the developing world.

The poverty of India is well known. About 30 percent of all Indians are still poor and illiterate. Poverty exists everywhere—in the dirty cities crammed with unsafe factories and shanties and in the countryside filled with thatched huts. Poverty means less than a dollar a day, inadequate sources of drinking water, little or no medical care—and no chance for education. Poverty means low-birth-weight babies and a lifetime of malnourishment.

When I traveled around the country, I witnessed the poverty in the cities and in the countryside. But I also saw the great improvements made by the Indian government in nearly every field. The road system was much better. The transportation system—railway, buses, planes—all had made India a more modern state. In absolute numbers, more people had moved from poverty to subsistence, from subsistence to middle class. The number of people then part of the upper middle class was nearly equal to the total Indian population at the time of India's independence from Britain—about 400 million. Education in India both for the masses and for the elites was vastly improved over what the British had left behind in 1948. High technology—invented, perfected, exported—was about to take off as one of India's best-known efforts to join the top rank of nations in the modern world. To conclude that India's approach to modernization through state planning had not led to positive results appears vastly exaggerated. Considering that India had remained a relatively open and democratic society, the progress made by the country since independence was impressive indeed. The World Bank would agree with this positive assessment.

Rajiv Gandhi was determined to open the Indian economy to the forces of change in the world. Taking advantage of India's sizable educated middle class and excelling in high technology lay at the center of his strategy. He asked me to help get American assistance for this concerted effort to pull India out of the economic doldrums.

For years, the United States had refused to provide advanced technology to India because of fears that critical information would find its way to the Soviets. The lead man for the United States was Reagan's senior science and technology advisor, Robert Dean. "Cousin Robert," as I called him jokingly, convinced Reagan to sell the state-of-the-art Cray supercomputer to India for its meteorology program. The hope was that the sale would lay a strong foundation for a new era of collaboration.

Unfortunately, there was little follow-up on the Indian side. The Reagan administration may have expected that the Indians would now turn to the United States for the acquisition of military equipment, thereby reducing Indian reliance on Soviet arms. That did not happen.

What did occur was that the Indian expatriates in the United States, who had risen to managerial levels in information technology, convinced their corporate chairmen and Rajiv Gandhi that the United States and India were natural partners in this field. Thus in late 1985, Texas Instruments, represented by its president accompanied by his Indian-born expert, was the first American company to come to India to start the information technology venture in Bangalore. To receive and send messages, Texas Instruments built a huge dish that enabled the company to outsource some of its programs to India. Other companies followed, first from America later from other countries. Rajiv Gandhi's keen interest in modern technology, linked with Indian experts in the United States and American private companies that saw the potential of India's know-how, started the extraordinary success story that made India a leader in the modern computing world.

India's challenges in international affairs—steering a course as an independent power—have always been complicated by the way the Asian subcontinent was carved up at the time of independence. When Great Britain ended 350 years of colonial rule in 1947, the Indian Congress Party and the Muslim League agreed to carve two nations out of the 562 princely states of the subcontinent. India had wanted to maintain sovereignty over the whole subcontinent but was forced to cede Muslim areas to a new nation called Pakistan. India took over the more numerous Hindu states and provinces, while Pakistan took control over the predominantly Muslim states. In effecting the transition, a massive migration took place. About five million Muslims moved from the new India to the new Pakistan, and 3.5 million Hindus and Sikhs moved from Pakistan to India. Violence during the transition cost more than a million lives. Pakistan was split into two regions, one on each side of India. Ultimately, as a result of the war in 1971, the eastern section broke away and became Bangladesh.

Although religion was the primary source of division between India and Pakistan, neither nation has escaped large-scale internal religious strife. India is primarily Hindu, yet it contains one of the largest and fastest-growing Muslim populations in the world—over 200 million. Even in a state dedicated to religious freedom, the existence of such a large minority creates some uneasiness. Both

Hindus and Muslims feel the sting of discrimination. Efforts to address the concerns of one group inevitably arouse the resentments of the other.

India and Pakistan have been bitter rivals from their birth. The two nations have fought three wars over their half-century of existence, two of them over Kashmir. They have engaged in constant border skirmishes that threatened to expand into all-out warfare. Until recently, each side distrusted the other to its core. India is a secular state; Pakistan is a Muslim state. India is a democracy; Pakistan has most often been dominated by military dictatorships. India has been a nonaligned nation with links to Russia; Pakistan has often been aligned with the United States. India first tested its nuclear capabilities in the 1970s; Pakistan developed its nuclear capabilities in the 1980s and 1990s and did not explode its first nuclear bomb until the first years of the twenty-first century.

So what's the best way to survive in such a complex setting? For India, the answer has always been nonalignment. In his farewell address, George Washington warned of the danger of entering "permanent alliances" with other nations. As the United States established its economic and political system, other American leaders warned that siding with Europe's warring factions would drain the new nation of resources and energy. But for some reason, the United States refused to allow other emerging nations the prerogative of avoiding entangling alliances. The formulation that John Foster Dulles came up with in the bitterest days of the Cold War—*Either you're with us or you're against us*—has governed U.S. foreign policy for a century.

After winning its independence from Great Britain in 1947, India steadfastly maintained its right to be nonaligned in the struggles between the United States and the Soviet Union. From the beginning, India advertised its willingness to do business with anyone in the world, as long as it served India's national interests.

Over the years, India became the worldwide leader of the nonaligned movement. Mostly a Third World alliance, the nonaligned nations met on a regular basis to explore ways to maneuver around the volatile issues separating the United States and the Soviet Union.

Fatal Embraces 177

You would think that the United States would be India's greatest ally. Since its independence, India has been the world's largest democracy. With a population exploding above one billion diverse peoples, India has managed to hold regular elections and make peaceful transitions to new governments. Over the years, India has struggled with ethnic and religious violence, poverty, dynastic ambitions, ecological and demographic crises, and intense military rivalry with neighboring Pakistan. But through it all, India has remained democratic. To paraphrase Frank Sinatra, if democracy can make it here, it can make it anywhere.

The United States should have a strong stake in this ongoing experiment in self-rule and has historically had strong relations with India. For years the United States has traded extensively with India and sold it military equipment. But India's determination to remain nonaligned angered U.S. administrations and drove India into the arms of the Soviet Union. Starting in 1972, the Soviets sold India weapons and cooperated on a wide range of international issues. India has also forged its own path on issues ranging from nuclear proliferation to the war in Southeast Asia to apartheid in South Africa.

Prior to leaving Washington for my new posting in New Delhi, I was briefed by different departments and agencies about this concern over India's reliance on Soviet weaponry and its frequent adoption of international positions parallel to those of the Soviet Union. "See what you can do about it," I was told.

In New Delhi, as I got to know Rajiv Gandhi and his wife Sonia, I would raise these subjects with him. He knew from the beginning that I was favorably disposed to helping India's efforts to modernize its economy as much as I could. On international affairs, my reputation for moderation and tolerance for nonalignment had preceded me. Hence, in our private conversations, I might make suggestions on how to improve India's economic performance, or bring its nuclear policy into line with international treaties, or introduce balance into arms procurement. In those discussions, I was not trying to be arrogant or overbearing, but rather to help Gandhi while staying in tune with Washington's instructions.

"Who are you to tell us how to run our economy?" he would ask, as much in sorrow as in anger. "Who are you to tell us whether we can make arms deals with the Soviet Union? Who are you to tell us we cannot pursue our own nuclear policy?'

Gandhi rejected the notion that India tilted toward the Soviet Union. The construction of Soviet arms factories in India was intended only to give India control over its own destiny—not to take sides with the Soviets. Had the United States been willing to build arms factories in India, Gandhi said, India would have preferred that alternative. During my time as ambassador, India "leased" a Soviet nuclear submarine so that the Indian Navy could learn how to operate such advanced naval vessels. The failure of the United States in 1971 to provide weapons and parts to India when requested or needed had meant that India would turn to those countries that provided and sold arms "without political strings attached."

Even more sensitive than the Soviet arms connection was the problem of the foreign policy positions adopted by the nonaligned movement. Many critics felt that the nonaligned movement was too sympathetic to Yasir Arafat and the PLO. As a leader of nonaligned nations, India played a prominent role in supporting Arafat's efforts to obtain a home for the Palestinians. In those days, Arafat often wore a military uniform and carried a pistol as symbols of his fight. Because of their own struggles for independence, Indians empathized with the Palestinian cause. Arafat was invited to visit India on several occasions.

Everything Arafat did—in India, Lebanon, Syria, Egypt, and the occupied territories—could and did set off tremors in American politics. The Israeli lobby in the United States exerted more power than any similar cause. A nation then of 4.4 million people (now over 7 million), with ties to several major power centers in the United States, Israel maintained a close relationship to the foreign policy establishment in the United States.

Did all these factors influence Gandhi to change course on these issues? Personally, I doubt it. India, like most major powers, will always do what its leaders believe is in the country's own long-term national interest. One might find ways to convince India to come part of the way on some issues, but Indians are certain enough of their own history, culture, and destiny that they will not bow to foreign pressure.

In a world of competing powers, nonalignment can be a difficult course to follow. The major superpowers—as well as other blocs of less dominant states—almost always insist that other nations choose sides. And when an important nation like India decides to be neutral, other powers may construe it as opposition.

Earlier, I explained that the decisive change in U.S.-Indian relations had taken place during the Bangladeshi War of Independence in 1971, when the United States had sided with Pakistan, refused to honor India's requests for spare parts and ammunition, and deployed an aircraft carrier off Calcutta. These decisions showed that Washington policy makers at the time did not understand India's temperament and psychology, or perhaps did not care. From 1971, U.S.-Indian relations were no longer based on mutual trust. Pakistan became the preferred U.S. partner in South Asia; and India reinforced its links with the Soviet Union.

India's position went something like this:"If you want to be our friends, offer us opportunities for collaboration. The more you offer us, the less reason we will have to collaborate with the Soviets. We will not abandon the Soviets, but we are happy to be friends with you, too."

India's response to the U.S. policy of "balancing" India and Pakistan was to assert its concern that Pakistan's military program fostered instability; that Islamic fundamentalism threatened to rile the Muslims within India; and that this threatened the stability of South Asia and beyond—from Afghanistan to Turkey to Bangladesh. As long as Iran burns with Islamic radical revolutionary fervor and there is instability in the Gulf heightened by the Iran-Iraq war, India has a strong interest in supporting only a limited modernization of Pakistan's defense establishment.

I found myself in the middle of the India-Pakistan problem from my earliest days in New Delhi because of the growing alliance between the United States and Pakistan. Pakistan was acting as the principal staging area for the Muslims fighting the Soviet Union's occupation of Afghanistan, and the United States was eager to provide Pakistan with weapons for the guerrilla war in Afghanistan.

One of the most prized pieces of military equipment in those days was the AWACS, shorthand for Airborne Warning and Control System. Built by the American company Boeing, the AWACS is a plane that provides up-to-the-minute surveillance of battlefield conditions and events. The system can provide detailed information from up to 400 miles away. The AWACS can be used offensively to scope out the enemy before deciding when and where to attack. It is perfectly reasonable to assume that a country with this system has a greatly increased capacity to attack distant enemies.

The other weapon that Pakistan was considering buying was the Ml Abrams tank. The Ml offers stronger armor, better navigational systems, and greater maneuverability in difficult terrains like desert than earlier models. Built by General Dynamics, the tank had not yet been tested in wartime conditions but would later play a major role in the Persian Gulf War of 1991. Pakistan's General Zia said that he could not afford the military toys we were offering and would pass on the Ml tank if he had to choose.

Gandhi complained to me—and to Reagan—about our supplying Pakistan with missiles, AWACS, and other military technology. "The supply of AWACS aircraft to Pakistan would trigger a qualitative new phase in the arms race in our area and enhance tensions to dangerous levels," he wrote to me.

Gandhi also criticized American support for Pakistan's nuclear program. He rejected the idea that India's existing nuclear capabilities had to be balanced by Pakistan's activities. "Pakistan's military-controlled and clandestinely acquired nuclear weapons capability cannot be seen in a bilateral context with India," he said. "The risk of nuclear weapons proliferation in our region is posed by Pakistan and that is where it must be addressed."

The American tilt toward Pakistan troubled enough lawmakers that Congress passed legislation—the Pressler Amendment—in 1985 that would require the United States to cut off all assistance to Pakistan if it proceeded with plans for a nuclear bomb. But Pakistan nevertheless moved full speed ahead with building nukes.

A tendency of some American policy makers to equate the nuclear programs of India and Pakistan especially irked Rajiv Gandhi: "India detonated a nuclear device in 1974, using enriched plutonium, to demonstrate its ability to master complex advanced technology." Gandhi argued vehemently that India's status as a world power—and as a democratic nation with peaceful designs for nuclear technology—put it in a different league from Pakistan. India was six times bigger than Pakistan, it had the brainpower and the industrial capacity to be a full-fledged nuclear power, and it always planned to develop nuclear power for energy.

The Indian nuclear program began over forty-five years ago, long before the first talks for the international Non-Proliferation Treaty. India has been criticized for refusing to sign the Non-Proliferation Treaty, but its leaders have always found the treaty fundamentally flawed, arguing that it discriminates against nations that use nuclear technology for peaceful purposes. India also complains that China gets favorable treatment under the treaty just because it tested a nuclear device before India.

India's baseline nuclear program sought to produce plutonium and then use the plutonium in breeder reactors. India's main nuclear energy program is not enriching uranium, as is Pakistan's. India is reprocessing its spent fuel to recover plutonium in order to reduce its waste storage problems and to use the plutonium in its fast-breeder reactor program. However, less than half of India's plutonium production is used in its one small breeder reactor at Kalpakkam. The rest, India argues, is an inventory to be used in a new generation of commercial-scale breeders under design.

Pakistan's nuclear program has always been oriented to the development of weaponry—and has always been secret—as Prime Minister Bhutto repeatedly stated in the 1970s. In contrast, India's program has been open to outside scrutiny, and the government has published the program's financial and technical details. Foreigners have been allowed to visit Indian nuclear facilities.

Pakistan has obtained materials secretly and illegally, and it does not allow outside inspectors to see its facilities. It has neither the ability nor a declared program to build numerous nuclear power stations. The large enrichment facility at Kahuta appears to operate for the sole purpose of building weapons. Pakistan produces enriched uranium, the ideal fuel for nuclear armaments. It has never demonstrated a need for an inventory of either plutonium or enriched uranium.

I understood Rajiv Gandhi's arguments about the lack of moral equivalency of India and Pakistan on nuclear issues. "If the U.S. chooses to equate India with Pakistan," I cabled Washington, "Gandhi says it will be 'impossible' to improve relations with the United States." I convinced Under Secretary of State Michael Armacost to have the U.S. Senate reverse a resolution treating Pakistan and India equally on nuclear matters that the committee had originally adopted on the advice of State Department experts.

The positions of India and Pakistan on safeguards are philosophically different. What concerns Pakistan is India's nuclear capability.

When I arrived in India in 1985, the Soviet Union had occupied Afghanistan for six years. More and more Soviet soldiers were being killed. The Soviets found out, as others before them, that Afghans are not pushovers and that despite many tribal differences, the one sentiment Afghans shared was that they did not want to be governed by foreigners. Soviet President Mikhail Gorbachev, eager to reform his country through *glasnost* and *perestroika*, showed more willingness during the next three years to pull out troops and participate in an international process for creating a new government.

As the Muslim insurgents mounted a guerrilla war against the Soviet Union in Afghanistan, the CIA established a strong working relationship with ISI, Pakistan's intelligence agency. ISI got all the money, while U.S. Special Forces advisors and the ISI trained guerrilla fighters under CIA management.

Weapons and funding came from a number of sources, including the United States, Pakistan, and Saudi Arabia. (After the Soviet withdrawal from Afghanistan, these well-trained veterans, in turn, trained guerrilla recruits for insurgency movements in countries such as Algeria, Egypt, Indonesia, Lebanon, the Philippines, Tajikistan, and Yemen.)

According to Steve Coll, U.S. support for the Afghan guerrillas escalated in 1985. CIA Director William Casey saw the war as a chance to weaken the Soviet Union. After Casey's trip to Pakistan in October 1984, the Reagan administration issued National Security Decision Directive 166, which provided military expertise and technology—like Stinger antiaircraft missiles—to the Afghan rebels. That directive ratcheted up the original intelligence funding approved by President Carter in 1980, and authorized stepped-up covert military aid to the mujahidin.

Over the years Israel's intelligence agency, Mossad, has worked closely with and against the U.S. government. The Iran-Contra deal had a significant Mossad involvement, as did the blocking of U.S. efforts to reduce the flow of heroin and cocaine from Colombia to the United States. According to Israel Shahak, a retired professor of chemistry at the Hebrew University in Jerusalem and a survivor of the Bergen-Belsen concentration camp, Israelis laundered U.S. drug money for the drug bosses of Colombia and Panama—despite publicized U.S. efforts to intercept it.

Were Mossad or other arms of the Israeli government involved in the U.S. support of Afghan guerrillas? In the 1980s Mossad set up shop all over the world, especially in places where Israel could demonstrate it could help in supporting U.S. foreign policy objectives. In those days, no initiative was more important than opposing Soviet expansion into Afghanistan.

Israeli support for U.S. activities in Pakistan aggravated U.S.-India relations at a time when they should have been flourishing. India reflected American values—democracy, secular government, and the development of a stable balance of power in the Far East—far better than did Pakistan.

Gandhi's letter of January 28, 1987, addressed to President Reagan, sets forth in straightforward terms India's position on Afghanistan and Gandhi's attitude toward the United States:

> Our position in Afghanistan is, as you know, that the country should be allowed to chart an independent, non-aligned course, free from intervention and interference. I reiterated this to General Secretary Gorbachev. I also conveyed to him the gist of what you had written to me. The General Secretary left me with the impression that the Soviet Union would like to withdraw its forces in a realistic timeframe from an Afghanistan which would be non-aligned and not unfriendly to the Soviet Union. I hope that a peaceful resolution will not elude us for long. Quite apart from other factors, an early settlement would be in India's interest.
>
> Pakistan has been exploiting the situation in Afghanistan to acquire higher levels and types of arms. Most of these have little or no bearing on any possible conflict on the Afghan border. I am glad that you have agreed to keep our concerns in mind on Pakistan's perceived requirement of enhanced early warning capability on its mountainous western border. There were disconcerting reports on the possible supply of AWACS aircraft to Pakistan. This would

trigger a qualitative new phase in the arms race in our area and enhance tensions to dangerous levels.

In your letter, which Secretary Weinberger carried during his visit to India, you had rightly pointed out that peace required true nuclear restraints. We remain very seriously concerned about Pakistan's nuclear weapon program. Pakistan's military-controlled and clandestinely acquired nuclear weapons capability cannot be seen in a bilateral context with India. The risk of nuclear weapons proliferation in our region is posed by Pakistan and that is where it must be addressed.

We attach great importance to our relations with the United States. We would like to strengthen our ties by expanding our existing cooperation and moving into new areas of cooperation in high technology and also in defense. After the discussions which Secretary Weinberger had in India, it may be possible for us to move further and establish greater linkages in the areas of defense cooperation and technology transfers.

Indians and Americans disagreed about what an eventual Russian withdrawal meant for the region. The Indians saw Afghanistan as a perfect candidate to be a nonaligned state. Americans saw it first and foremost as a defeat for Soviet arms and a step in containing Soviet encroachment in South Asia.

I was in the middle of a flurry of letters between Reagan and Gandhi about the transition period in Afghanistan. Both expressed support for a coalition government, for giving the Afghan people a right to select a new government, and for an orderly exit of Soviet forces. They also seemed to agree on the dangers of a fundamentalist regime taking over Afghanistan. As Gandhi said in a July 20, 1988, letter: "By its very nature, fundamentalism cannot be reconciled with the basic values which both of our countries cherish: democracy, equal rights for all citizens, equal status for women, and other such human rights."

But the two differed on the makeup of the coalition government. The Soviets and Indians favored leaving Najibullah in charge for the transition period, with a broad-based coalition in the cabinet.

Reagan resisted Najibullah, insisting that he did not have the support of the Afghan people, and called for as short a transition period as possible, the better to sweep Najibullah from power.

Another difference had to do with how Afghanistan would fit into the new global balance of power. Gandhi insisted that Afghanistan become a nonaligned nation, free of the competition between the United States and the Soviet Union. Reagan sometimes used the language of nonalignment, but in reality he wanted to make sure that Afghanistan was closer to the United States than to the Soviet Union. In the end, Reagan backed off the idea of a coalition government entirely.

In September 1988, the mujahidin showed a growing capacity to coordinate their activities, which scared India, raising the specter of a radical Islamic state, allied with its enemy Pakistan. Such an alliance would not only pose a traditional military threat to India but would also serve to destabilize internal Indian society, with its roughly 200 million Muslims.

My friend Arnold Raphel, the U.S. ambassador to Pakistan, agreed with me that the future of Afghanistan could shape the relations between India and Pakistan for a generation. In a message in the summer of 1988, Raphel wrote that Americans too often thought of Afghanistan mainly in terms of the Soviet withdrawal.

Both Islamabad and New Delhi saw the possibility of a major strategic reshuffling, he noted, with a strong Islamic bloc stretching from Turkey to Pakistan, with Afghanistan a full and supportive member, confronting a Hindu India with its large Muslim minority. In Zia's words, a reconstituted Afghanistan created the possibility that "India will know it can never threaten us again while we have to be worried about our back." Raphel concluded his memo: "For most Americans, the Soviet withdrawal is the victory. For our South Asian friends, it is only the first act in a much larger drama."

Remarks by General Mirza Aslam Beg, one of the leading military figures in Pakistan, reflected the volatility of the region. Alleging a "triangular conspiracy consisting of the USSR, Afghanistan, and India aimed at destabilizing Pakistan," Beg said that "Pakistan and Afghanistan are now one. Two nations but one people." He looked forward to building a "strategic consensus" with Pakistan, Afghanistan, Iran, and Turkey—part of what he called a "grand design" for the region. Today, General Beg is retired and no longer close to Americans. To the contrary, he is an outspoken critic of American policy toward the South Asian subcontinent.

Just as troubling, the fundamentalists who were gaining ground in Afghanistan showed a tendency to work with terrorists all over the world. In the military effort to oust the Soviets from Afghanistan, the United States supported all who wanted to help in this endeavor. Volunteers came not only from Pakistan but from many Muslim countries around the world, including Algeria, Egypt, Iran, Jordan, Morocco, Palestine, Saudi Arabia, and Yemen. All were welcomed and financed from Saudi or American sources. There is little doubt that some of these fighters against the Soviet occupation of Afghanistan later turned into terrorists and took the law into their own hands for causes diametrically opposed to the interests of those who had financed them in the Afghanistan fighting.

By August 1988, I had reached a strange point in my career. After serving for three years as ambassador to India—a position I never sought, but enjoyed immensely—President Ronald Reagan had decided to bring in a new ambassador. The normal tour of duty for ambassadors is three years, so the desire for a change was not uncommon. But rather than wait until the election, key actors in the administration had already chosen John Hubbard, a former president of the University of Southern California. Indian leaders and media were confused about the rush to change diplomats.

I told President Reagan and Secretary of State George Shultz that I would step aside as ambassador if they wished me to do so. All they had to do was ask. I had appreciated the opportunity to serve—and to speak up as vigorously as I had—and I recognized that Reagan was the man elected to run the country, not me.

Around that time, I got a visit from an old and dear friend, Patricia Byrne. Pat and I had known each other since 1953, when we served together in Saigon. She told me that an American general had just arrived in Islamabad to brief the Pakistani military on the American military assistance program to Pakistan. This news was not unexpected. The United States had been working hard for years to strengthen its ties with Pakistan, which was its key ally in trying to contain communism from spreading in South Asia. In that endeavor, the United States supported all those who were fighting to bring about a withdrawal of Soviet forces from Afghanistan.

As ambassador to India, I had worked hard to convince higher-ups in the administration that a solution to Afghanistan—and the whole region—required a balanced approach. By 1987 the Soviets had already agreed to the principle of withdrawing troops from Afghanistan, but not yet to a timetable. And who was to govern Afghanistan after the Soviet withdrawal? The Soviets and India wanted a secular, neutral government in Kabul. I also thought this approach to be in the best interests of the United States. I feared that we were creating two monsters with our current policy. By arming the fundamentalists among the mujahidin, we risked creating an extremist government that would oppose basic Western values of tolerance and human rights. By arming Pakistan with highly sophisticated weapons, I believed we were alienating India and undermining the stability of South Asia.

At four o'clock in the afternoon of August 17, I received the first of several phone calls from Ronen Sen, Indian prime minister Rajiv Gandhi's personal secretary. He told me that the C-130 Hercules transport plane carrying General Mohammad Zia ul Haq had crashed. Zia had just attended a demonstration of an American-made Ml tank—a piece of equipment he did not want to buy but which American military contractors wanted to sell. Zia's plane had crashed on takeoff from the military air base outside Bahawalpur. Sen called with updates every fifteen or twenty minutes.

From the moment I heard the news, I suspected that the plane crash was not an accident. But my most immediate concern was who was on board with him. After the second or third phone call from Ronen Sen, it was clear that the U.S. ambassador to Pakistan, Arnold Raphel, and the head of the U.S. military aid mission, General Herbert M. Wassom, were on Zia's plane. But why? According to my information, both had flown up to Bahawalpur on the embassy plane to witness the tank demonstration. Why had they not returned on their own aircraft? What had happened to their bodyguards?

My search for answers ultimately led to my early retirement from the Foreign Service. The more I pushed for answers, the more officials from the Reagan administration pushed back. My continuing concerns ultimately led me to arrange consultations in Washington in September. But the meetings that had been agreed to in high-level messages never took place.

When I arrived at the State Department, I was told that meetings about the Zia affair and U.S.-Indian relations were not on. That surprised me, because the State Department had sent me messages setting up specific top-level appointments. It was clear the administration wanted to put the assassination in the past and move forward with its existing policies toward India, Pakistan, and Afghanistan. That, I hasten to add, was the administration's right and prerogative.

But then I got the shock of my life. I was told that doctors had signed papers that branded me as psychologically unsound. I had a choice: Go to my family's ski chalet in Switzerland, or get medical care in the United States. Either way, I was not allowed to return to India for the time being.

In the summer of 1988, a quiet struggle had been going on behind the scenes among Pakistan's military elites, American arms suppliers, and countries across the region. At stake was the balance of power in Asia. The question was what kind of conventional military would Pakistan have—and how might that military be used against neighbors?

As noted, America wanted to influence the struggle by selling arms to Pakistan. General Zia considered buying two systems in particular—the AWACS plane and the M1 tank.

When Ambassador Raphel reported on June 6, 1988, that Zia had decided against the purchase of the Ml tank, we were surprised. Washington was upset. But General Zia did not have unlimited resources. A nuclear program and a war require a lot of money. At a small dinner for Congressman Charles Wilson, on June 5, 1988, at Zia's residence, Zia told Wilson that the price of the tank was too steep. Pakistan would use its resources instead on the AWACS.

As soon as Zia said no to the M1, there was pressure to reconsider. Advocates for Ml mobilized in Washington and Islamabad. They organized a demonstration of the tank's capabilities on August 17. Zia reluctantly agreed to fly to Bahawalpur to see a lone tank fire its cannon in the desert. Major General Mahmood Durrani, the commander of the Pakistani Armored Corps and Zia's former military secretary, pushed hard for Zia to see the demonstration. Durrani argued that the entire army command would be on hand for the demonstration, implying that Zia's absence would be taken as a slight.

The demonstration was a disaster. None of the ten tanks worked as advertised. If anything, the event seemed to be a demonstration of why Zia should not buy the tanks even if he had the money to do so. But the issue soon became moot when Zia and his companions—including some of his top generals and Ambassador Raphael—were killed in the crash of the plane carrying them back to Islamabad.

After *Pak One* was airborne, a controller in the Bahawalpur tower asked the plane's commander, Mash'hood Hassan, his position. Mash'hood radioed back: "*Pak One*, stand by." After that, there was no further response. Controllers on the ground became alarmed. Efforts to contact Mash'hood grew desperate. *Pak One* was missing only minutes after it had taken off.

Meanwhile, at the river about nine miles from the airport, villagers saw a plane lurching in the sky, as if it were on an invisible roller coaster. After its third loop, it plunged directly toward the desert, burying itself in the soil. It exploded and became a ball of fire as its fuel burned. All thirty-one people on board *Pak One* were dead. In the course of that evening of August 17, Ronen Sen mentioned to me that a satellite had observed, and perhaps even filmed, the way Zia's plane took off, lurched, and then crashed.

To my mind, the most likely explanation for the crash is that a nerve gas bomb planted in the C-130's air vent was triggered to go off when pressurized air was fed into the cockpit. A gas manufactured in the Soviet Union would have done the trick, but so would a host of other nerve gases. According to a technical expert at the U.S. Army chemical-warfare center in Aberdeen, Maryland, the American-manufactured VX nerve gas is odorless and easily transportable in liquid form. A tiny quantity would be enough, when dispersed by a small explosion and inhaled, to cause paralysis and loss of speech within thirty seconds. Its residue would be phosphorous. The chemical analysis of debris from the cockpit of Zia's plane showed heavy traces of phosphorous.

In late August 1988, I tried to make sense of all the data I got from the Indians, our mission in Kabul, my own staff, Washington, and ambassadorial colleagues in New Delhi. I first conferred with British ambassador Allgood. Prior to his posting in India, he had served in the British cabinet, responsible for MI6. We enjoyed a close personal relationship, but when I asked him to help me untangle the different pieces of information on Zia's assassination, he became silent and offered no help whatsoever.

My Canadian colleague was also not helpful, nor was our New Zealand colleague, the conqueror of Mount Everest, Edmund Hillary. My French colleague, André Levin, listened to all I had to say about a possible serious cover-up, but said only that he would pass on my concern.

Accusations and counteraccusations swirled around for weeks. Who killed Zia? The Indians? The dissatisfied Pakistani military? The Afghan Secret Service? The Russians? American agents? When I saw Prime Minister Gandhi, he first opined that an explosive device had been placed in a fruit basket that was put on board Zia's plane. This device could have triggered another reaction within the plane that may have accounted for the silence of the crew in answering the calls from the control tower and the "rudderless plane falling to the ground."

I also discussed the crash with General K. Sundarji, chief of staff of the Indian Army. A likeable man, Sundarji was a graduate of the Command and General Staff College at Fort Leavenworth, Kansas. In his long career, he had commanded Indian troops in a U.N. operation in the former Belgian Congo and served in all the wars and skirmishes between India and Pakistan. Sundarji was known as the "scholar warrior" among his friends. He died in February 1999.

At first, Sundarji linked Zia's death to the situation in Afghanistan. He did not think that the Soviets were behind it. He did not think the Afghan Intelligence Service had the means to pull off the assassination. But he had personal reasons to suspect Mossad. In 1986 and 1987, Sundarji had clashed with Mossad when Indian troops were deployed to Sri Lanka to oppose the Tamil secession movement in northern Sri Lanka, in response to a call for assistance by Sri Lanka's president. Sundarji told me he had discovered that dozens of Mossad officers were working with Sri Lankan forces.

Sundarji had a healthy respect for Mossad, whose primary function, he thought, was to oppose Pakistan and any Islamic nation increasing its military potential. The arrival of Indian forces in Sri Lanka forced the Mossad officers out.

I met with General Sundarji and his wife Vani on June 25, 1993, when they were our guests at our apartment in Paris. Naturally, the conversation turned to the assassination of President Zia five years earlier. Sundarji told me in a solemn voice: "You [the Americans] did it." I am not sure he meant that we had actually been directly involved in carrying out the deed rather than in the behind-the-scenes planning and cover-up. Neither the U.S. ambassador nor the U.S. general was supposed to be on Zia's plane, he believed, having flown up to the demonstration at Bahawalpur on the American Embassy plane. Rather, their presence was due only to Zia's last-minute invitation.

Did India have a hand in the Zia crash? I don't know. Rajiv Gandhi was certainly not involved. Intelligence units and others in India might have played a role. I didn't think the Indians were involved, but maybe they were. Did the Russians do it? The Afghans? Was Israel involved? On July 19, 1988, Reagan had written to Zia, praising his regime for the progress Pakistan made under his leadership in developing durable broad-based democratic institutions. Given that the letter was written one month before Zia's death, I find it difficult to believe that the United States was involved in his assassination, as some foreign voices have claimed.

Why did I conclude, as I eventually did, that the Israeli intelligence agency Mossad had played some role, though surely not alone? Perhaps I just strung together a number of events that led me to the following accusation: (1) In New Delhi I received several visits from Representative Stephen Solarz and later from Representative Tom Lantos, both firm supporters of Israel. Both men thought that, as a refugee from Nazi Germany, I would automatically support Israel and willingly side with Israel whenever needed. But this assumption was dead wrong and showed a complete misunderstanding of my outlook on life. I represented the United States of America, and for me, Israel is a foreign political entity. I had made this clear over many years in the U.S. Foreign Service and had even explained it to the Senate Foreign Relations Committee in the confirmation hearings for my appointment to various ambassadorships. (2) In their visits to New Delhi during my tenure, both Solarz and Lantos were not emphasizing the need for a Soviet withdrawal from Afghanistan. Rather, they were actively promoting (a) the upgrading of the Israeli vice consul in Bombay to full consul, considerably extending his jurisdiction to include the site of an ancient Jewish synagogue in southwestern India; (b) having Prime Minister Gandhi meet Israeli Foreign Minister Shimon Peres in New York to balance India's links with PLO leader Arafat; and (c) trying to avert Pakistan's becoming a nuclear state. All this was cloaked in a strongly pro-Indian stance in any Pakistan-India squabbles when discussing these subjects with Rajiv Gandhi and other Indian leaders.

Add to this concoction a certain pro-Israeli bias of some Indian elements who saw in Israel the favorite ally of the United States, and you end up with these same people believing that by supporting Israel they are ingratiating themselves with the policy makers in Washington.

I must also admit that my experience in Lebanon had taught me to distrust the Israeli intelligence apparatus. I have already described how Mossad provided American weapons to try to kill me in Beirut, because I had carried out the president's instructions to work with the Palestinians. Perhaps this incident had left a mark on my psyche.

Who, I asked myself, stood to gain the most from the assassination of Zia? I thought first of Israel, because Zia was a conservative Muslim fundamentalist and the Pakistani determination to obtain the nuclear bomb had made him an opponent of Israel.

As U.S. ambassador to India in the second part of the 1980s, I was eager to bring the United States and India closer together. I saw increased trade and especially increased cooperation in high technology as a way of achieving this objective. During my three years in India, I returned several times to Washington on consultation. Each time I used the occasion to meet with immigrants from the Indian subcontinent. I encouraged them to play an important role as bridge builders to tighten links between their country of adoption—the United States—and their country of origin—India. I carried this message to cities on both coasts, wherever large Indian immigrant communities had invited me to speak. These "new Americans," like myself some fifty years earlier, liked this message and took action. They looked around the United States to find out which groups in the country had powerful lobbies in Congress and could influence legislation. They quickly concluded that the pro-Israel lobby and their friends in Congress, like Representative Solarz, were particularly powerful in Washington and at the same time well disposed toward India. Perhaps they also thought that, in view of my own past, I would concur in this evaluation.

And so, over time, the extremely successful Indian immigrants, who have the highest income of any immigrant group, established a close relationship, even an alliance, with the pro-Israel bloc in Congress. Successful Indian immigrants went to see their representatives and senators and supported them, especially those who were pro-Israel. This alliance continues today, more than twenty years after I first arrived in New Delhi. But today, Israel has become an important provider of advanced weaponry to India, including drones manufactured under U.S. license in Israel. Arms exports from Israel to India amounted to a couple billion dollars by 2005.

Add to this group the American evangelical fundamentalists, who are known for their pro-Zionist sentiments. All three groups are strong supporters of Israel in Congress, regardless who is prime minister in Israel or for that matter who is prime minister in India.

My friend Robert Oakley had been dispatched to Islamabad to replace Arnie Raphel shortly after August 17, 1988. On August 31, two weeks after Zia's demise, he told me about his August 29 meeting with Pakistan's new Army chief of staff, General Beg. General Beg had reaffirmed that "Pakistan and Afghanistan are now one," two nations but one people. Oakley reported: "General Beg denied the importance of the upsurge in Islamic fundamentalism and said that there would be no fundamentalist government in Afghanistan."

Did General Beg's views coincide with those of the American administration in Washington? Beg told Oakley that Iran was "another emerging reality" and that closer relations between Iran and Pakistan would help dilute Iranian fundamentalism. Beg looked forward to the "strategic consensus" of Pakistan, Afghanistan, Iran, and Turkey that he saw as a "grand design." No formal pact would be necessary, but such a consensus would create a new regional power equation, Beg believed, and provide the United States with new options for dealing with India, the Soviet Union, and the Middle East. Oakley wisely questioned some of Beg's statements.

At the same meeting, Oakley's military advisors urged Beg to make up his mind on the Ml tank purchase. The United States wanted to show its support for Pakistan by actions and not just words. Buying the tank would send a signal. My reading of the message under reference implies that Beg agreed to proceed with the tank purchase. Oakley's military aide, General Pfister, pointed out that there were a number of other systems—like the Cobra helicopters, TOW missiles, and launchers—that would demonstrate U.S. support for Pakistan and "would probably not encounter congressional opposition."

But who were those members of Congress that might oppose the shipment of American arms to Pakistan? Some Pakistanis blamed "pro-Indian lobbies" in the United States. But a number of members were concerned about Pakistan's military ambitions, including its quest for nuclear capability. These legislators opposed arms sales to Pakistan. I doubt legislators worried about India's reaction to the sale of arms to Pakistan, since they knew that India relied exclusively on Russian weapons, that India already had exploded its first nuclear bomb in 1974, and that it relied on its own know-how and industrial capacity for its nuclear capability. At the same time, Pakistan's quest for a nuclear deterrent was seen by some as an effort to build an "Islamic bomb"—opposed not only by the United States but also by Israel.

On September 10, I cabled Washington asking if I could return to Washington to meet with top officials in the White House and State Department. I wanted to tell them that our good relationship with India was in peril because of the U.S. tilt toward Pakistan and our determination to support the fundamentalists rather than the secularists in Afghanistan. I also wanted to share with my superiors in Washington my assessment of who may have been behind the assassination of Pakistan's president.

Everyone knew my concerns, but we did not seem to be communicating. I thought I had to meet people face to face and have a tough, detailed conversation about these topics. When you send cables back and forth, there's sometimes a tendency to talk past each other. Issues get couched in careful diplomatic language. The parties can elude each other's questions and concerns. On September 10, I received a reply from Assistant Secretary Richard Murphy expressing gratitude for my willingness to come to Washington to see Shultz, Webster, and other high-level officials.

My wife Martine advised against the trip. In all our years together—even in war zones like Vietnam, Cambodia, and Lebanon—she never advised me against going anywhere for any reason. But she had a premonition about this trip. She thought that the people in Washington were so resistant to my advice that I might suffer some extreme consequences if I continued to press my case. My time in India was almost over—the Reagan administration had already decided to replace me with John Hubbard—and top officials had had enough of my concerns.

A few days before leaving New Delhi, I communicated several concerns to Secretary Shultz, notably that "our relationship with India is in a nose dive unless there are some changes made." I complained about the administration's timing of Hubbard's nomination to replace me as ambassador. I liked Jack a great deal; he was not the problem. But with the president serving out his final two–three months, and with such serious ongoing crises in South Asia, I thought a recess appointment unwise. Finally, I told Shultz that I would give the president my resignation any time he asked. I prepared two memos before the meeting—"What can be done to send the right signals to India?" and "Some random thoughts of Ambassador Dean on South Asia."

Some ominous signs appeared in my last few days in India. For some reason, service on the secure telephone lines between India and the United States went dead. Day after day I tried to get through to the State Department, but could not do so. Nobody told me what was wrong or what could be done to fix the lines. And when the State Department made arrangements for my flight to Washington, I was listed as John Gunther, not John Gunther Dean. And a CIA agent accompanied me on the trip.

When I arrived at Dulles International Airport, I finally began to learn what was happening. I was told I would not be meeting with Secretary of State Shultz, CIA Director William Webster, or anyone else about India, Pakistan, and Afghanistan.

The next day, I went to the State Department to see George Vest, the director general of the Foreign Service. He informed me that I was not going back to my post in India. And unless I volunteered to go to my wife's family vacation home in Switzerland I would be placed under medical care in the United States.

The State Department used a phony appraisal of my "strain" for its report. Dr. David Kosh, a regional medical officer in New Delhi, had written in the late summer that I was "under stress" and that he worried about "possible personality changes." That was the evidence the State Department used to establish that I was mentally incapacitated. Dr. Frederick Summers, the neurologist at the U.S. Embassy in New Delhi, expressed doubt about State's appraisal—for which he was summarily punished. In 1992, the former head of the State Department Medical Service, a Dr. Goff, confirmed to me that my medical clearance had been withheld "for bogus reasons."

Washington's actions surprised me. By questioning my sanity, which they backed up with reports from psychiatrists and other medical doctors with whom the State Department Medical Unit had made appointments, the State Department took away my medical clearance.

Kept out of Washington and New Delhi, I could not speak with inquisitive journalists trying to find issues for the upcoming November elections. The department's first thought was to send me to an asylum. Fortunately, that idea was discarded, and I was sent to Switzerland for "recuperation." I had orders to stay there until I received word to return to New Delhi to pack up our personal belongings and leave.

This was the kind of technique that the Stalinist regime used to silence its critics in the Soviet Union. I could not imagine that these methods could be employed by an American administration on one of its Senior Foreign Service officers.

I flew from Washington to Switzerland, where I reported to the Swiss police. My wife and one of our sons joined me for the forced period of rest. This strange "confinement to quarters" lasted until the end of October. State Department officials telephoned regularly to make sure I had stayed put. An assistant secretary of state and a top aide even paid a visit to make sure I did not stray. Finally, Washington told us we could leave Switzerland.

We returned to New Delhi in late October to pack up and leave. My Indian friends and colleagues were all very nice. The Indian president gave us, as a farewell present, an oil painting that I presented to the American residence. It depicted the five continents of our earth. In front of each continent were grieving women in tears.

I returned to Washington after the New Year. I was assigned a huge office in the State Department, near the secretary's suite. But I had no specific duties. My superiors kept me busy with appointments with psychiatrists and doctors from the department's medical unit. I also went to specialized laboratories, which scanned my brain. I took a number of "intelligence tests," as if I had suffered some kind of brain damage at my last posting.

My career was over. I made it known, since no new assignment was offered, that I was willing to resign from the Foreign Service. Suddenly, the department acknowledged that I was in top physical and mental condition. My medical clearance and my security clearance were restored.

The funny thing is that if anyone had told me that my service was no longer needed and that it was time to end my Foreign Service career, I would have accepted it. I would have been unhappy, but I would have accepted it. I have always been loyal and followed the instructions of my superiors. I understand that presidents and secretaries of state have more complicated lives than ambassadors, and that sometimes they need to reject the advice of diplomats. I considered myself privileged to have served five presidents as chief of mission. I would leave if asked.

Apparently, it was not enough to just ask me to leave. I also had to get cut off—completely—from anyone who might want to hear my thoughts about the controversies on the subcontinent of Asia. It was too much of a risk to set me free, where I could talk to newspaper reporters or old colleagues from the Foreign Service or officials from India or any other government. For some reason, the administration had to muzzle me.

Upon retirement I was awarded the State Department's Distinguished Service Award. I also received a letter from Secretary Shultz, commending me for "the unprecedented success in improving relations between the United States and India, a significant achievement of the Reagan Administration."

Years later, I learned who had ordered the bogus diagnosis of mental incapacity against me. It was the same man who so effusively praised me once I was gone—George Shultz.

It was not the purpose of this chapter to rehash the war to oust the Soviets from Afghanistan. Others, in particular Steve Coll in his book *Ghost Wars* (2004), have already done that very well. But what does require explanation is how warriors the United States supported in Afghanistan turned so violently against the very hand that fed them. The answer centers around the rivalry between two Afghan fighters—Gulbuddin Hekmatyar, a Pashtun, and Ahmed Shah Massoud, a Tajik.

In 1985 when the United States decided to use the C.I.A. to escalate U.S. covert action in Afghanistan, it threw its support, together with that of Saudi Arabia, behind the fundamentalist Hekmatyar. Others favored the secular nationalist Massoud. While Massoud played the major role in ousting the Soviet military from Afghanistan, he was also willing to find a way of working with pro-Russian elements inside and outside Afghanistan after the Soviet troop withdrawal. Hekmatyar remained firmly opposed to working with pro-Russian elements.

In August 1989, six months after the Soviets had pulled out of Afghanistan, the *Washington Post* published an article by Steve Coll entitled, "U.S. facing a dilemma in arming rebels—most effective group is the most extreme." The article points to Hekmatyar, "who had been lashing out publicly at rival rebel groups and at the governments of the U.S. and Iran." Coll then raises the question of whether it was advisable for the United States to provide the fundamentalist Hekmatyar with more arms.

It is true that Massoud was more willing to work with the former Russian enemy than was Hekmatyar, and he maintained that policy until he was assassinated in September 2001. As a matter of fact, several months before his assassination, he attended a regional security conference in Moscow.

Key to the confrontation between the two Afghan fighters was that Pakistan President Zia had favored Hekmatyar and shared with him the conservative view about the role of Islam in society, as did General Beg, who had taken over the military reins following Zia's death in the suspicious fatal plane crash in August 1988.

What does all this amount to? The United States—with the help of Saudi Arabia—financed and armed the Muslim fundamentalist faction of Hekmatyar. This group turned into the Taliban, which in turn became an adversary of the United States.

But who won the war against the Soviet-backed leadership in Kabul? Hekmatyar? He only contributed to that result. It was Massoud who entered Kabul on April 29, 1992. As the French newspaper *Le Monde* wrote on May 2, 1992, in its article entitled "Commander Massoud makes his entry into the capital Kabul," "The fighting which has lasted four days has just ended in the center of Kabul by the defeat of the fundamentalist Gulbuddin Hekmatyar."

While the entire world press focused on the moderate, secular Massoud as the true victor of the war, the United States maintained its support for the fundamentalist Hekmatyar until well after the fall of Kabul. The decisive factor for this policy appears to have been that Hekmatyar was solidly anti-Soviet and Massoud was not as determined in his anti-Soviet policies. Secretary of State George Shultz had secretly walked into Kabul with Hekmatyar when the city was freed of the Soviet puppet regime. But it was Massoud who became defense minister in the Afghan government that took over from the Soviet-supported regime, while Hekmatyar eventually ended up going into exile as a determined enemy of his former U.S. sponsors.

Why this long explanation? Because it is essential for the American public to realize that we—the United States—backed the Afghan fundamentalists who turned against us. And we turned against them in later years. Some of the anti-American terrorists who committed horrible acts against the United States are the same warriors who fought with U.S. and Saudi support in Afghanistan. It was the anti-Soviet policy that dominated U.S. decisions on whom to support in the Afghanistan war, and if that required "sitting down for supper with the devil," so be it.

Part and parcel with the Islamic revolution was concern about terrorism. The world had not yet figured out a smart way to think about—and confront—global terrorism, a perennial part of global politics. A strategy used by the ideologically charged and militarily weak to confront dominant powers, terrorism has taken on a more devastating form as modern insurgents have gotten their hands on more and more lethal weaponry, used it with greater impunity, and threatened more and more innocent people. And in the 1970s and 1980s, a number of states sponsored terrorists to do their bidding. With millions of dollars in funding and access to secret intelligence, terrorists have been able to create widespread upheaval.

Rajiv Gandhi openly worried about what his country could do to fight terror. We talked on May 13, 1986, about the limits of state power against terrorism. Could India use its military forces against Pakistan if Pakistani terrorists got caught in India? His remarks implied that he was opposed to this approach.

The Afghan civil war would continue without end, but the Taliban, a strict fundamentalist sect, had taken over control of about 90 percent of the country by 1996. The Afghans welcomed the Taliban, for the people had become weary and cynical about their corrupt warlords and the continual warfare, supported by foreigners.

Some of the weaponry we supplied to Pakistan and the Afghan resistance later hurt us. Stinger missiles provided to the Afghan resistance became a political danger to American civilian aircraft in the hands of terrorists after the Soviet military withdrawal from Afghanistan. Even during my days in South Asia, the American embassies in Islamabad and New Delhi kept close watch on how many Stingers were in the hands of the Afghan resistance, what shape they were in, and what groups actually held them.

As long as the Stingers were used against the Soviet military, nobody appeared to have any qualms. But what if the Afghans sold them to others for cold cash once the Soviets had left Afghanistan? In July 1993, the *Los Angeles Times* reported that the CIA had requested $55 million to buy back hundreds of Stinger antiaircraft missiles that the United States had supplied to Afghan rebels. That sum—more than five times a previous allocation for a covert Stinger repurchase program—was offered by the Clinton administration because of fierce competition for the missiles on the international black market. U.S. agents were finding themselves outbid for the shoulder-launched rockets that now fetch as much as $100,000 a piece. The article went on to link anti-American terrorist activities to the Afghan resistance movement. "Even if the United States can recover many of the missiles, new versions from other countries are likely to flood into the market," the *Times* reported.

Will the fundamentalist revolution continue to thrive? Will terrorism be checked? Can a diverse nation such as India remain a vibrant democracy? Can the arms race—especially the nuclear arms race—be controlled? Can neighbors with years of enmity find a way to get along? Can the dirty business of the world—arms, drugs, sex trafficking—be controlled? Can diverse groups live together in peace?

My experience in India affirmed that we can pass all of these tests. But it requires courage, because underlying all these questions is a complex and secret world of dealing and double-dealing that makes straight and honest decision-making difficult.

Whenever a difficult challenge arises, such as selling arms, sharing technology, or addressing religious and ethnic extremism, the tendency is to look for the solution that damps down the most immediate problem. Need to fight the Soviets in Afghanistan? Arm mercenaries to do the job, regardless of their background or interests. Need to fight terrorists? Align with whoever promises immediate action, even a brutal military dictator.

The Zia assassination put us in a difficult position in Afghanistan. The pro-Russian government headed by Najibullah stayed in power for a lot longer than people expected. We ended up fighting some of the same people we had earlier financed when they fought against the Soviets.

The most damaging aspect of the whole affair is that a number of countries see the Zia assassination as just another example of the U.S. protecting the Israelis.

Nothing that happened checked Pakistan's efforts to get the bomb. They have the bomb now. And because of Al Qaeda and Taliban attacks, we again embraced a military dictatorship in Pakistan, because the president of Pakistan was sitting on a powder keg and we needed to make sure it didn't explode.

How to end the chapter on my last Foreign Service assignment, for me a sad ending to a career of more than forty years of service dedicated to the nation? I could be vindictive, angry, greedy for compensation, looking to get even. Instead, I leave it to time to let truth prevail. I don't think anybody in the State Department or in the U.S. government—then or today—believes that I was mentally deranged when I said loud and clear that President Zia was assassinated and it was not mechanical failure of the plane that caused his death. Other voices have joined mine in suggesting that foreign intelligence agencies—probably working with some dissident Indian or Pakistani elements—caused Zia's assassination. That event was also the beginning of the fallout between the United States and Pakistan. The increase in anti-American terrorism may also have its roots in the way the United States handled the foreign fighters who fought successfully the Soviet occupation of Afghanistan but were no longer needed—or valued—after the Soviet military withdrew from that country. Further, I have no doubt that the assassination of Zia and its aftermath contributed to the deterioration in U.S. relations with the Muslim world, and possibly even to the linkage Muslims everywhere make between U.S. politics and Israeli policies in the Middle East.

I am not a whistle blower but I am attached to having the truth prevail on issues that affect the reputation of the United States. Hence, when I received a written request by the former American president Jimmy Carter to donate my documents and papers to the U.S. National Archives, I complied. I felt that this was the correct way to let others—historians, researchers, diplomats, academicians, librarians, scholars, politicians, and journalists—examine the documents and make up their own minds where the truth lies.

I prefer to end the chapter on India on a happy note.

It is the story of a Gilbert Stuart life-sized painting of George Washington I brought to New Delhi and which hung in the U.S. ambassador's residence during my tenure, from 1985 to 1988. It became an attraction both for American tourists and Indian intellectuals interested in their own history. American Express tours added the residence of the American ambassador to their town excursion for tourists, who saw the impressive portrait for what I hoped it would be: a personification of the history of U.S.-Indian cooperation.

Toward the end of the eighteenth century, American merchants from New England sailed often to Calcutta for trade of mutual benefit to the newly independent American colonies and the old but still British–ruled India. One well-to-do Indian merchant in Calcutta, when asked by his American merchant partners what he would like to receive as a sign of their friendship, replied: "Send me a painting of your liberator, George Washington, who has made you free." And so the American merchants had the Gilbert Stuart painting of George Washington made in America and then gave it to the Calcutta merchant. It stayed in that merchant's house for about 150 years. But the humid, warm climate was not good for the canvas. When after World War II the inventor of the bazooka, a naturalized American of Czech origin, visited India with a lady friend, he bought the painting from the merchant's house and had it restored to its original glory. It ended up eventually at Washington and Lee University in Lexington, Virginia. As it happens, the family of my wonderful daughter-in-law owned an art gallery in New York. They were especially knowledgeable about American paintings and succeeded in negotiating with the university the loan of the Stuart painting to the U.S. State Department for the duration of my tour of duty in India.

The painting of George Washington, on display again in India after more than 150 years, truly reflected a bond between the United States and India. For Americans, the painting of "The Liberator" was a symbol of America's message of freedom to the world. And for the Indians, it was a symbol of the aspirations of their own hard-won freedom and progress to inspire all those who have come out of colonialism.

A Final Word

As I sit down with my family to celebrate my 80th birthday, I ask myself what has been the leitmotif of my life. And I come up with the same answer I gave as a young man— serving my adopted country, the United States of America, to the best of my ability in the discipline I chose for my career: diplomacy. For forty-two years I served both Democratic and Republican administrations with equal zeal and dedication. On one issue, that of integrity, I found it difficult to compromise. I was raised with a number of universal values and American traditions on which I was unwilling to compromise.

When I grew up in the Middle West in the late 1930s and early 1940s, I really believed in the veracity of the 1883 poem by Emma Lazarus, "The New Colossus," inscribed on the Statue of Liberty:

"Give me your tired, your poor,
Your huddled masses, yearning to breath free,
The wretched refuse of your teeming shore,
Send these, the homeless, tempest-tost, to me,
I lift my lamp beside the golden door!"

I saw in the torch held high by the Statue of Liberty, a beacon of hope not only for our country but for many people around the world. Yes, I believed as a youngster and still today that the American flag is a symbol of our country, and while I never needed to wear a replica of the flag on my lapel, I did in Cambodia carry out the American flag over my left arm because I did not want anybody—foreigners or Americans—to desecrate the symbol for which it stands.

For all these years I have continued to have faith in American traditions, which I believe are also admired around the world: respect for the law, honesty, tolerance, a sense of justice, and equality. Perhaps I also bought into the myth that America has some kind of a mission, a role to play, to peacefully propagate these values around the world.

As a representative of the American people I tried to live these values in my daily occupations. A foreign statesman told me years ago: "Other countries bestow the leadership on you Americans; you do not seize it unilaterally. The United States, a country with much power and wealth, owes a lot to those with less." The British use the term *noblesse oblige* for the same concept. However it is expressed, the United States as the most powerful nation since World War II must set a good example if we want other countries around the globe to acquiesce in U.S. leadership. If we seize this leadership unilaterally, we are no longer a truly democratic nation but risk being accused of authoritarian behavior in our international relations.

As a member of the United States Armed Forces during World War II and in the Vietnam conflict, I learned that the only way to lead people is by setting a good example. In representing my country, I can only lead by doing the right thing myself, not by exhorting others to do the right thing. When one is the boss—in any profession or position, civilian or military, private or public sector—one must set a good example. I tried to do that in my career. I leave it to others to determine whether I succeeded in this challenge.

In retrospect, I found the approach we took to foreign affairs shortly after World War II more satisfying than our recent rather egocentric policies. As a member of the Marshall Plan cadre in the early 1950s, I was part of the Economic Cooperation Administration (ECA). Yes, we emphasized peaceful economic cooperation with other nations. The Europeans liked this policy except for those nations who feared that this approach would undermine their economic and political system. The ECA was replaced with the Mutual Security Agency, with the emphasis on "mutual" rather than unilateral. The goal of the United States was to share security problems and not impose our views unilaterally. Perhaps not all projects were shared on a 50-50 basis, but nevertheless all initiatives were designed to benefit mutually all parties.

Until quite recently, we did not put ourselves above the law in our diplomatic relations with the world community. To the contrary, we helped create international organizations where we placed ourselves on the same level with other great powers: the United Nations and the many specialized U.N. agencies like ILO, UNESCO, UNIDO, WHO, and others. We only withdrew from certain international organizations in isolated cases, and we usually paid our dues, even if sometimes with delay. When did we start thinking that the United States was above the law and regulations that the world community—including the United States—had accepted over time? During recent years we have withdrawn from all kinds of treaties and conventions generated by organizations that we had helped to found. On what basis do we now consider ourselves above the law?

Today I sometimes wonder whether we are applying the rule "do as I say but not as I do." Have we adopted dual standards in foreign affairs–those for the mighty and those for the weak? Some foreigners accuse us of hypocrisy. Are we not in reality living all together in one world, where we in the United States are just the most powerful among many countries on this small planet Earth? Isn't it time for us to revert to a virtue we tried to practice in the past, that of respect for the law? And what about tolerance? Do we today show respect to all races and religions, or are we merely mouthing it?

When I left India and went into retirement, my Swiss colleague in New Delhi came to the airport to say farewell. I still remember the advice he gave me on that occasion: "John, don't forget, diplomats are peacemakers, and you should continue to live that role." True, whenever I could, I tried to find a nonmilitary solution to a conflict: at the Vietnam peace talks in Paris; in the transition from colonialism to nationhood in West Africa and Southeast Asia; in Lebanon in regard to the Israeli-Palestinian conflict; and in India trying to find a new beginning for Afghanistan after the Soviet military withdrawal from the country. Was not Afghanistan in reality a U.S-Soviet military confrontation and part of the Cold War?

I am today still inclined to believe that America should devote a greater portion of its financial resources and abilities to avoiding military solutions and to using negotiations and diplomacy to the maximum. Our aim should be to avoid the destruction, misery, and loss of life wrought by the use of force. This does not mean neglecting our military establishment. But it does imply using diplomacy first and military force as a last resort.

If we have to have an adversary, as some politicians claim, why not adopt some of the ideas expounded a century ago by Harvard professor George Santayana, when he suggested that we find ways of channeling our energies to work with nature and protect the environment, for example by planting trees or harnessing water power Are the concepts behind the organizations such as WPA and CCC, established by Franklin D. Roosevelt in the 1930s, still valid today? Fighting poverty or natural disaster can be as great a challenge as military confrontation. Is not more gained for our country and for humanity by our helping the victims of the earthquake in Kashmir than by building more antimissile defense systems? And against whom? Russia? China? Unfortunately, powerful elements in our country still believe that we must confront the Russian Federation that emerged with the disappearance of the Soviet Union. Others call for opposing China's march to modernity, because they fear the Chinese may become an effective challenger to America's predominant role in the world. Do we really have to create an opponent in order for the United States to function? I hope not.

It all comes down to doing the right thing, not just mouthing good intentions. In putting down a coup d'état in Laos and putting my own life on the line, I succeeded in helping Laos complete the intra-Lao negotiations that put an end to twenty years of warfare. In carrying out my president's orders in Lebanon, I did not ingratiate myself with some elements in the Near East but I did help make the Palestinians valid interlocutors in the search for a peaceful solution to the Israeli-Palestinian conflict.

Diplomats remain the frontline defenders of America's national interests outside our borders. Only if diplomats fail should military options be considered. As we look toward a future marked by troubled times, when our country has never been less popular, Americans, and particularly our political leadership, should seriously consider one principal issue. Is setting a good example by acting decently and in a manner consistent with the rule of law and the other traditional American values that we purport to embrace likely to be a more successful strategy than seeking to impose our will by force and threats of force? Which course will better serve the interests, well-being, and happiness not only of the American people, but also of the rest of the world?

Compare the goal of global domination pursued in recent years, without notable success, to the goal of again inspiring the world by our traditional values and adhering to them. Surely regaining the respect and admiration of mankind through the example set by our behavior is the nobler and more moral goal for a great country and a great people—one of which all Americans could be proud.

Index

Abdo, Johnny, 138
Abdullah (king of Saudi Arabia), 147
Abramowitz, Morton, xi, 156, 162
Afghanistan: drug trafficking in, x, 171; India's stance on, x, 183, 184, 185; Islamic fundamentalism in, x, 171, 184, 185, 186, 187, 193, 194, 198–99, 200; and Pakistan, x, xiv, 171, 179, 183–84, 185–86, 193; Soviet troops in, x, 170–71, 179, 182, 183, 184, 185, 186, 200, 202; U.S. involvement in, x, 171, 179, 182, 183, 185, 198–99, 200–201, 202
Africa: colonization of, 36–37, 112; decolonization in, 25, 34–35, 37–38, 42–43; JGD's posts in, 34–46; nonaligned movement and, 45; polygamy and, 41–42; post-WWII status of, 25, 29; separatist movements in, 43; U.S. policies in, 25, 35. *See also* Benin; Ghana; Guinea; Liberia; Mali; Togo
Agent Orange, 59
Agnew, Spiro, 84
Albertus Magnus, 21
Ananda Mahidol, 159
Angkor Wat, 60, 87

Aql, Basil, 139
Arafat, Yasir, 132, 136, 137, 139, 142, 178, 192
Armacost, Michael, 181
Armitage, Richard, 101
ASEAN (Association of South East Asian Nations), 151, 156, 166, 167
Ashkenaczy family, 2–3
Asia: post-WWII status of, 25, 29
Assad, Hafez al-, 142
AWACS (Airborne Warning and Control System), 179–80, 183–84, 188

Bamako (Mali), JGD as chargé d'affaires in, 42–46
Bangkok (Thailand): JGD as U.S. ambassador in, 149, 150–54, 157–58, 159, 160, 161, 163–66, 167; JGD's earliest visits to, 149
Bangladesh War of Independence (1971), 172, 175, 179
Bao Dai, 30, 33
Beg, Mirza Aslam, 185–86, 193–94, 199
Beirut (Lebanon), Saudi influence in, 140–43
Belgium: African colonies and, 37; JGD's ECA posting in, 27–28;

NATO headquarters in, 28; Thailand and, 156
Benin, former slave trade in, 42
Bhumibol Adulyadej (king of Thailand), xiii, 58–61, **126**, 166, 167
Bhutto, Zulfikar Ali, 181
bombing, JGD's views on, 72–74
Brademas, John, 23
Brazil, slave trade and, 42
Breslau (Germany), 1–2, 9
Britain: African colonies and, 36-37, 38; India and, 112, 175, 176, 202; Israel and, 136; in Southeast Asia, 156; in WWII, 73
Brown, Fred, 55
Brüning, Heinrich, 13, 23
Buck, Paul, 14
Buddhism: in Laos, 66, 67; in Thailand, 150, 166–67
Bush, George H. W., x–xi, xiii, 90, **129**, 169
Byrne, Patricia, 186

Cambodia: JGD as ambassador to, xii, xiii, 80, 83, 84–85, 89, 91–93, 95, 97–113, **119–21**, 169, 170, 205; JGD's hopes for, 46; Khmer Rouge in, xiii, 31, 81, 86, 89, 91–92, 95–96, 97, 98, 100, 102, 103, 105, 109–11, 162; Kissinger and, 84, 89; Laos and, 66; neutral status and, 31, 32, 87, 88, 94, 95, 96, 97; Nixon "secret plan" and, 52; peace negotiation efforts and, xiii, 16, 84–85, 89–90, 91, 92–93, 94, 97–99, 100, 103, 104, 166–67; post-WWII status of, 28–29, 30–32, 101; in pre-Vietnam War era, 87–88; refugees from, 161–62; regional interconnections and, 136; 167; U.S. bombing of, 83, 86, 89, 95; U.S. exit from, xiii, 99, 102–9, **121**, 205; U.S. land mines in, 59; U.S. policies and, 76, 94, 97, 112, 167; Viet Cong and, 49, 54, 85–86, 95

Carter, Jimmy, xiii, xiv, **130**, 135, 138–39, 180, 202
Carter, Rosalynn, **130**
Casey, William, 182
Central Intelligence Agency (CIA), 25, 56, 90, 182, 198, 200
Cham Museum (Danang, Vietnam), 59–61
Chamoun, Camille, 135, 141
Chamoun, Danny, 141
Charles (French general), 45
Cheever, Daniel S., 23
Chiang Kai-shek, 30, 41
China, People's Republic of (PRC), 30, 32, 33, 41, 69, 77, 86, 90, 91, 94, 96, 97, 112, 149, 157, 166, 170, 171, 181, 208
China, Republic of, 30, 41, 166
Chou Enlai, 90, 93
Church, Frank, 56
Churchill, Winston, 32
Cold War, 25, 26, 29, 32, 34, 37, 47, 48, 74, 86, 112, 137, 151, 166, 167, 173, 176
Coll, Stephen, 182; 198
communism: in Africa, 46; ideals of, 67; in Indochina, 31–32, 34, 49, 52, 65–66, 69–70, 74, 77, 86, 94, 151, 161; in post-WWII Europe, 26; U.S. policies and, 25, 29, 34, 46, 47, 65, 66, 72, 77, 86, 91, 94, 98, 167. *See also* Domino theory; Khmer Rouge; Pathet Lao; Viet Minh
Conant, James B., 22

Index

containment: coalition governments and, 74, 75; as Cold War strategy, 25, 86
CORDS (Civil Operations and Revolutionary/Rural Development Support), 53–61, 62
Curtis, William, 131, 132

Dallin, Alexander, 16
De Gaulle, Charles, 28, 32, 37, 45, 53, 101
De Santos (Benin village chief), 42
Dean, Catherine (daughter), 131, 132–33
Dean, John Gunther: birthplace, 1–2; career goals and, 8, 205; as CORDS regional director, xii, 53–61, 62, 206; as emigrant to U.S., 6–12, 111, 161, 191; as graduate student, 22–24; Harvard University and, 8, 9, 11, 12–15, 20, 21–24; and Jewish identity, 1, 2, 3–4, 146–47; marriage of, 28, 29; as Marshall Plan administrator, xii, 25, 26–29, 30, 34, 206; in military service, 15–20, 26, 206; name change and, 6–7; parents of, 2–3, 4, 5–12, 23, 24; personal credo of, 205–6; school days of, 3–4, 6–7; U.S. citizenship and, 6, 15
Dean, John Gunther, Foreign Service career: as activist diplomat, xii–xiv, 76, 169–70; assassination attempt on, xiii, 131–34, 136, 192; in Cambodia as ambassador, xii, 80, 83, 84–85, 89–93, 95, 97–113, **119–21**, 169, 170, 205; in Denmark as ambassador, xiii, 59, 113, **122**; early retirement and, xii, xiv, 187–88, 195, 197–98, 207; in India as ambassador, ix–xi, **127–30**, 169–71, 174, 177–78, 179–80, 181–82, 184, 185, 186–88, 190–93, 194–97, 201, 202–3; in Laos as DCM/chargé d'affaires, xii–xiii, 34, 65, 68–81, **117–18**, 149, 208; in Laos as political officer, xii, 34, 66; in Lebanon as ambassador, xiii, **123–25**, 131–47, 169, 192, 208; in Mali as xiii, chargé d'affaires, 42–46, **115**; xiii, medical clearance removal and, 194–97, 198; in Paris as political officer, 47–48, 49–51, 52–53, **116**; "recuperation" in Switzerland and, 196–97; scientists and, 17; in Thailand as ambassador, xiii, **126**, 149, 150–54, 157–58, 159, 160, 161, 163–66, 167, 169; in Togo as consul, xiii, 34–36, 38–43; in Vietnam as CORDS regional director, 53–63
Dean, Josef (father), 2; death of, 24; as emigrant to U.S., 6, 7–8, 9–10; JGD at Harvard and, 13, 14, 20; JGD's life lessons from, 9, 10, 23, 25; Nazi persecution and, 5, 6, 12
Dean, Lucy Ashkenaczy ("Mutti"), 2–3, 4; emigration to U.S. and, 5, 6, 7, 9, 11; and JGD's Togo posting, 38
Dean, Martine Duphenieux (wife), ix, 27-28, 29, 35, 42, 62–63, 70–71, 88, 108, **116, 125**, 132, 143, 149, 150, 195, 196
Dean, Robert, 174
Debré, Michel, 53
Decolonization, 25, 28–29, 34–35, 37–38, 100–101, 175, 203. *See also* Cambodia; Guinea; Laos; Mali; Togo; Vietnam

Democracy in America (Toqueville), 111
Denmark: JGD as ambassador to, xiii, 59, 113, **122**; Thai security issues and, 156
Dien Bien Phu, French defeat at, 33, 34, 49, 101
Dienstfertig, Josef (father). *See* Dean, Josef (father)
Dienstfertig, Lucy Ashkenaczy ("Mutti"). *See* Dean, Lucy Ashkenaczy ("Mutti")
Dienstfertig, Wolfgang (brother), 4, 5–6
diplomacy, essentials of, xiii–xiv, 86, 92–93, 96, 135–36, 137, 143, 169, 207–9
domino theory, 34, 47, 69–70, 86
Donovan, William Joseph ("Wild Bill"), 150
Draper, Morris, 138
drug trade, in Afghanistan, x, 171; in Thailand, 151–53, 161, 165–66; U.S. efforts to combat, 151–53, 182–83
Dukakis, Michael, x–xi
Dulles, John Foster, 32, 75, 176
Duphenieux, Martine. *See* Dean, Martine Duphenieux (wife)
Durrani, Mahmood, 188–89

Eagleburger, Lawrence, 99
Economic Cooperation Administration (ECA), 25, 26–28, 206
Eisenhower, Dwight D., 32
embassies, U.S., agency coordination in, 151–52
Enders, Thomas O., 84

Fahd (prince of Saudi Arabia), 142
Faust (Goethe), 20

Federalist Papers, The, 11
Ford, Gerald, xiv, 84, 90, 97, 98, 106, 108, 109, 113, **122**
Fort Belvoir (Va.), 15–16
Fort Hunt (Va.). *See* Post Office Box 1142
France: African ex-colonies and, 35, 36, 37–38, 40, 41, 44–45, 112; in Indochina, 25, 29–30, 31, 33–34, 49, 53, 59, 60, 67, 68, 87, 88, 101, 106, 112, 149, 170; JGD's graduate studies in, 22–23; post-colonial policies of, 101; post-WWII status of, 26, 32–33; Thailand and, 156; in WWII, 11–12
Franklin, Benjamin, 10
French Sudan, 42–43. *See also* Mali

Gandhi, Indira, 172–73
Gandhi, Rajiv, xii, **128**, 169, 173, 174, 175, 177–78, 180, 181, 183–84, 190, 191, 192, 200
Gandhi, Sanjay, 173
Gandhi, Sonia, 177
Gemayel, Amine, **125**
Gemayel, Bashir, 135, 145–46
Geneva Conference (1954), 31–32, 34, 50, 66, 101
Germany: Brüning chancellorship in, 13; and fall of France, 11–12; as former colonial power, 38, 40; JGD's feelings for, 12; philosophy in, 23; Weimar Republic era, 5, 18. *See also* Breslau (Germany); Nazis
Ghana, former slave trade in, 42
Ghost Wars (Stephen Coll), 198
Giscard d'Estaing, Valéry, 93
Godley, G. MacMurtrie ("Mac"), 68, 72, 74, 75
Goodman, Herbert, 23

Gorbachev, Mikhail, x, 171, 182, 183
Gordon, Lincoln, 26
government contracting, graft in, 28
Greece: Marshall Plan and, 26–27
Guantánamo Naval Base, U.S. prison at, 57
Guinea, 37, 43, 44, 46

Habib, Philip C., 51, 103, 146
Hamilton, Alexander, 10–11
Hariri, Rafic, 144
Harriman, W. Averell, 25, 26, 51, 53
Hartman, Arthur, 14, 26
Harvard University: JGD and, 8, 9, 11, 12–15, 20, 21–24
Hassan, Mash'hood, 189
Heffley, Carl, 61
Hekmatyar, Gulbuddin, 198–99
Herter, Christian, 40
Hilger, Gustave, 18–19
Hillary, Edmund, 190
Hitler, Adolf, 5, 18, 74
Ho Chi Minh, 30, 33, 48, 52
Ho Chi Minh Trail, 48–49, 59, 85–86
Holbrooke, Richard, 51, 53
Houghton, Amory, 38
Howland, Richard C. (Dick), 75
Hubbard, John, 186, 195
Hudson, Eugene L., 56
Humphrey, Hubert H., 52

India: economic issues and, 173–75; geopolitical data on, 171–73, 175–77; internal conflicts and, 170, 171, 175–76, 201; JGD as ambassador to, ix, **127–30**, 169–71, 174, 177–82, 184–88, 190–98, 201, 202–3; nonalignment and, 172, 175, 176, 177, 178–79; nuclear program in, x, 176, 178, 180–82, 194; regional conflicts and, ix, x, xiv, 170–71, 176, 179, 200; Soviet Union and, 172, 174, 176, 177, 178, 179, 194; U.S. foreign policy and, 172, 176–80, 181, 183–84, 187
Indochina, 25, 28–29, 72, 149; containment of communism in, 74, 86. *See also* Cambodia; Laos; Vietnam; Vietnam War
infrared technology, 16
Institut des hautes études internationales (IHEI), 22
insurgent warfare, logic of, 30
intelligence work: illegal tactics in, 56–57; personal hardships of, 25–26; scientific knowledge and, 16–18
Iran, and regional "strategic consensus," 193–94; U.S. hostage crisis in (1979), xiii, 138–39
Iran-Contra scandal, x, 182
Islamic fundamentalism, 171, 179, 184, 185, 186, 187, 192, 193, 194, 198–99, 200, 201
Israel: Afghan guerrillas and, 183; and arms sales to India, 193; and attack on JGD in Lebanon, 133–34; and criticisms of JGD, 145–46; regional conflicts and, 136–37, 138, 139, 141, 145–47, 170; U.S. lobby for, xii, 178, 191–92, 193, 201, 202; Zionism and, 144, 147. *See also* Mossad
Japan: in Indochina, 29, 30, 67–68, 88; and Thailand, 156–57; in WWII, 12, 16, 19, 88, 156
Javits, Jacob, 80
Jazelli (lawyer), 6
Jews: in Breslau, 1, 3; Dienstfertig/Dean family as, 2–3, 5, 6, 8,

146–47; Nazi persecution of, 3–4, 5–6, 12, 21, 110
Jihad, Abu, 139
Johnson, Lyndon B., 47, 50–52, 62, 85
Juin, Alphonse, 48

Kaltenborn, H. V., 11
Kansas City (Mo.), Dean family in, 7–12, 39
Kashmir, 176
Keeley, Robert, 106, 107
Keita, Modibo, 43, 44–45, 46, **115**
Kennedy, John F., 32, 47, 137, 151
Kennedy, Robert F., 47–51, **116**
Khalidi, Walid, 139
Khmer empire, 60, 87
Khmer Rouge, 31, 81, 86, 88–89, 90, 91–92, 93, 95–96, 97, 98, 99, 100, 101–2, 103, 105, 109–11
Khomeini, Ruhollah, 139
Khoury, Michel, 144–45
Khrushchev, Nikita, 137
King and I, The (Broadway musical), 154, 159
Kissinger, Henry, xiii, 52, 53, 84, 87, 89, 90–91, 93, 97, 100, 103, 112–13, **119**, 172
Kosh, David, 196

La Piana, George, 20, 21
Lantos, Tom, 191, 192
Laos, 66–68; attempted coup in, xiii, 77–81, 208; communist takeover in, xiii, 81; JGD as DCM/chargé d'affaires in, xii–xiii, 34, 65, 68–81, **117–18**, 149, 170, 208; JGD as political officer in, xii, 34, 66, 71, 149; JGD's hopes for, 46; Nixon "secret plan" and, 52; peace negotiations in, xii–xiii, 73–77, 78, 80, 81, 93, 208; post-WWII status of, 28, 29, 30, 31–32, 101; POW search scams and, 163–64; regional interconnections and, 136, 149; U.S. bombing in, 72–74; Viet Cong and, 49, 54, 72; warring factions in, 65–66, 68, 72; World Bank loan to, 81. *See also* Pathet Lao
Le Duc Tho, 53
Lebanon: assassination attempt on JGD in, 131–34, 136, 192; currency of, 144–45; geopolitical importance of, 143–44, 146; JGD as ambassador to, xiii, **123–25**, 131–47, 169, 208; political factions in, xiii, 134–35, 136, 145–46; Syrians in, 141, 145
Levin, André, 190
Liberia, 35
Lindbergh, Charles, 8
linkage, in U.S. diplomacy, 76, 86–87, 89
Lodge, Henry Cabot, Jr., 53
Lomé (Togo), 38–39
Lon Nol, 88, 89, 91, 92, 93–95, 96, 99, 100, 102, 103, 104, 105, **120**
Long Boret, 85, 96, 109–10
Lumumba, Patrice, 43–44

M1 Abrams tank, 180, 187, 188–89, 194
MacArthur, Douglas, II, 50, 51
Madison, James, 10–11
Mai Van Bo, 49
Mali: JGD as chargé d'affaires in, xiii, 42–46, **115**; location of, 44
Malraux, André, 43, 44, 46
Manac'h, Etienne, 49–51, 53, 90, 93
Margrethe II (queen of Denmark), **122**
Maronite Christians. *See* Phalangists

Marshall, George C., 21–22, 24, 26
Marshall Plan: in Europe, 21–22, 24, 26–27, 45; in Indochina, 29. *See also* Economic Cooperation Administration (ECA)
Martin, Graham, 109
Massoud, Ahmed Shah, 198, 199
McCarthy, Eugene, 51–52
McCloskey, Pete, 56
Meloy, Francis E., 132
Middle East: Carter's involvement in, 139; regional complexities of, 136, 146; weapons sales to, xii
military personnel, JGD's respect for, 54–55, 56, 57–58
Miller, Robert H., 23
Mongkut (king of Siam), 159
Mossad (Israeli intelligence service), xii, 133–34, 139, 182–83, 190–91, 192
Murphy, Richard W., xi, 195
Murphy, Robert, 27–28
Mussolini, Benito, 21

Najibullah, Mohammad, 184–85, 201
Nasser, Assad, 140
nationalism, in ex-colonial countries, 25, 49
NATO (North Atlantic Treaty Organization), 28
Nazis: and Jewish persecution, 3–4, 5–6, 12, 21, 110, 136, 161; Lindbergh support for, 8; in WWII, 12, 14, 19
Negroponte, John, 51, 53
Nehru, Jawaharlal, 171, 173
"New Colossus, The" (Emma Lazarus), 205
Nixon, Richard, xiv, 52, 59, 60, 62, 72, 75, 76, 85, 89, 90, 95; China and, 91; Watergate scandal and, 83–84, 97
Nixon Doctrine, 86
nonaligned movement, in Africa, 45; India and, 172, 175, 176, 177, 178–79
nuclear weapons, 17, 19, 201; in India, 176, 178, 180–82, 194; in Pakistan, 170, 176, 180–82, 184, 192, 194, 201
Nuremberg laws, 3, 4

Oakley, Robert, 193–94
Olmsted, Thomas, 106
Olympio, Sylvanus, 39–42, 46; wife of, **116**

Pakistan: and Afghanistan, xiv, 171, 179, 185–86; India and, ix, x, xiv, 170, 172, 175–76, 177, 179–82, 183–84, 185, 200; Iran and, 193, 194; military program of, ix–x, 179–80 183–84, 186–87, 188, 191, 194; nuclear weapons and, x, xii, 170, 176, 180–82, 184, 192, 194, 201; regional "strategic consensus" and, 193–94; U.S. policies and, 172, 176, 179–80, 181, 182, 183, 186–87, 188, 194, 201, 202. *See also* Zia ul Huq, Muhammad
Palestine Liberation Organization (PLO), 132, 134, 136–37, 138, 139–40, 170, 178
Palestinians, xiii, 134, 135, 136, 139, 141, 144, 146, 178, 192, 208
Palmer, Jack, 102
Papandreou, George, 27
Paris: JGD as political officer in, 47–48, 49–51, 52–53, **116**
Pathet Lao, 32, 65–66, 69; in peace negotiations, 73, 74–75, 77, 78, 80, 81, 150

peace, requisite conditions for, 65, 70, 137–38
Pearl Harbor, bombing of, 12
Pentagon Papers, 83
Perot, Ross, 163
Persian Gulf War (1991), 157, 180
Petersdorf (uncle), 5
Petschek, Max, 23, 24
Phalangists, 135, 141, 145–46
Pheng Pongsavan, 74, 76, 77
Phnom Penh (Cambodia), U.S. exit from, 99, 102–9
Phoumi Vongvichit, 74, 77, 78, 79, 80
Plaine des Jarres (Laos), 69
Portugal: African colonies and, 36, 37, 112; slave trade and, 42
Post Office Box 1142 (Fort Hunt, Va.), 16, 18, 19
Potomac River, JGD's swim across, 19
POWs, search scams and, 163–64
Prem Tinsulanonda, 155–56, 157, 164

Raphel, Arnold, 185, 187, 188, 189, 193
Reagan, Ronald, 69, xi, xii, xiv, **128**, 135, 137, 139, 150–51, 157, 169, 170, 174, 180, 182, 183, 184, 185, 186, 187, 191, 195, 198
Realpolitik, 17–19
Rice, Condoleezza, 16
Rockefeller, Nelson, **122**
Rogers, William P., 40
Roosevelt, Franklin D., 12, 14, 19, 30, 32, 208
Ross, André, 77
Russian Federation, 208

Santayana, George, 208
Sarkis, Elias, 135, 144
Saudi Arabia, 143, 147, 170, 171, 182, 186
Saunders, Harold, 138
Savang Vatthana (king of Laos), **118**
Schanberg, Sydney H., 99, 103, 107
Schlesinger, James, 103
Schlicke, Heinz, 16, 20
Schelling, Thomas, 26
segregation, in Kansas City, 9
Sen, Ronen, 187, 189
Senegal, and French Sudan, 42–43
Shahak, Israel, 182–83
Shaher, Ali, 140–43
Shoesmith, Thomas, 23
Shultz, George, xi, xii, **127**, 186, 195, 196, 197–98, 199
Sihanouk, Norodom, 30–32, 87–90, 93–94, 96–97, 106
Sirik Matak, Sisowath, 91–92, 105, 107, 109
Sirikit (queen of Siam), 158, 159, 160
Sisowath Monireth, 88
slave trade, in Africa, 42
Sokom Khoi, 104–5
Solarz, Stephen, 191, 192, 193
Soldatov, Alexander, 137
Soulier, Jean, 165–66
Souphanouvong, 66, 68
Southeast Asia. *See* Cambodia; Indochina; Laos; Vietnam
Souvanna Phouma, 65, 66, 68, 70–72, 73, 74, **117**; attempted coup against, xiii, 77–81, 150; death of, 81
Soviet Union: African involvement of, 37, 43, 44; as Ho Chi Minh backer, 33; as Khmer Rouge backer, 86, 96; Middle East and, 136, 137; post-WWII status of, 26, 29, 32; Reagan and, 137; Stalinism in,

18–19, 196; U.S. détente with, 90, 91, 97, 112
Sparkman, John, 89
Stalin, Joseph, 18–19, 93
Stalingrad, battle of, 14, 18
Stern, Otto, 4
Stern, Paul, 4
Summers, Frederick, 196
Sundarji, K., 190–91
Sundarji, Vani, 191
Syria: global politics and, 136, 178; and Lebanon, 134, 135, 137, 142, 145, 146, 170

Taliban, x, 199, 200, 201
Tasca, Henry, 26
Tehran (Iran), U.S. embassy hostage crisis in, 138, 139
Teresa, Mother, **130**
Terrorism, 17, 32, 57, 92, 131, 137, 186, 199–201, 202
Texas Instruments, 175
Thailand: AIDS epidemic in, 159, 161; Asian trade partners and, 156; and Cambodia, 87, 93, 155; Cambodian refugees in, 161–62; drug trade in, 151–53, 161, 165–66; geopolitical data on, 154–58, 167; JGD as ambassador to, xiii, **126**, 149, 150–54, 157–58, 159, 160, 161, 163–66, 167, 169; JGD with Marshall Plan in, 149; and Laos, 68, 80, 149, 150, 155, 170; MIA-POW scams and, 163–64; post-WWII status of, 30, 32; religious issues in, 166–67; royal power in, 155, 158–61; sex trade in, 153–54; U.S. relations with, 150–54, 156, 157–58, 162, 166, 167; in WWII, 156
Thanat Khoman, 156, 157
Thao Ma, 77–78, 79–80

Tito, Josip Broz, 45–46
Togo: colonial history of, 38, 39–40; Foreign Office of, 40–42; former slave trade in, 40; JGD as U.S. consul in, xiii, 35–36, 38–42; U.S. role in, 35-36, 39–40
tolerance, as fundamental value, 3, 9, 206, 207
Toqueville, Alexis de, 111
Touré, Sékou, 37, 43
Trinh, Nguyen Duy, 48, 49
Truman, Harry, 32
Turkey, Marshall Plan and, 26–27; in regional "strategic consensus", 193–94;

United Nations: Israel and, 136; refugee data from, 161; Togo and, 38, 39
United States: core values of, 10, 11, 57, 67, 111, 183, 184, 205–9; election of 1968 in, 51–52, 53, 91; election of 1988 in, x–xi, xii; foreign policy failures of, 111–12; global aspirations and, 100–101, 206, 209; sociopolitical tensions in, 47

Van den Heuvel, William, 49
Vance, Cyrus, 51, 53, **123,** 138
Vdovine, Andrej, 77
Venizelos, Sophocles, 27
Vessey, John W., Jr. ("Jack"), 68–69
Vest, George, xi–xii, 196
Vientiane (Laos), 66, 71, 149
Viet Cong, 49, 52, 54, 56–57, 58, 61
Viet Minh, 32, 33, 68
Vietnam: archeological museum of, 59–61; Cambodia and, 86, 87, 162, 170; communist takeover in, 81, 109, 157; JGD as CORDS regional director in, 53–63, 72,

206; Laos and, 68, 69, 87, 149, 170; post-WWII status of, 28, 29, 30, 31, 33–34, 101; regional interconnections and, 136; U.S. involvement in, 32–33, 34, 66, 83, 98; U.S. land mines in, 59
Vietnam War: aftermath of, 157, 163–65; Agent Orange in, 59; as avoidable conflict, 32; JGD's family and, 62–63; JGD's views on, 56–59, 61–62; Nixon "secret plan" and, 52, 91; peace talks and, 49–53, 62, 97; Phoenix program in, 56–57; U.S. bombing and, 48–49, 50, 51, 52; U.S. linkage policy and, 76, 86–87, 89; U.S. public opinion on, 48, 62, 83, 112; Vietnamization policy in, 85
Von Braun, Werner, 16

Waldheim, Kurt, 90
Walid, Abu, 139
Warburg, Max, 20
Waring, Robert O., 132

Washington, George, 176; portrait of, 202–3
Wassom, Herbert M., 187
Watergate scandal, 83, 97
Webster, William H., xi, 195, 196
Weinberger, Caspar, 184
Weyand, Frederick C., 56
Wilson, Charles, 188
World War II: appeasement in, 74; decolonization following, 25, 28–29, 34–35; devastation of, 20–21, 22, 25, 28; Germany in, 11–12, 14, 18; at Harvard, 14–15; infrared technology and, 16; Japan in, 12, 16, 19, 29, 30; JGD's military service in, 14, 15–21; Soviet role in, 19

Yalta Conference, 19
Yugoslavia, 45

Zia ul Haq, Muhammad, ix-x, xi, xii, 180, 185, 187-92, 193, 198-99, 201, 202
Zionism, 2, 144, 193

www.ingramcontent.com/pod-product-compliance
Lightning Source LLC
Chambersburg PA
CBHW020755160426
43192CB00006B/331